GRUESOME TIDE

GRUESOME TIDE

A Ben Grant Story

Eric J. Collenette

WILLIAM KIMBER · LONDON

First published in 1988 by
WILLIAM KIMBER & CO. LIMITED
100 Jermyn Street, London SW1Y 6EE

ISBN 0-7183-0672-4

Photoset in North Wales by
Derek Doyle & Associates Mold, Clwyd
and printed in Great Britain by
Biddles Limited, Guildford, Surrey

There is a tide in the affairs of men,
Which, taken at the flood, leads on to fortune;
Omitted, all the voyage of their life
Is bound in shallows and in miseries.
William Shakespeare 1564-1616

I

Chatham Barracks on the afternoon of the twenty-eighth day of May 1940 is a busy place. Something big is going on and no one seems to know exactly what. I am here because I am part of an advanced party of submariners sent to prepare our boat for re-commissioning after a refit. It is a frustrating time as we try to keep out of the dockers' way, for they can become very touchy if we seem to be interfering in their work. Each morning I go down to the dockyard and scramble through a maze of pipes and hoses to find every corner of the boat in a state of flux, with brown-overalled workmen disembowelling her innards. One ill-judged move on our part and they will walk off at the drop of a spanner.

As yet the war doesn't seem very real. Apart from a couple of false alarms and an initial panic when school children and mothers-to-be were evacuated to the country, everything is quiet and normal. Much of our time is spent twiddling our thumbs, and I am bored and despondent. So, when a red-faced lieutenant comes along shouting for volunteers I don't even bother to ask for details. I would do anything to get out of the stagnant atmosphere of barracks and find a little action. Against all my natural instincts I shuffle off across the parade-ground to find out what I have let myself in for.

'Where you orf?' It is Stoker Petty Officer Albert Finney of the revolving eyeballs, rum-soaked breath and quivering frame. He is lolloping alongside me as though one leg is shorter than the other. If ever the temperance societies wanted an anti-booze advert, Finney is their man. He is a disjointed, debauched mess, whose spirit-pickled bones are held together inside a loose-skinned frame that sags all over the place. He can make any place look untidy just by being there, and his only redeeming feature is his affinity for diesel engines. Once installed in the oily cavern of a submarine's engineroom he merges with the metallic surroundings like an extra piece of machinery. You have only to walk into a public bar to know Albert is about for he exudes a permanent aura of diesel-fumes even when he is dressed in his shore-going togs.

'I've volunteered,' I say in a subdued tone, hoping he might not hear properly and go off on another tack.

'Volunteered!' The word echoes back from the blank walls as he stops in his tracks, staring wide-eyed.

I press on fast, ignoring the startled looks of passers-by and trying to leave him astern, but he keeps pace with a series of crab-like movements, leering at me, with his face working in a mixture of disbelief and suspicion. 'You – volunteer!' He snorts, waiting for me to admit that I am joking.

I say nothing. We both know that only idiots volunteer, and anyone who does so without knowing what it is all about is overdue for a spell in the nuthouse. His eyes narrow and an evil smile expands across his face, creasing his wrinkled features so that he looks like a conniving gnome.

'You crafty bastard! You're on ter somethin', ain't yer?' he accuses gleefully, falling into step, determined to stay with me. I stop in my tracks and turn to face him as he shuffles inside his loose uniform.

'I'm telling you, I've volunteered,' I gulp hard before taking the plunge. 'I don't know what for: I've just got to get out of this bloody place for a while.' I turn away from him, avoiding his incredulous eyes. 'There is no ulterior motive, Albert. That's the truth.'

For a moment he allows me to gain a few yards while he nurses his disbelief, then with a cackling laugh he lumbers after me. 'I'm comin' wiv yer,' he chortles. 'You crafty sod! I've never known yer stick yer neck aht fer nuffin'.'

He is still muttering when we are taken in buses to Sheerness and met by a Wavy-Navy lieutenant-commander, wearing a grey, roll-necked sweater under his uniform jacket and a harassed expression. He listens while I reel off my credentials and introduce Finney.

'Do you think you could manage that?' he asks, pointing at a small vessel nudging the wharf. It looks like a cross between a Thames barge and a small coaster.

'What is it?' I ask cautiously.

'It's a skoot, spelt s-c-h-u-i-t-j-e in Holland, where they come from. Most of them are bigger than this, and we've put officers in them, but you can have this one if you think you can manage. I've got a couple of reservists to help.' He takes a rolled-up chart from under his arm. 'You can have this, but hopefully, you will not require to use it. All you need do is follow the crowd.'

'Follow them where, sir?'

He looks slightly embarrassed. 'Oh, didn't I explain? You are going to Dunkirk. Those are your two crewmen.' He indicates a couple of bodies standing disconsolately on the covered hatches. I look beyond them at the small, squat rabbit hutch of a wheelhouse and the fag-end of a funnel poking up behind.

'All right, sir,' I hear myself saying.

'Good,' he says with a sigh of relief. 'You will go down to Ramsgate to take on supplies before sailing across the Channel. Best of luck, and thank you, chief.'

'Fuckin' 'ell!' explodes Finney when the officer is out of earshot. His eyeballs are jumping about wildly as he echoes my thoughts. 'What yer got me inter this time?'

Ignoring him I go down to the two men brooding on the hatch. One is a gangling youth with an outsized cap slopped over his big ears. His thin mouth is pulled up on one side to give his face a lopsided twist.

'What's your name?' I ask gently, for he looks as if he will blow away if I breathe too hard on him.

'Maundy, sir. But everyone calls me Seth.'

'Septic you mean,' snipes the other man caustically,

dragging my eyes in his direction. He has a hard face with an unsmiling mouth and cruel eyes. There is something cold and calculating about him that I do not like. I swing back to Maundy in time to see the hurt on his face. 'You can speak for yourself, laddy, and you won't call me "sir". Chief or coxswain will do. What is your full name?'

He looks down as though he is used to being bullied, reluctant to open up to anyone.

'Come on, lad,' I urge. 'I need your full name for this.' I show him a Next of Kin form; known to all and sundry as a 'This is not a will' form, because that is what it reads in black capitals across the top.

'Septimus Maundy,' he mutters *sotto voce*. He has suffered with that name, and heartily sick of it. I can either leave it there and let him sort it out for himself, or I can bring it out into the open so there is no more bait for his mordacious companion.

'Where did you get a name like that?' I ask in a friendly tone, trying to draw him out.

He reacts to my grin. 'They found me on Waterloo Station at seven o'clock on Maundy Thursday, so that's what they called me.' He grins sheepishly. 'He's right though; everyone calls me Septic, and I don't mind really. I'd just rather be called Seth.'

Nothing I do will ever change that. Once the lower-deck gives you a handle it sticks forever. I turn to the other man. I'll bet no one ever dared to give this bloke a nick-name. 'And you?' I snap at him.

He scowls back contemptuously. We hate each other on sight. 'Royal is my name,' he sneers. 'Jack Royal. You will find that I've done my time at sea.' His tone is hostile as he tries to stare me out; but he doesn't stand a chance.

'Have you now,' I say when his eyes flicker away. 'Well, "admiral", I'll reserve judgement on that until later, when I've seen just how much you do know. Fill in this form and then go forward with Maundy to single-up ready for slipping.'

They go off and I am left to gaze out into the growing

dusk where other *schuitjes* are coughing into life before sliding out into the mainstream. Our diesel joins the chorus and settles to a steady rhythm with a wisp of exhaust puffing from the funnel. A keen wind blows in from the estuary, helping to peel our bows away as the headropes are let go. The jetty slips quietly aft as I spin the wheel and sidle out into the queue, taking my place between two other *schuitjes* in a line being led out by two trawlers.

Soon we have a healthy bow-wave building up under our fore-foot as we pick up speed and thrust the murky water aside. There is something magical in an estuary even on an evening like this, and I can't help but fall under its soft spell as we move out across the smooth surface. 'I was a seascout once.' Septic's nasal voice cuts through my thoughts as he leans in through the door, wearing a stupid grin.

'Keep your eyes peeled and your ears open for aircraft,' I snarl, wiping his grin away. Can't afford to get too pally or I'll find myself wet-nursing him.

He backs out deflated and I'm left to myself again. The *schuitjes* are shadowy entities, shapeless in the deepening gloom of late evening. Orders are passed from ship to ship verbally, over a megaphone, for few of the vessels have a signalman on board. We arrive at Margate without mishap and take on water and food for the troops stranded on the beaches. We are to sail two hours before dawn, each ship carrying a hooded sternlight. We are warned not to lose the ship ahead or we could break the chain. It is all a bit of a shambles really. Made all the more hazardous by a multitude of miscellaneous craft dodging about all over the place at will.

We work hard all night loading the supplies from a lighter and fuelling-up. So it is something of a relief when we finally get under way and sail eastwards towards a new dawn that will soon replace the man-made version that lights up the horizon above the port of Dunkirk. The sound of war is muffled by distance and breeze, but it comes blustering across the sea, silencing our talk and shutting our thoughts and fears inside ourselves. Suddenly I am aware that Royal is standing in the shadows outside the wheelhouse. I lean over and slide the door open.

'Can you steer?'

He shifts his stance, turning his heavy bulk toward me. 'Yes.'

'You had better take a spell then. Just follow the light ahead.'

Without further comment he comes in and grasps the spokes. Within five minutes I am satisfied that he knows what he is about. His thick fingers are no strangers to the feel of a helm, and I watch him coax the *schuitje* with skill, running clear of the land. There is no need of a chart to show our destination for when the sun peers over the world's edge a huge pall of black smoke lifts into the sky to form an awesome beacon. The trawler takes us on a zig-zag course through the channels between sand-banks and along mineswept sea-roads.

I feel the need to break the spell. 'You've steered a ship before.'

It is a stupid statement. Anyone with half an eye can see he is experienced, but I use it as an opener, hoping he will loosen up. He studies the compass for a while, then looks up to squint at the dawn, adjusting the helm to line up on the ship ahead. It is the act of a responsible seaman, checking his course, taking his marks, so that if we lose touch with the others he will know where to steer. My curiosity mounts, along with my impatience, when he makes no response.

'I asked you a question, Royal,' I snap.

He darts a glance at me, and for one instant I know he is about to give me a mouthful, but he takes hold of himself and looks back at the bow . 'I told you; I've been to sea before.'

I am becoming tired of this one-sided conversation. 'Look, Royal, I am entitled to know what I can expect from a member of my crew.'

'What's it matter so long as I do my job?'

'It matters a lot. Christ knows what we will find when we get there. Finney I know about. I can trust him without question. Maundy will need watching all the time. I know nothing about you. Bloody hell, I'm not asking for your life's history!'

His lips purse and I can see he is relenting a bit. He doesn't take his eyes from the lead ship and his fingers move on the polished spokes like a virtuoso. When he speaks it is as though he is vindicating some inborn, festering hate.

'I was first mate on a coaster owned by a pious, bible-punching louse named Ely Spring. He calls all his ships after biblical women and I ended up on the *Sister Ruth*. Each cabin had its prayer-book, and grace was said after every meal. We signed on every dead-beat we could find in the name of Christianity. Jailbirds, perverts – anything we could drag out of the dockside pubs.

'We carried cargoes that no other ship would touch. Some so volatile that if one of the crew farted she could explode. The ship was well overdue for the scrapyard and her skipper lived out of the bottle. Ten days ago – it seems more like a century now – we ran her on the rocks off Cornwall. I say "we" because it was my watch, but instead of being on the bridge where I should have been I was helping the cook to overpower our worthless master who was in one of his periodic alcoholic fits. We managed to drag him below to his cabin where we strapped him into his bunk and let him stew in his own juice, but by the time I got back to the bridge we were almost on the reef.' He goes silent as he relives the scene and I can see his knuckles turn white as he grips the spokes. 'There was nothing I could do!' he almost whispers.

'We lost two firemen, an engineer, and the skipper. No one remembered he was still tied up in his sweat-bag. I doubt if he even woke up before the water got to him; we were all too busy scrambling for the boats, and breaking them out of their stowage; God, they were welded in with paint and dirt! In the end most of us climbed over the rocks and shallows to get away from her before she broke up and sank.'

He takes a long look at me then, and I get the feeling he is watching to see how I will take the next bit. 'The crew were a lot of bloody chancers; out to save their own skins. You know, the kind that never misses an opportunity to land some poor bastard in the soup, especially if he outranks them. I was their prime target; a first mate who made the lazy sods sweat. A natural victim for their plebian hate, and they ran true to form. The bloke on the wheel didn't want to admit that he had slacked off in my absence so he got together with his mates and they piled the blame on me. I was on the beach, waiting to be called to book for losing the ship and causing the skipper's death when they asked for volunteers, and I jumped in with both feet.'

'You have not been found guilty yet. You could have a ship of your own with your qualifications. You might make a name for yourself and get off the hook when the Enquiry comes.'

His face suddenly takes on a vicious twist. 'That's none of your fucking business! My reasons are my own, and I've told you all I need to tell you. The form I signed puts me under the Navy's authority for this trip only, so don't push me too far.'

I have an uneasy feeling inside. I believe only half of what he says, but I must leave it there for now. If I could I would get rid of him, for he makes me feel uncomfortable. However, right now we are moving in towards the stench of battle with a host of other craft and already the long, flat expanse of coastline with its drab, square, sea-side houses and featureless landscape is growing out of the haze. I take the wheel and study the scene across the bow.

From here it looks to be a chaotic shambles. a sight that leaves us speechless as we run in to the beaches. The oppressive pall of black smoke dominates the port and town, and the dunes are veined with straggled lines of queuing men, zig-zagging in abstract patterns over the grey sand while the men wait their turn to be picked up. Already the wreckage of abandoned craft litters the water's edge,and the masts and funnels of sunken ships sprout like petrified trees in the shallows. The air is thick with sooty smuts and flying ash, and a black rain mottles the surface, mixing with floating oil to form islands of undulating scum where corpses wallow like dead fish.

It is a sickening panorama, made even more harrowing by the weak cries that carry out to us from the dunes as we glide by. All the time the incoming surf threatens to take hold of the small boats and swing them beam-on to the swell, spilling out their scared passengers. The bedlam of war howls and thumps above it all, making it difficult to think. Shells fall continuously into the harbour, for the Germans are already as close as Gravelines, only about ten miles away, and they have the range down to a fine art. Heavy smoke screens the evacuation from the Luftwaffe as yet, but it adds to the grim scene of destruction with its sombre shadow that seems to creep out over the sand like a scourge.

I am looking for a spot on the beach where I can ease the bows into the surf and make it easy for the troops to wade out to us. I cannot afford to go in too close even with our shallow draught, for when the extra weight of the men comes on she will bed into the sand and I'll never get her off again. I notice Naval officers with drawn pistols controlling the men. Sections of the area are under control of Beach Officers and they are having their work cut out.

I am too engrossed in my task to notice a destroyer's motorcutter come alongside and keep pace with us while an officer leaps across the gap onto the well-deck. The wheelhouse door slams back onto its stoppers and I snap a startled look at a tall, dark-featured lieutenant as he enters my domain. Like me he prefers his uniform cap to a steel helmet, and wears it with the peak set squarely above his intelligent brown eyes.

'Where are you taking this ship, chief?' he asked briskly.

'Into the beach when I can find a gap, sir. The East Mole

looks too congested at the moment.'

'Did you bring any cargo?'

'Yes, sir, and drums of water.'

'Excellent! They need water above all else at the moment. They are drinking from the radiators of wrecked vehicles.' He points towards a spot filled with floating debris and several bodies. 'Take her in over there. Run her right up onto the sand and leave her. Don't worry about the flotsam; she'll carry the lot with her if you go in fast enough.'

'I'll rip the bottom out of her, sir,' I protest.

'No matter. We are going to abandon her anyway. Too many soldiers are being drowned in the shallows or from upturned boats. We will use this old tub as a jetty. I have already lost one whaler and I do not intend to risk any more boats until the mob is under control.'

I brace up. This is my command. Time-honoured tradition says that I give the orders, and no one can tell me to ditch her, no matter what rank he holds. He darts a sideways glance and sees the determination on my face. 'Do it, chief,' he says gently. 'The destroyer can do three trips to your one with four or five times the number of troops. We badly need a jetty. Those makeshift abortions the army is making out of bren-carriers and trucks are death-traps where they have not been securely anchored.'

I look forward to where Royal and Maundy are waiting for my signal to drop the anchor if necessary. They are out of earshot and I feel I am letting them down, but something in Martingale's tone makes up my mind. We are in a small vacuum while all hell breaks loose about us and I nod agreement. It is as if the decision is being made for me. There is an aura about him that merits respect and I know instinctively that he is to be trusted. I can see he has come up through the ranks, which goes some way towards persuading me, but it is more than that. I know I can go all the way with this bloke, and it is not because of his two stripes.

I stick my head out of the door to yell at the men on the

fo'c'sle. 'Hold on forrard – I'm running her up on to the sand!'

They exchange puzzled looks, but I have no time for lengthy explanations now. I shout down the voicepipe to Finney, telling him to open the throttle wide, then get the hell out of the engine-room. 'We are leaving her on the beach,' I tell him.

I ignore the flood of obscenity that spews out of the voicepipe and concentrate on the beach, aiming the bow for a spot where the wreckage is thinnest and trying to ignore the bodies that roll away as we drive in through the surf.

'You'd better have this.' My hand closes automatically on the shiny butt of a service revolver and I look up into his face. 'Our biggest enemy is panic, chief,' he explains. 'Most of the men are well-disciplined, but there is an element amongst the crowd that would wreck everything, given a chance. Back in Dover they refer to many of these as "useless mouths". They are the pen-pushers, drivers, staff personnel, and administrators; mixed with a fair sprinkling of deserters. The fighting troops have only just started to leave. You may need that gun when they start to clamber aboard. By the way, what's your name?'

I stuff the pistol into my belt. 'Grant, sir. I'm coxswain of the submarine *Scavenger*.' That last bit is pure swank and I sense him smiling.

'Good,' he says gratefully, 'then I can rely on you to do what's required without a lot of damn stupid questions. My name is Martingale, and I am first lieutenant of *Brigand*. That's her over there.' He indicates a modern destroyer steaming slowly through the mess with boarding nets rigged over her side and helmeted squaddies lining her upper-deck. She is under way even though there are rafts and boats alongside, being towed along by their painters while their passengers clamber aboard. It is not the best way to embark tired soldiers, but she is extremely vulnerable and will not wish to overcome the inertia of a standing start if an attack comes. Her big engines will send her surging forward at the first sign of trouble. Her gunners and lookouts scan the skies for the first sight of enemy aircraft. She looks mean, lean and powerful, like the officer standing at my side.

No more time for contemplation. The last few yards are eaten up as the *schuitje* finds an extra burst of speed. Finney climbs out of his hatch to stand for a moment in oily silence, studying the situation, wiping filthy hands on a wad of cotton-waste. 'I've lifted the governor,' he grunts casually, then belches into the atmosphere.

She rides up onto the sand and comes to a juddering stop with a gush of sooty smoke from her funnel. The engine loses its steady pulse and raises its voice in protest as it races out of control. The deck vibrates, setting our teeth chattering while Finney grins in evil delight. The noise culminates with an ear-splitting screech and a sharp explosion. We are stuck firmly in the sand and already the troops come wading out; intent on boarding her.

That is the last thing I want. The whole purpose behind running her in like this is to bring them over the side with dry feet once the ladders are rigged. That way we can feed them aft in orderly fashion as the boats come in. Now, if we don't stop them, they will swarm over the sides like bloody pirates; laden down with waterlogged battledress and carry heavy equipment. They could easily become overwhelmed in the surf as their mates press in on them from behind, and it is inevitable that some will drown, or be trodden underfoot.

'Hold it there!' I roar, leaping down into the waist to run forward with my revolver cocked in my right hand.

Everyone freezes when they see this raving maniac charging towards them, yelling and waving a loaded revolver like Buffalo Bill. I jolt to a halt, feeling rather stupid as I look down at their anxious faces. Nevertheless, it has done the trick and stopped their mad rush, so I press home my advantage. 'Get back to the beach,' I order in a more controlled voice. 'Form up in a queue or we'll pull out and leave you.'

Sheepishly they wade back to dry land and I notice the welcome appearance of several officers and NCOs arriving to take command of the situation. Martingale is beside me, picking out the senior man and shouting instructions to form a chain of the fittest to discharge some of the cargo. Others form up in order and begin to embark over the bow in batches of eight. Discipline is restored and the procedure seems to be working. Miraculously the enemy is occupied elsewhere for the time being. Although when I look towards the harbour I notice that the smoke is being carried out to sea by the change in the wind, leaving us wide open to air attack.

'Royal!' I bark, and he looks at me with a half-insolent expression on his face. 'No need to replace the hatch-covers when you unload; we can use them as life-rafts if necessary.' He nods at me with an off-hand leer, making my blood boil.

'That's a good idea, Grant.' Martingale calls as he follows me aft. 'I think it's time I returned to my ship. I'm sure you can manage well enough without me. Don't stand for any nonsense from the Army. The Navy is in charge once they leave the beach, and the key to success is organisation.'

We issue life-jackets as the troops come over the bow, and some enterprising body has heated up a thick soup in our small galley so that each man gets a ration as he comes aft. You'd think it was venison the way they scoff it. Later I find out that Finney and one of the destroyer's cooks are responsible, having filched the ingredients from the hold, along with other items I pretend not to notice.

Most of the soldiers wear steel helmets; fewer carry arms. All look haggard and hollow-eyed as we shepherd them into the boats. The destroyer's cutter runs a shuttle service with a pair of carley-rafts in tow, leaving a couple of empty ones behind each time so that they can be loaded while she makes the trip. It is agonisingly slow, but it is the best we can do. Elsewhere on the beach there is a woeful shortage of small craft to ferry the troops out. Mostly ship's lifeboats and naval cutters and whalers. The long queues never seem to shorten, and the overworked craft make long journeys through the shallows to waiting ships.

The scene is unreal, like a painting by a mad artist who has used his brush to spatter every colour he can find over a background of blue sky and grey sand. An abstract portrait of insanity, with no pattern nor form, where men and vehicles strew the area like insects on a corpse. The troops filter aft with a mixture of ribald comment and grim silence. Some of the more vociferous ones complain of their treatment, and urge their mates on with a barrage of mindless oaths and threats, but mostly they are willing to be led in rotation, guided by our lads, who have to use force on the more dejected ones who would stand like zombies if left alone.

Still the sky stays clear above us, but the beaches are unveiled now, providing an open target for the Luftwaffe when it comes. It will be as easy as a fairground shooting gallery for them when they do turn up. In the meantime the shelling goes on and we try to close our ears to it, control our nerves and feed the troops aft patiently, making certain our over-anxious sailors do not over-load the cutter or the rafts. One swamped whaler or carley raft could wreck the whole smooth-running process now.

The excruciating howl of the first diving Stuka takes hold of my innards with invisible talons as I look up to see a whole gaggle of them dropping out of the sky towards the harbour. They don't peel off like other aircraft; just drop their noses and fall screaming out of the sky in vertical dives like black vultures. Every ship erupts with a cacophony of anti-aircraft fire, joining in with the army guns on shore to mottle the sky with flak. It seems impossible that anything can survive that lot, but the bastards keep coming on, dropping their bombs and pulling out to soar away in triumph.

All we can do is work. Move the squaddies along as quickly as possible. Encourage or curse them when they hesitate. Shutting our minds to the awful prospect of a bomb landing amongst this lot. Inter-service relations have never been so good, but heaven help any 'Brylcream Boy' who turns up in his sky-blue today. Anything that flies gets fired at, and many gunners would be just as happy to shoot down a stray Lysander in mistake for a Stuka, for they look very alike when stared at through a gun-sight; and there's every chance that some brass-bound bastard who is responsible for landing us in this bloody mess is sitting up there looking down at the chaos he and his kind have created.

A sudden burst of sound grabs my attention and I look forward to see a scuffle taking place beneath the fo'c'sle. Royal and Maundy are shouting down to a noisy mob of soldiers standing up to their waists in the drink. I hurry forward to stare down. The men in the water have red crosses on their arms and are asking to bring stretcher cases on board. I can see a whole line of them ranged along the sand.

'Use the hatch-covers!' I shout, happy that some use can be found for them at last.

'Belay that order!' The sharp command comes from a burly lieutenant-commander who wears a steel helmet and brandishes a revolver, which seems to be the naval dress of the day. His voice cuts through the babble like a knife. 'Those stretcher cases are to be left ashore. Get them back up the beach at once!'

The medics look from him to us in protest. Some of the wounded lift their heads and stare up at us with pleading eyes. 'Come on!' the relentless voice of the officer insists. 'Get moving – get them out of here at once!'

'Hey!' Royal's gruff voice yells back. 'What the hell!'

'Stow it!' I snap at him. I can see the reasoning behind the brutal order. We have no room for seriously wounded on this trip. They occupy too much space and require too many hands to take care of them, and manhandle them down into the rafts and boats. It is down to blind economics. The cold truth is that fighting men are at a premium, and there is no room for compassion on a day when humanity takes second place to hard-nosed pragmatism. On this beach, beneath a sick cloud of filth with the abominable noises of war resounding about us it is the survival of the fittest, and soulless men with gravel voices are taking command.

As I turn to go aft, a Messerschmitt skims along the whole length of the beach, cutting a swathe through the brown horde as they scatter in terror either side and grovel in the sand. In that awful moment I feel a terrible doubt. A sensation of utter despair as though it is the final symbol of defeat. I can visualise the pilot's face in my mind's eye, see his grinning mouth as he watches the soldiers splay out like toys beneath his guns, and for the first time I know there is a chance we could lose the war against the grey machine that gobbles up everything in its path. Right and wrong, courage, patriotism; they mean nothing against the sheer might of this hideous machine, for it feeds on its own rotten bile.

A hot anger surges up inside me to overpower the despair as I scramble aft. If there is a God, or any justice, we will rid the world of the stink of this evil. In that moment I have passed through a barrier. All doubt is gone. I know that nothing as vile as this can survive.

'Chief!' The shout comes from the coxswain of the motor-cutter. He is beckoning to me from the stern. 'Come on, chief. This is our last trip.'

I make sure my blokes are following and move aft past the reproachful eyes of the squaddies. 'Lucky bastards!' their looks say. 'You're going home to Blighty and leaving us here in this hell-hole with the hounds of death at our heels.'

Stony-faced we clamber down into the sternsheets of the cutter to stand in silence as the coxswain takes her out in a wide sweep towards the destroyer. She is lying dead in the water now. Taking her life in her hands as she picks up the remainder of the survivors from the rafts and whalers. It is better to take the risk of stopping and get the job done quickly so that she can get the hell out of here, back to her own element.

The cutter's falls are lowered to the water-line ready for us to hook on for hoisting. I can see Martingale and his seamen clearing a path through the milling throng on the upper-deck so that the falls can be led forward to the capstan. It is difficult, for the squaddies are reluctant to go below, and a certain amount of none-too-gentle persuasion is required.

I grab the forward block as it swings past my left ear, handing it down through the square cockpit in the canopy so the bowman can shackle it on. He raises his arm to show he is secure and the coxswain hooks on aft before raising his own hand. A sharp order from Martingale and the slack is taken up on both falls before being 'married' so that the boat lifts on an even keel with water dripping from her bilges. Already *Brigand* is surging ahead, dragging the rafts along as the soldiers frantically scramble to get aboard.

'You any good with a Lewis gun, chief?' a PO with the crossed gun-barrels and crown of a GI on his sleeve is asking, almost before my feet touch the deck. 'We lost a couple of men earlier on – I could do with an extra gunner.'

The badge on my lapels must tell him that I am in the wrong branch, but he also knows that I'm a submariner, used to jumping into other men's shoes. I have handled a Lewis before, and I don't want to stand about doing nothing when the action starts so I nod quickly. 'I'll manage,' I tell him, 'but don't expect me to get anywhere near the target.'

He grins. 'Don't let that worry you. All we can do is hope to scare the shit out of them and put them off their aim. Come on, I'll show you where the weapon is and give you a crash course so you don't slaughter too many of our own lads. You will be close to the compass platform, so you'll see what's going on,' he chortles, patting my shoulder. 'It ain't gonna be for long. They are pulling us out. These new destroyers are too precious to risk in this madhouse.'

II

I reckon every man on the upper-deck believes the Stuka's nose is aimed directly at him. We had watched in awe as they came in clover-leaf formation as if they were on display, then one by one dropped their snouts to select their targets. To me on the starboard Lewis gun it seems the diving aircraft is threaded on an invisible wire stretched taut from the edge of the smoke to the centre of my gun-sight. My guts dissolve as I try to hold steady and squeeze the trigger. In theory it should be impossible to miss, for the target is coming straight at me, and I do not even need to allow for deflection; just point the barrel at the plane and watch the tracer home in on the cockpit.

Theory makes no allowance for the maniacal scream of diving sirens, or the way the evil, black silhouette fills the sky. I can see the flicker of guns on the leading edges of the wings, and in my mind's eye, the fanatic hatred on the pilot's face, for I know I am facing a skilled opponent; better trained than any other pilot in the world. The same dedicated type of cold-hearted bastard that shot up the beach a century ago. I know he is staring at me with his cruel eyes as I wait with my puny little gun, and nothing exists but the duel between us.

I grit my teeth and hold my aim. I see his wings waver and realise that my barrage is unnerving him. I see the silver shape of the bomb leave his belly early to arc down towards the stern and explode in our wake. I feel his black shadow sweep over me as I strive to follow him; swivelling fast as he swoops away in a climbing turn. I keep firing until the magazine runs dry, and I remain frozen with my finger squeezing the useless trigger long after the Stuka's stern-gunner fires his parting burst.

It's a miracle that only one man is hit by the burst – it is a tragedy that the man is *Brigand*'s captain. He had been leaning over the side of the bridge urging his sailors to hurry with the last few survivors struggling knee-deep in swirling water as the rafts were dragged along by the destroyer. The ropes were stretched to breaking point, and the rafts in danger of being swamped, but there was a desperate need to get the ship away as the aircraft plummeted out of the sky. The soldiers were clumsy and weighed down with their gear, exhausted and unpractised at scrambling up boarding-nets. The seamen worked like demons to drag them over the side as the ship picked up speed. Weakened and frantic in their efforts to stay alive, some brought about their own execution as they fell back into the swirl of our slipstream and were sucked into the maelstrom of *Brigand*'s propellers.

In the midst of this torment the skipper was struck down by a bullet smashing into his spine, leaving a huge crater in his chest where it emerged. He fell lifeless to the deck with his anxiety still registered on his face.

A shout goes up for the first lieutenant, and Martingale arrives breathless onto the compass-platform to take command. One brief skyward glance shows we are safe for the moment. My Stuka is a dark vulture heading eastwards with a plume of smoke issuing from its tail, and the big Juno engine stuttering.

'I hope you catch fire, you bastard!' I scream at it. 'I hope you fry slowly all the way to hell!'

I am shaking uncontrollably. My hands clasping the Lewis in a painful grip. I can claim a hit but I feel no elation; only an all-consuming hate for the animals responsible for all this. Looking towards the bridge I see Martingale taking charge without fuss. Stepping into his demanding role like a natural born leader. He is a professional and has already shrugged away the shock of losing his skipper, to take hold of his emotions and concentrate on what has to be done. Slowly it dawns on my numbed brain that I must reload.

That helps me to control my nerves, and the shaking stops. I search the sky for the next attacker as I fumble with a new magazine. To the west flames are licking the underside of the heavy smoke, providing a dramatic background to the crane jibs leaning drunkenly above the wrecked buildings. The wind still carries the smoke out to sea and I can see the endless line of men on the east mole waiting patiently to board ships as they come in under the barrage. The Luftwaffe are having a field day as they approach almost unopposed to select their targets.

Dozens of vessels churn through the mess, each one anxious to pick up its quota of soldiery and get to hell out of this insanity. They are a conglomeration of cross-channel steamers, trawlers, destroyers and a hotch-potch of smaller craft more suited to the sheltered waters of tributaries or harbours. All the time the abominable cacophony blasts our eardrums, and the sky stays mottled with flak.

Looking towards the beach, it is hard to define where the sea ends and the beach begins. The area is littered with abandoned boats and rubbish. As yet the front-line troops have not arrived, and there is disorder amongst the less disciplined groups. Shameful displays of self-preservation that has to be quelled at gun-point in some cases. Most of them are headquarters staff, but there are also men who have deserted and thrown down their weapons to run. They have looted shops and houses en route, and stolen from their own mates. They make a wild mob, clammering for places in the boats, and willing to stampede over anyone to get aboard. They make it bad for the majority who try to maintain calm and form up in orderly lines.

One thing shines through it all. A respect for anyone in naval uniform. Once they are picked up they are convinced their troubles are over, and faithfully place their lives in our hands. It is a humbling experience as we watch them pack into every available corner and prepare

to enjoy their trip home. We have to persuade them to go
down the ladders, for Martingale insists on stowing as
many as possible below deck to keep our stability. We cram
them into the engine-rooms and stores, and stuff them
into any space big enough to take a man. Anything to get
them off the upper-deck. I try to shut out the vision of
what could happen if we are struck by a torpedo.

'Aircraft green two five! Angle of sight four five!' The
lookout's report coincides with the thump of the Bofors
and the heavier bark of the main armament. I am fighting
a losing battle with the magazine, and the more I struggle
the worse it gets. I curse the blasted thing. I can't think of
anything more frustrating than a useless gun when the
enemy is falling out of the sky and I beat my anger out on
the hard black casing. It is one thing to stand there and
squeeze the trigger, but I am a fumbling idiot when it
comes to clipping on a reload. I look round desperately for
someone to show me how it is done, but they are all much
too busy with their own affairs.

A chorus of protest comes as Martingale increases
speed, dragging the last, half-filled carley-raft along.
Inevitably the rope parts and it rolls away, spilling men
over the side while others wave angry fists at us. One
panic-stricken squaddy makes a vain effort to leap for the
guardrail and anxious hands reach out for him, only to
watch helplessly as he falls back screaming into the wash.
We close our ears to him as he is swept aft into the white
water at the stern. The ship's propellers have a gluttonous
day today.

There is room ahead to make our turn, and Martingale
stands over the binnacle voicing helm orders to the
coxswain below. He ignores the bedlam of the guns and
the menace from the sky, for he needs to concentrate on
the manoeuvre. We all pray that the swing will spoil the
aim of the bombers as they poise for another attack. I go
on struggling with the blasted magazine, cursing my
incompetence and my fumbling hands.

It must be a simple operation for anyone who knows the

drill. Some snappy catch or other that I cannot find. The aircraft are coming in and I hammer my fist on the drum in frustration when I hear the scream of engines.

This time they are hell-bent for the mole and the clutch of vessels moored alongside. A paddle-steamer thrashes her way astern with her deck crowded with troops, all watching the incoming Dornier with hypnotic trepidation. She slows to a stop as her skipper goes ahead on one wheel and astern on the other to pivot her towards the open sea.

The bomb hits her amidships, throwing up a huge fountain of wreckage and dirty water. She staggers, reels, and begins to settle. Her skipper must be a quick thinker for her paddles are already turning in unison to drive her towards the beach. He is intent on running her up onto the sand, but it is a vain gesture, for the green ocean is pouring in through the gaping hole forward and she is sinking upright to deck-level with fire and smoke spewing from her bows. An avalanche of panic-stricken soldiery sweeps aft like a tidal-wave over her decks.

'We can make our turn now, sir,' I hear the navigator remind his new captain. He is anxious that we do not miss the opportunity.

'Forget it,' replies Martingale sharply. 'We are going alongside the paddler. You will have to squeeze the troops in tighter; put them in the boiler-room if necessary.' He lifts his head to yell, 'Get some fenders over the side forward!' and ignores the sharp look of the yeoman who is holding the signal ordering us to pull out immediately.

I have given up on the Lewis. It seems to be well and truly jammed, and there is no one available to help me. I stand transfixed as we move in gingerly towards the smoking wreck. Pongoes are milling about like scared ants; desperately pressing into their mates in their efforts to escape the fire in the bow. Suddenly someone sees a destroyer nosing in towards them and his wild cry brings a full-throated response from his oppos. Trampling everything and everyone underfoot they swarm aft towards the poop-deck. A tall column of spray lifts to starboard and collapses inboard to drench the struggling men as a shell bursts alongside. The navigator goes right up into the bows with a drawn revolver, shouting down into the crowd, urging them to stay calm as the last few yards are eaten up.

Now there are NCOs and officers forcing their way through the mob, striving to make themselves heard above the racket. Their sober, angry barks penetrate the incoherent ravings, gradually restoring order, and the chaos subsides when the troops realise that the ship is no longer sinking, and the fire, although still burning fiercely, is taking time to eat its way aft.

'Aircraft attacking dead astern, sir!' This time it is a sub-lieutenant shouting the message as he perches on the director-platform, waving an arm wildly to point at yet another Stuka hurtling down at us. We see the bomb leave its bay and plunge unerringly into X gun deck, penetrating the thin plates into a wardroom filled to over-flowing with Army officers. It explodes with a thunderous detonation, hurling death and destruction in all directions. The deafening howl of the aircraft swamps all other sound as it climbs away in triumph, leaving behind a smoking ruin on *Brigand*'s stern, with the 4.7 inch gun leaning over the side amidst the crimson-streaked carnage. No one has survived on either of the two after guns, and bodies of sailors are twisted into an untidy pile with those of the officers.

'Get the men moving, pilot!' Martingale's voice is drained of emotion. There are screams from aft but they must be ignored; left to those whose duty it is to attend to the butchery. Right now the only thing in the first lieutenant's mind is getting his command away. Even the sound of exploding ammunition from ready-use lockers must be disregarded, along with the knowledge that two whole racks of depth-charges wait with their lethal contents poised to erupt.

A bare-headed sergeant stands on the bulwarks of the

paddler, bellowing at the men with a voice that lifts even above the uproar. He is feeding the soldiers up to our lads, using his fists when necessary, while an army captain backs up the navigator with his own revolver, calming the frantic men as they are torn between the smoking threat creeping up from behind and the exploding menace of the destroyer. Some run about like headless chickens, needing to be over-powered and dragged aft by their more stable mates. Others jump overside, only to realise with horror that the sea is too deep, and their screams turn into gurgling sounds of despair as they are swept away.

A bridge telephone whines and a subby grabs the receiver. He waits a moment while Martingale passes more orders down through the voicepipe before chanting his message. 'Damage control report, sir. Wardroom gutted – X and Y guns out of action – fire under control – cannot estimate number of casualties.'

'Very good,' comes the laconic standard response.

The smoke drifts over us, choking us with its oily stench, but hiding us from marauding aircraft. Its stinking filth is everywhere, clogging our nostrils and burning our throats, but we bless its comforting blanket and the momentary relief it brings as the last survivors are dragged on board.

'Half ahead together!'The screws bite and *Brigand* judders with the vibration as she slides astern in a long curving turn. Martingale watches her lean bow arc across the burning wreck of the paddler and the grim panorama of the beach, until it points eastwards to take us out towards the Kwinte Bouy; ten miles off Ostend. This is the longest of the three routes across the Channel. The shortest, past Calais, is not possible: The Germans have it covered from shore with their artillery. The next is through the Ruytingen Channel, between the outer and inner Ruytingen Banks, too risky for our over-loaded destroyer. Therefore it has to be the longest route, round the Kwinte Bouy, then west to the North Goodwins.

We are coming abreast of La Panne, where the muffled

rumble of battle drifts out to us as we drift slowly by. The sound is interspersed with the heavier detonation of big guns and bombs. Our wake surges in amongst the flotsam at the water's edge, causing bodies to bob amid the debris in the disturbed sea. In one place it catches the stern of a ship's lifeboat, spilling its human contents out when it is hurled on to its beam-ends.

Now Martingale has eyes only for the distant buoy; his face is set in a deep frown as he watches it come closer. It is a very important buoy; so important it is permanently lit even in these times, and the Germans are only too aware of this vital turning point. Their E boats lurk in the vicinity, waiting for just such a juicy target as we offer. We advertise our approach with the cloud of smoke pouring from our stern, and there isn't an E-boat commander worth his salt who will miss the chance to sink us and our cargo of men. Already there are wrecks lying about with garbage spewing out across the area, and my heart is pumping fast as we shape up for the turn.

Steering straight for the buoy *Brigand*'s lookouts and gunners search the haze for the first suspicion of a low silhouette. Every gun is loaded and primed, every red- rimmed eye tuned for the first sighting. I hear the judder of the director above my head as it rotates in small arcs; its powerful optics watching for the first target to appear. The troops sense the tension and withdraw into themselves as their initial elation at being picked up evaporates and is replaced with gut-knotting anxiety. They see the strained expressions on the sailors faces and try to read a clue to what lies ahead. We have to force ourselves to watch the sky, for our eyes are drawn to the area beyond the buoy, and the smoking remains of ships that have failed to run the gauntlet.

'There they are! Two of the sods!' The unorthodox shout comes from a scruffy individual hitherto unnoticed as he stands in the background. All eyes swivel to follow his outstretched arm as a more formal report comes from a lookout to confirm his sighting. 'Two torpedo boats – red one five and closing!'

The ferry skipper grunts and lowers his arm again as everyone launches into the drill. His old, tired face is set in a grim mask as he watches the activity. His ship is gone, and with it part of his soul. He knows that at his age his ferrying days are over, and the tumult going on about him has little effect on his desolate world.

'Stand-to surface port – bearing red one five – target is an E-boat – All guns follow director!' A and B guns train onto the bearing, their muzzles lifting and falling to the roll of the ship as they range on the target. There is a mirage effect today that lifts the vague shapes of the E-boats clear of the surface to give them a surrealistic image. They appear to skim over the water with huge bow-waves lifting either side of their bows: squat, evil-looking beasts, with the gaping mouths of their torpedo tubes staring out at us, wide-eyed and menacing.

'Shoot!' A and B guns bark simultaneously, and the acrid tang of burnt cordite wafts over me.

'Blast!' Martingale spits the word. 'There's no room to swing in the channel with those bloody wrecks dotted all over the place. We need to alter course to bring the pom-poms to bear.'

I can see his problem. We need the space to take evasive action when the torpedoes come. The course we are on is a suicidal one, and there seems no way to avoid presenting a perfect set-up for the Germans. With only A and B guns available and the pom-pom hidden behind the mass of superstructure the E-boats have it all their own way.

'Full ahead both!' he orders suddenly. 'Port ten!'

Even a slight swing will spoil the aim of the E-boats. He ignores the navigator's warning shout as he brings the bow across to the inside of the buoy. At point-blank range the guns blaze away. Their crews are well-trained professionals with cold nerves, who have gone through the mind-bending drills of Whale Island that turn men into automatons. Layers line their pointers up with those of the director. The interceptors close. Gun-ready lamps wink, and after the warning gong sounds the barrels belch flame. The leading boat disintegrates in an eruption of vivid yellow and red; the bow splays open like the skin of a banana.

Now the pom-pom can bear and the raucous chatter of the multiple barrels joins in the chorus, pouring a stream of shells in a low arc across the opalescent sea.

'Shift target left!' The smoking muzzles of the big guns train round even as their loaders ram in shells and cartridges.

'Torpedo tracks – dead ahead!' The lookout's scream snaps Martingale's head round to see the two tell-tale lines of bubbles converging on *Brigand*.

'Midships!' he orders to stop the swing. 'Meet her – steer three two zero!'

I hear the navigator suck in his breath even from here as both tracks run down our port side with six yards to spare. The other E-boat leans into her turn now – wide open to our guns. The four-sevens roar in a concerted salvo, while the pulsating rhythm of the pom-pom persists as the layer brings his target into his sights. A flicker of flame grows out of the soft belly and spreads aft for a second before enveloping the whole craft with a blinding sheet of flame as she is blasted out of the water.

Cheering soldiers hardly notice the jolt as *Brigand*'s keel ploughs a furrow through the soft mud and her port screw is wrenched out of its bracket. Her speed carries her on into clear water beyond the sand-bank, but already Damage Control is reporting buckled plates and ruptured seams, with water pouring into the bilges. Now our speed drops dramatically as we skew into a tight turn. Unless this is quickly rectified we will run back into the shallows again.

The starboard propeller threshes madly as Martingale attempts to drag us back into deep water, but despite full rudder we still swing the wrong way, arse-first this time, so that we are in danger of digging our working parts into the mud. Ominously the whine of her engines dies and all vibration ceases. *Brigand* wallows in the water, her passengers subdued and silent again as they sense a new danger. The sultry sun beats down on the blank surface of a limpid sea, and we wait with taut nerves for the next attack.

Twice we go ahead with the rudder hard-a-starboard to counteract the screw, dangling eveything possible over the side to create some drag. Twice we run aground, and eventually Martingale has to admit defeat. Our radio screams for help and we try to control our nerves while we wait for a tug to come and rescue us.

Suddenly the GI is beside me. I offer up the magazine for him to clip into place, and he does it automatically. I can see that his mind is on other things. 'You'd better have these,' he grunts without looking at me, handing over a set of dog-tags. I stare down at the embossed details. The name reads 'Jack Royal'.

'I'd better go down,' I say, easing out to pass him. He places an arm out to stop me. 'Don't bother; you won't recognise him. There are a lot like him down there, with their faces burned away.'

I feel a surge of guilt for my first reaction is gratitude, for if someone had to die, I'm glad it was Royal. I can hear the weariness in the GI's voice as he concentrates on the Lewis. As far as I am concerned Royal was a nonentity, a man with a past that had turned his attitude bitter and morose; not the type of bloke to mix well with his messmates. I shrug the thought away. 'My other blokes are okay then?'

'Christ knows!' he mutters solemnly. 'We won't be able to sort out that lot until we get back to Dover.'

We get down to another crash course on Lewis guns so that I am able to change my own magazines in future. When he is gone I am left alone with my sweaty maulers clamped on the warm metal, staring out into the heat-haze, hoping the Germans will leave us alone for a while.

Fate seems to have had its fill of us today. We are spared any further visitations, and the tug comes blustering up with a bone in her teeth. She circles us once to give her skipper time to weigh up the situation, then she pushes her squat stern against ours and in short time we are being towed ignominiously arse-first towards Dover. The Germans miss their golden opportunity to despatch one of His Majesty's best destroyers. We pass through the heads into the bustle of the harbour and shout through the loud-hailer for a place to berth. Another harbour tug comes to help her mate push us tidily against the wall, and Martingale rings down 'Finished with main engines'.

The squaddies begin to disembark while our blokes go below to examine the damage. I leave the Lewis slumped on its stand and go over to the other wing to stare down onto the jetty where tired men are shuffling into disconsolate lines under the stern eyes of their sergeants who attempt to re-kindle a little military swank into them. Further aft stretchers are being carried across to waiting ambulances. Some of the inert shapes have blankets drawn up over their faces, and no doubt Royal is amongst them. I close my mind to that and look away from the grim procession. All the while the deep grumble of distant gunfire rolls in from the Channel, sounding as though the Continent is suffering the biggest guts-ache of all time.

My eyes are drawn to a separate party of squaddies drawn up away from the rest. Something about them makes me stare even harder, and then I realise these men are in full marching order. Each one carries his rifle and wears his helmet squarely as a tall sergeant struts along the ranks muttering at them. His back is ram-rod stiff, and his rifle is slung smartly over his braced shoulder. I squint at his shoulder-flashes to see which Guards regiment he represents. It tells me he is from the Middlesex Regiment, and as I watch he begins to talk to them in a low coaxing voice. 'Come on, me lads. Bags of swank. Remember who you are. 'Awkins, you are standin' like a pregnant duck – brace up, fer Gawd's sake!' He stretches his body tall. 'Company – *Shun!*'

Heels slam together. They waver, red-eyed with fatigue, but they are attracting the attention of watching sailors

and soldiers. The sergeant waits while they gather
strength for his next order. 'Left turn – Quick march!'

They move off, hob-nailed boots hitting the ground
cleanly, arms swinging. Their sodden uniforms shapeless
on their tired bodies and salt-stained boots moving in
unison, they go like a phalanx of zombies past the rabble
who belong to no one, and can only stare derisively at this
pointless display of military pride.

Something lodges in my gullet, threatening to choke me
as I watch the small unit disappear round the corner. I
stare after them long after they have gone out of sight, and
I can still see them in my mind's eye. I feel like spitting at
the shambling horde of griping afterguard who have to be
driven like sheep to their waiting trucks. These are the
men who are unstiffened by battle. Untried and untested;
sickened by the futility of something that has gone
desperately wrong. Some bury their shame, for they have
the awesome knowledge that when the chips were down
they threw away everything, including their pride, and
ran. Some will shake the guilt away, even convince
themselves that theirs was the intelligent way and there is
no place in a real world for military swank. Others will live
with the nightmare all their lives and wake sweating in the
darkness with terrible visions imprinted on their minds.

The small column of infantry have no such misgivings.
They have no cause to be ashamed. They were pushed
into something they could not fully understand, and they
have done all that could be expected of them. Theirs is not
the all-consuming pride of the Guards, nor the fanatical
zeal of the enemy, but they behaved like soldiers right up
to the end and marched proudly away to prepare to fight
again.

I am totally lost in my contemplations as I lean over the
side; oblivious to what goes on behind me until
Martingale's voice comes from beyond the signal-lamp.

'I'm sorry, sir,' he is saying in a solemn voice. 'To lose
one's ship – I cannot begin to imagine how you must feel.'

I peer round the corner in time to see the old ferry

skipper go down the ladder. His tired footsteps are replaced by a brisker pair on the steel rungs as the head and shoulders of a lieutenant heave into view. He looks utterly out of place in a smartly cut uniform. I withdraw into my own little corner, an unwilling eavesdropper to their conversation.

He has a plummy voice that goes well with his immaculate uniform, and there is an admonishing flavour to his tone. It is difficult to retain one's dignity on the war-stained bridge of a scruffy destroyer; littered with the remains of her ordeal and the residue of a shattered army. His place is obviously on the bleached quarterdeck of a flagship with a telescope tucked under his arm or a pink gin in his hand. Beside him Martingale looks like the skipper of a tramp steamer.

'You are required to present yourself at Dover Castle tomorrow at oh-nine-three-oh to make a full report to Captain Luff. In particular, he will wish to learn your reasons for disregarding a direct order to pull out from Dunkirk. I will arrange transport for you if you can be ready at oh-nine-three-oh. You should bring with you a full list of damage and repairs needed to make *Brigand* ready for sea. I would advise a concise report, with no unnecessary embellishment. Captain Luff has no time for erroneous ramblings.' At no time during this spiel does he look directly at Martingale.

'Do I have to wear sword and medals?'

The sarcasm is lost on this bumptious sod. 'That will not be necessary Only a nucleus of the ship's company will remain in *Brigand*; the remainder are already being assigned to other duties.'

'May I ask where they are going?'

'I haven't the full details to hand, but I do know that some are to replace men in one of the V class destroyers. There has been a little trouble, and the medics have classed some of her ship's company as being unfit for duty.'

'Oh, what sort of trouble?'

I can hear the lieutenant shuffle uncomfortably. 'I do not know the full details, but it seems they are reluctant to sail back to Dunkirk without a break. Therefore, we are replacing some of her crew and resting her overnight. There has been similar disturbances on some of the ferries; and several RNLI lifeboat coxswains have refused to go because they say their boats are unsuitable for operating on the beaches. The war brings out the best and the worst in us, Martingale.'

'Yes, well you'd see that; tucked away in your nice little office, you are in a much better position to know what it is all about,' sneers Martingale. 'They are probably right about the lifeboats; they are not suited to running up in the shallows, and no use to anyone lying on their beam-ends in the surf.'

The sarcasm still doesn't register; this bloke must have a hide like a rhino. 'That is a matter of opinion. The fact remains that other members of *Brigand*'s ship's company are to go to the ferries, and we are putting three badgemen and leading hands in charge of the lifeboats, with naval crews.'

'Where does that leave me?'

'You will remain here until Captain Luff can see you.'

'Kicking my bloody heels!' protests Martingale. There is a bloody emergency on, lieutenant. Everyone is needed – can't the post mortem wait, for Christ's sake!'

The prim staff officer is getting piqued. 'We cannot run the Navy to suit you, sir. If I may speak bluntly for a moment, you have already exceeded your authority by not withdrawing from Dunkirk when you were ordered out. If you had obeyed orders *Brigand* would not be in the state she is in now. We would have a valuable front-line destroyer available, and you would probably be in top line for a command. As it is, I will tell you quite frankly, I doubt whether you will be given as much as a trawler.'

I tense for an outburst from Martingale, but he must have seen something in the other man's face that warns him to remain silent. You could hang a hat on the atmosphere as they face each other, and finally it is the shore-based man who backs down. He mumbles something about expressing only the views of his seniors and turns to leave. 'Initiative is one thing, Martingale. You must believe that we cannot have individuals taking ships all over the place at will.'

'All I see is a picture of a beach swarming with the cream of British manhood, waiting to escape death or capture, lieutenant. I do not see the sense of holding inquisitions when there is work to be done.'

The other man has reached the top of the ladder. 'That is not your decision. I look forward to seeing you in the morning.' His feet clatter down the ladder, leaving behind a void to be filled with the noise of distant gunfire and the softer, echoing sounds of the harbour. Away to the east the sky glows an unearthly mixure of yellow and red to reflect the sunset behind me. The first shadows of evening dilute the colours of the harbour, turning everything to sombre shades of drabness. A cross-channel steamer blares a deep-throated warning as she enters through the gate, asking for a place to berth so that she can unload her crowded decks. A metallic voice replies and she moves in like a ghost ship towards the pier just astern of us. There is something mysterious about her in the twilight as she sidles against the wall.

Beneath my feet I feel the vibration of our generators pumping warmth and light throughout the broken ship, and I watch the ferry's masts come into line and blend with the black background of the town. There is a funereal quality now, as though the full tragedy of what is taking place across the water registers at last on this side of the Channel, to be felt in the very fabric of the port. The gloom settles like a cloak, and black figures of disembarking soldiers pour like liquid down the gangways to line up in disconsolate groups, ready to be marched off to their trains. I find I can no longer bear to watch, and I turn away, to come face to face with Martingale.

'You've been here all the time,' he accuses.

'Yes, sir.'

'Eavesdropping on officers' conversation?'

'You could say that, sir.'

He studies my face for a moment. My skin must look sallow and violet like his in the half-light, with deep-set, hollow eyes, red-rimmed with exhaustion. Night is coming in fast now, turning our faces into cratered skulls as it casts its depression across the scene. The blacked-out buildings made a sad backdrop to the great drama being played out here in the harbour. The darkness holds on to the sharp barks of the sergeants as they bellow at their men, while the deep rumble of distant war merges with the whisperings of the restless water round the hull. He turns to place both hands on the rail, staring out into the shadows.

'You said you were a submariner, Grant?'

'Sir.'

'Eavesdropping must be a natural hazard in those tin-cans, I imagine. There must be few places to hold confidential conversations.'

I don't answer. He is building up to something and I do not wish to interrupt his thoughts. A heavy rumble of sound rolls in from the sea: I dread to think what it means. The glow continues to paint the eastern sky, pulsating like the dying breath of a stricken beast. Vessels creep in and out of the port like black phantoms. Bustling tugs nudge larger ships in and out of their berths. The crews of two destroyers are so exhausted the harbourmen take over and shift them without help. In some cases they have to wrench the hawsers from the numbed hands of the crew who can hardly stand.

'It is all over in France now, Grant. In a few days the whole of Germany will be celebrating. Swastikas flying from every vantage point, and Aryan faces glowing with pride and joy. Hitler, Göring, Himmler, and all the gang will receive the unqualified accolade of a nation who will be more convinced than ever that they are the super-race, and totally invincible. Their Führer has dragged them out of their shame and despair to victory and glory. Without doubt they are the greatest military power on earth. Right now the English Channel must look like a very fordable stream. If we do not get our army back we may as well begin negotiating with our new Führer.' His voice gets harder. 'I do not intend to spend another night and half a day twiddling my thumbs waiting for a stupid bloody enquiry.' He hammers his fist hard on the rail and goes silent for a moment.

'I'm concerned about me and my lads, sir.' I say quietly. 'We are not part of *Brigand*'s company, and at a loose end at the moment.

He looks at me intently, as if my words have formulated a new idea in his head. 'That's true, Grant. I doubt if they have any record of you here. What do you intend to do: go back to your submarine?'

I think for a second or so. 'No, sir. *Scavenger* is not due out of dock for another week yet. I will have to report somewhere I suppose. I've lost one of my blokes, but I still have a stoker PO and a young OD if I can find them. There must be someone in authority to give us another berth. I wouldn't mind taking one of those lifeboats across.'

'How would you like to stick with me? I can use you as an excuse to have another go at the lieutenant. Maybe together we can persuade him to change his stance. If not, frankly, I'm not above taking things into my own hands and worrying about the consequences later. "In for a penny," as they say.'

I don't even hesitate. There is something about this bloke that I like. If I am going to chance my arm I'd just as soon do it with him. 'I'll go and find the others, sir. We can get some grub together and meet you wherever you say.'

He is full of enthusiasm now. 'No, Grant. We will go to see this feller together. Find your chaps by all means. Tell them to get the grub, while you come with me. I'll give you five minutes, then meet me at the brow.'

'Aye aye, sir.'

Finney is crashed out on a bench in the POs' mess and responds with his usual laconic indifference. 'What's wrong with just sittin' 'ere and waitin' fer them ter come and find us. What's got inter yer these days, Ben? You've got the volunteering bug.'

'It's better than being roped in with a crowd of pusser-bound general service sheep, isn't it?' I insist. I need him with me this time, because he is part of my world.

'What do yer want me ter do?' he asks guardedly.

'Round up Maundy and get some grub, then meet me at the brow in about an hour from now.'

'What about that bloke Royal?'

'He's dead,' I say flatly. 'I'm not keen to take Maundy, but he will be out on a limb if we leave him here.'

'Royal dead!' he exclaims, coming to life at last. 'Bloody hell!' He looks shocked. 'Not that I liked the bloke much.' He swings his legs off the bench and stares thoughtfully at the deck. 'I caught 'im lookin' at the bodies when they was stretched aht on the deck. Liftin' the blankets as if 'e was lookin' fer someone. Queer bird 'e was, but I didn't reckon on him gettin himself killed.' He shakes his head slowly. 'There are some sods yer reckon will never get killed; mostly the ones who wouldn't be missed anyway. 'E was one of that sort as far as I'm concerned.'

'There's no need for that kind of talk; he's had it now.'

He looks up. 'Yeah, I know. He gave me the fuckin' creeps though. Twice I fahnd 'im nosin' rahnd those bodies when 'e thought no-one was lookin'. He backed orf sharpish when 'e saw me lookin' at 'im. I reckon he was some kind of pervert, and I don't believe all that shit abaht the Merchant Navy either.' He clamps his scruffy old cap over his oily hair and stands up. 'I'll go see if I can find the other useless bastard.' He fires one final shot. 'We could be sittin' back in barracks now, yer know.'

I watch him slope off, scratching his backside as he shuffles down the passage. I climb up to the upper deck where the last few pongoes are crossing the gangway. It is totally dark now; the blackness thick and heavy. Martingale is waiting for me when I step ashore, and we go off together without speaking.

*

Lieutenant Dalby is spluttering with indignation when he is rooted out of the hotel lounge by a terse message scribbled on the back of the card he gave Martingale back at the ship. This is the first time I get a good look at him, and what I see doesn't impress me. He has a round, polished, pink face and small button-mouth that pouts all the time. Now he looks as though he has been scrubbed with a wire-brush for his cheeks are aglow with anger. In his soft, pudgy hand he clasps his card; and he is livid at the blunt wording scrawled in large capitals for all to read, including hotel flunkeys and underlings like me. The message demands an immediate interview with someone in authority, and Lieutenant Martingale is no diplomat when it comes to dealing with pompous captain's secretaries.

'I cannot possibly disturb Captain Luff now. Do you think you are the only one he has to deal with?'

'No,' grates Martingale heavily, 'but except for yourself I seem to be the only officer unemployed at the moment, and I have no intention of sitting on my arse while the cream of the British army is stranded in Dunkirk.'

Dalby's face goes puce. 'My God, you are an arrogant swine! Luff and his staff have been working non-stop for over fifty hours. He has been ordered to take a rest, and it is my job to see that he gets it.' His face seems to collapse, and for the first time the fatigue shows through his facade. Martingale sees it too for his manner changes abruptly. 'All right, Dalby. Forgive my rudeness. We are all under strain, but I can't sit here like this.'

Dalby slumps. 'We are all under stress, Martingale.'

'Nevertheless I would like to see someone now.'

Dalby sighs. 'That is impossible.'

'Then I must go up to the castle. If you cannot help me I must find my own way.'

'Without a pass you will not get past the gate, let alone into the Dynamo Room. You are wasting your time and your breath.'

Martingale snatches the white card. 'I'll use this, and my uniform. I am determined to get a message through somehow, believe me. I will go to Admiral Ramsay himself, if necessary. I am sure he would be concerned to learn that his officers and sailors are kicking their heels while he is desperate for manpower.'

Dalby is quivering now, puffing himself up like a blow-fish. I have no sympathy for him. Lack of sleep is the least of the problems for those involved in the evacuation. He can snore his fat head off once he has sorted our problem out. 'Don't be ridiculous,' he scoffs. 'There is a certain protocol to observe. That card means nothing.'

Martingale adopts a threatening stance; thrusting his face inches from the other man's. 'If you keep me arsing about here until mid-morning I will stir up the biggest stink you've ever known, lieutenant.' He draws back a little. 'Anyway, Chief Petty Officer Grant and his party are waiting for their orders. I would go with them if necessary, if that is all that's on offer.'

Dalby crumbles. He looks from Martingale to me then back again. His voice is weak now. 'All personnel should report to the regulating office at the harbour,' he blusters lamely. 'However, wait here please. I will make a telephone call.' He waddles off, leaving us to shuffle uncomfortably in the plush surroundings.

I am conscious of my dirty uniform. The big, ornate double-doors constantly swing open to allow a two-way stream of traffic to flow through. Civilians, officers; they crinkle their sensitive noses when they come close. We have brought the stink of Dunkirk with us and it sours the elegant atmosphere of the foyer.

When Dalby returns we are surprised to see a smirk of satisfaction transforming his features. 'Not only have I found you a ship, Martingale, but you can take these people with you as your crew. It isn't a destroyer, of course. I know you would not expect that. However, it is a command.' His smirk grows even wider.

'Oh?' Martingale queries in a suspicious voice.

'There is a TRV at Ramsgate. If you can arrange for a signalman and a couple of hands she is yours.' He waves a disparaging hand. 'Not as glamorous as a destroyer perhaps, but I'm sure that is of small concern to someone as eager as you are to get back to the war. Who knows, you might even regain some of your lost prestige if you play your cards right.'

The sod! I would thump his conceited face if I was Martingale. But the smirk is wiped from his face quickly when he doesn't get the reaction he expected.

'Great!' exclaims Martingale, clapping a grateful hand on Dalby's shoulder. 'Those torpedo recovery vessels are exactly what is required over there. The destroyers can't get within a mile of the beach, and these old buckets have hardly any draught at all forward when they are in ballast. Well done, Dalby. Grant will make an ideal number one, and if you will arrange transport I will take my yeoman of signals, a stoker, and a couple of seamen to back up Grant's men.'

Dalby is spluttering again. 'Surely you will need an officer for your second-in-command?'

'Why – are you volunteering?'

The lips tighten. 'You haven't a monopoly on courage, sir. My duty is here. I would go if I could, of course.'

He gets a placating pat on the shoulder. 'I'm sure you would,' smiles Martingale. 'It must be hell to stay here when everything is happening over there. As regards a second officer: not on your life! I don't want a wet-eared ex-yachtsman prancing about on my bridge when I can have a professional NCO up there. Grant is a submarine coxswain, and what he doesn't know about the job isn't worth knowing.'

Brimming over with self-esteem I follow him out. He

calls back over his shoulder to Dalby as we leave. 'I'll send you a list of names and numbers for your records, lieutenant. I wouldn't want anyone to be posted adrift. Thanks. You have been most helpful.'

I'd go anywhere with this bloke. I fall into step with him as we hurry back to the ship. It is difficult to pick our way through the darkness, but eventually we reach *Brigand* to find Finney waiting for us at the gangway with two civilians. The shortest of the two is wearing a gabardine raincoat and a trilby, the prototype version of a movie detective, but it is the angular one with the long, sad face that steps forward. 'Chief Petty Officer Grant?'

'That's me.'

'I am Inspector Thrush, this is Detective Constable Sully. I would like to ask you a couple of questions before you sail.'

'Oh?' I have the average citizen's suspicion of policemen.

'It's about Jack Royal; Petty Officer Finney tells me he is one of your men?'

'Was. He is dead now.'

He exchanges looks with his stubby mate. 'So we are told. We will need to confirm that, chief. Would you accompany me to identify the body?'

'By what I'm told his own mother wouldn't recognise him. He was blasted to hell by a bomb.'

'That's as maybe. You haven't seen the body then?'

'No, but I have handed in his dog-tags.'

'There shouldn't be any real problem,' he says quietly. 'However, just to satisfy me I would like you to have a look. You see I have a warrant for his arrest. I'm sure you realise that I can insist on your co-operation. I promise I won't keep you from your duty for long, chief. All I want is for you to look at the body and see if you can recognise something that makes you certain it is Royal. The bodies have all been taken to a church hall close to the docks.'

Martingale intervenes. 'We are on our way to our ship, Inspector. I suggest you take Grant with you now, and we will pick him up from there in thirty minutes.'

'Good idea, sir.'

The two rows of corpses are ranged along the walls with their feet towards the centre of the hall. There is no describing the smell, and my stomach is churning as we walk along the line until we reach the one with the label reading 'Jack Royal'. The stocky man lifts away the canvas and I steel myself to stare down at the charred mess that was once a face. No one could possibly recognise that horror. I can see that it is a human head because there is a gleaming set of teeth snarling at me out of what looks like a crushed strawberry.

The blanket is pulled right down to reveal most of the upper trunk, and there is still shredded remains of clothing welded to the flesh. That is how I know that the body is not Jack Royal. I am about to say so when I realise that if I do it will lead to complications, and I could miss the boat. I stare straight into Thrush's eyes. 'It could be anyone,' I say in all truth.

He is a persistent bastard and I don't get away with it that easily. 'There is nothing there to tell you it is not Royal?'

I stare down at the charred remains of black jersey that I know Royal was not wearing. 'Nothing,' I lie.

He is studying my face intently. 'When was the last time you saw him?'

'Before we got off the beach. I manned the Lewis gun on the bridge. The others stayed down on the upper-deck.'

'Right, chief,' he says soberly. 'I don't want to keep you from your war, I'm ex-navy myself. However, I must tell you that I am not satisfied with this, and if I find you have deliberately withheld information I will bring you to book. This is no time for closing ranks, Grant, even for a shipmate.'

'If you think anyone can identify that chunk of burnt meat, inspector, bloody good luck to you,' I grate. 'We will bring back another selection if you like.' I turn to walk away, and hesitate. 'By the way, what's the charge?'

'Murder,' he says bluntly.

III

Thursday dawns misty and calm. The buses got us to the ship just after midnight and Martingale insisted that we rest up for a few hours, so I allow everyone to sleep until five o'clock. Water is the urgent need of the troops in Dunkirk now, and we load hundreds of easy-to-carry cans of the precious liquid. Finney's new assistant recovers from his initial revulsion at the appearance of his boss and learns to respect the underlying expertise that hides beneath the oily exterior as they get to grips with their engine. On the bridge Petty Officer Borroughs, yeoman of signals, sets about organising his 'flag deck', and makes it plain that he will brook no interference from outsiders when it comes to communications. He shows his competence when he begins to decypher ambiguous signals from second-rate bunting-tossers who have been dragged prematurely from training school for the occasion.

We become part of a fleet of miscellaneous craft plodding towards France. The small convoys are merging so that it is impossible to tell where one lot ends and the next begins. Skeins of ships' lifeboats and naval whalers are towed along by anything with a reasonable engine, the huddled shapes of their lonely helmsmen peering anxiously ahead. Few have any arms on board, for every available Lewis gun and close-range weapon have been issued to tugs and escorts.

We go by the middle route this time; through the Ruytingen Channel, grateful for the blanket of low mist that shields us from the sky. As we make our approach we are appalled by the increased squallor that spreads like a

48

disease from the grey sands, spilling out to merge with a scum of floating garbage, while a large freighter drifts powerless amid the outlying shallows with her hull aglow with internal fires. Our TRV picks her way through sunken craft of all shape and size, trying to avoid hundreds of small boats plying between ship and shore with pitiful cargoes of exhausted pongoes.

Finney admits that he did not make too much of an effort to find Maundy, especially after he was interrupted by the police, and I'm not sorry to lose the inadequate reservist. Much as I disliked Royal, I have to admit that he was worth ten of his mate when it came to seamanship. Leading Seaman 'Chopper' Burgess is on the helm, responding easily to every command from Martingale as he coaxes us in towards the East Mole.

The awful stink of the burning port slithers out to us from under the black pall that spreads its oppressive shadow across the sombre scene. There are other ships grouped round the mole, and a staggered queue of men shuffling along in small batches, moving as though they are in a hypnotic trance, and allowing themselves to be badgered into line by naval shore-parties. The constant blast of shells have lost their power to terrify numbed minds as the Germans bombard the harbour with everything they have. They have been almost too clever, for they have the range so well calculated that their shells are landing in the centre of the pool and doing no real harm. Nonetheless, some do find their targets and blow big gaps in the mole which have to be bridged by anything that can be utilised for the purpose, and there are plenty of waterlogged bodies floating in the murky water beneath.

Martingale has to hold us off while a cross-channel steamer comes out astern with her decks thronged with men, and while we are hove-to a small dinghy ranges alongside with a tall, elegant major standing upright like an out-of-work admiral between the thwarts, and a sad little corporal manning the tiller. The major boards the

TRV and looks about him with an air of disdain as he contemplates the spartan conditions in our puny little ship with its high fo'c'sle, square wheelhouse and open bridge. For a moment it looks as if he is about to climb back into his boat, but he sets aside his prejudices and picks his way aft through the deck-gear until he comes face to face with Martingale.

His eyebrows dance up and down as he tries to ignore the scruffy appearance of the TRV's skipper. 'Beastly business, lieutenant,' he drawls between two loud explosions from the port, tapping the peak of his cap with a swagger-stick in response to Martingale's sloppy salute. 'Ghastly mess. Your fellows are doing a magnificent job of course – always trust the Navy. God knows what's happened to the light-blue wallahs.'

'We have some hot cocoa on the brew if you'd like some,' offers Martingale, as another unearthly crash reverberates across to us and we see a plume of flame and debris rise from the centre of town.

The major grits his teeth; striving to retain his composure amid the turmoil. He slaps the leg of his riding breeches with his stick.

'Ah, that's very decent of you, old chap. Much appreciated; but I cannot stay.' He leans his face closer with an air of confidentiality. 'There has bin some toing and froing between the top brass and the politicians, you know. Seems the froggies have bin complaining. From now on the two armies are to be evacuated on a fifty-fifty basis: "*Partage – bras dessus, bras dessous*", as Churchill says. In particular, five thousand places have bin offered to General de la Laurencie's troops for the way they held on and allowed our chaps to retreat from a section of the western perimeter.'

He stares wearily into Martingale's face and allows a haunted look to show in his eyes for the first time. 'This is no time for chauvinism, lieutenant. There has bin too much of that nonsense already in this affair. We would be much obliged if you will place your ship at the disposal of a

small unit of the Secteur des Flandres, who have shown
exemplary courage as the backbone of the French Defence
Force.'

'I understood the French had their own ships.'

'You can forget "them and us" now, lieutenant.' There is
a hard set to the major's jaw and a sharp edge to his voice
as he swallows his impatience. He has seen many days of
ignominious retreat, and all the squalid misery that goes
with it. Now his patience is running out. 'There are two
hundred *poilus* gathered near an upturned barge and I
have promised them a ship. Your people have agreed to
help me to honour that promise by offering your small
vessel.' He sways for a moment, and his face goes slack. 'I
have a personal interest in this, lieutenant. As a young
subaltern I stood in the Champ-Elysées on 14th July 1919
and watched the victory parade. It was preceded by the
Grands Mutilés with their hideous wounds. Those without
eyes were privileged to carry the ensigns. France lost
twenty-seven per cent of all men between the ages of
eighteen and twenty-seven – more than any other nation
except Serbia. No wonder they say the British will fight to
the last Frenchman. Churchill's order is not just a
diplomatic gesture as far as I am concerned.' His voice tails
off.

'Consider it done, sir.' Martingale nods soberly. 'Just
point us in the right direction.'

'I'll lead – you follow.' He smiles, and we watch him
climb down stiffly into the waist, straddling the gun'll
before stepping into his dinghy. It rocks alarmingly until
he settles himself once more with his feet astride; erect and
statuesque, with his baton outstretched like a war-leader in
an old-fashioned film. The bland little corporal nudges his
throttle automatically, his vacant features shadowed by an
outsized helmet as he pilots his flimsy craft through the
flotsam. There is nothing left in this mad world to excite
him, least of all the gesticulations of his theatrical master.

We pick up speed as we circle to follow. Soon we can
identify a cluster of men separate from the long lines of

khaki troops that stretch aimlessly across the dunes. Drawing closer we see that the French are fully armed and kitted, with rolls of bedding over their shoulders. They are formed up in ranks near to an upturned barge that serves as a jetty running out into the surf. There is an air of discipline about them as they wait in silence. Even when a Messerschmitt howls across the dunes with guns blazing they scatter without panic into shallow trenches, then reassemble again afterwards as though on parade.

The beach shelves gently, so we take it very slowly as we nose in, for even with our shallow draught there is not much clearance beneath the keel. However, the tide has risen since the barge was sunk, so there should be adequate water even when we have our passengers on board, and with care we should get off easily before the tide drops.

In contrast to other instances when concerted rushes by men who have no knowledge of the sea resulted in chaos these men seem to know what it's all about, and they are marched out in orderly files until they are shoulder-deep, to reach the barge. Even so they refuse to abandon their equipment or their rifles, despite the protests of our men, who know how little space we have on board.

Every inch of space on deck and below is occupied. Several wounded are carried below into the crew's quarters and stretched out on our bunks. The mist has cleared to leave a bright, sunny day and an open invitation to the Luftwaffe to attack the vast expanse of defenceless sand where squaddies grovel into the holes. Nothing shocks any more. The sprawling corruption that surrounds us no longer offends our senses, for they have been saturated by the continuous bellowings of outrage.

The men on the fo'c'sle wave to signal that we have everyone on board. The clank of the winch comes as we take up the slack on the kedge anchor we dropped when we came in. It is time I returned to the bridge and took the helm. Once we are clear and swinging to line up on course to go out towards the Ruytingen Channel we slip the kedge, and the screw takes over to push our blunt bows ahead. Martingale comes to stand by me, but he gives no helm orders, trusting me to steer a course through the traffic, grateful for every yard that slides under our keel. We have all had a gutful now; a blind acceptance of it all. Our only task is to get these men to Dover. After that perhaps someone will decide that enough is enough, and there is no purpose in these suicidal trips.

'*Capitaine!*' A French captain stands in the doorway; his face dark and oval, with deep, brown eyes and a heavy stubble. There is a quality in the man's expression that commands attention. His uniform is filthy and there are scorchmarks on his sleeve.

'Captain,' he persists in good English. 'Where do you take us?' The question is blunt, uncompromising, as though he knows he is not going to like the answer.

'Dover.'

His mouth tightens. 'Then what?'

Martingale thinks for a moment while I concentrate on the compass. 'I have no idea,' he admits quietly.

We are skirting a wrecked *schuitje*, and he has to watch me manoeuvre us past. A mass of cargo is washing out of her open hold and our blunt bow thrusts it aside as we bulldoze our way through. Once settled on course again he turns to the Frenchman.

'I did hear that some of your soldiers are being taken to Southampton and shipped to southern ports.'

'Why can you not take us to Cherbourg? We are all Frenchmen and wish to carry on fighting.' He draws himself upright, full of pride. 'My men and I belong to the Fortifié des Flandres. Unlike the British Army we have not been ordered to throw away our weapons and run.'

Martingale bristles. 'You are tired, sir. If you look you will see that most of our men have their rifles, and I have no doubt that our leaders know what they are about. What would you have us do: sacrifice a whole army for a gesture of defiance?'

'It is not your homes that are being over-run,' the

captain complains bitterly. 'Our generals say the Germans are stretched to the limit and need to regroup while they bring up their supplies before advancing. We have already attacked Calais and driven them back. If your army had not burned your vehicles and wrecked your tanks we could have pushed them back from the coast.' He looks desperately sad. 'Now France is on her own and more young men will die for a lost cause.' His face hardens. 'We have been abandoned, and the least you can do is take us to another part of France so that we can fight on.'

Martingale looks out across the devastation that litters the beach from the burning town to the Belgian border. All semblance of order seems to have gone, and every ship is engaged on its individual mission, trying to take on its quota and escape before it receives attention from the prowling Luftwaffe. There is nothing positive in all this; only the last throes of a beaten army scrambling away from the advancing grey hordes who must be even more convinced that they are invincible. They do not need any fanatic orations from their leaders to bolster them now. All they see about them tells them that they are the master race, and part of a New Order that will dominate the Continent from the Urals to the Atlantic. Every promise Hitler made is being fulfilled, and there will be jack-boots marching up the Mall by Christmas.

Martingale is being asked to stick his neck out again. To place his prospects of promotion at risk, and most likely wreck his whole career: a career not easily thrown away when he has struggled up through the ranks. The Navy might take the view that he had reasonable excuse for disobeying one order to save the men on the paddler, but to take his ship to France instead of Dover is beyond that. His orders leave no room for misinterpretation. If he defies the Admiralty this time he leaves himself wide open, and I can see the torment of his thoughts mirrored in his eyes.

He darts a quick look at the Frenchman. 'You are a military man. Would you ask me to disobey my orders?'

A ragged, scorched sleeve lifts and sweeps like a condemning pointer to take in the whole desolate panorama. 'Who is giving the commands today, captain? I can see no one.'

'Cherbourg is too far and we are unarmed except for a couple of Lewis guns and your rifles.'

Hope gleams in the Frenchman's eyes as he senses a weakening in Martingale's resolve. 'Abbeville then. Brigadier General Charles de Gaulle is there with the Fourth Division Cuirassée. Your own soldiers too. We could join with them.' For the first time his face takes on a pleading look. 'We could stop running, captain – put an end to this shame.'

We are following in the wake of a Southern Railway cargo ship as she leads us through the channel into the mouth of the Straits. There is little time left for deliberation. If we are to turn south it must be done now. Every nerve in my body is tuned for Martingale's decision.

'Port ten!' he grunts. 'Steer south by south-west.'

We are committed then; I expected nothing else, but as I spin the spokes there is a deep, empty feeling weighing heavy in my stomach. We are leaving the English coast to starboard and heading down through the tight gullet of the Dover Straits into the open Channel on our own. There is six days left now before *Scavenger* is due to come out of dock and sail for her patrol area: I hope she won't be going to sea with the 'spare crew' coxswain on board.

'Boat in trouble ahead, sir!' Chopper is pointing across the bow at a small cabin cruiser, dangerously overloaded, and wallowing powerless in the choppy water.

'Slow ahead!' orders Martingale. 'Let's take a look.'

I steer the TRV in close, taking care not to run down the cruiser, for she has only a few inches of freeboard and even our wash could sink her. I have little time to study her passengers, except to notice the man at the helm is dressed in naval gear. The remainder look like British squaddies, who scramble over the side smartly enough when we sidle up. Once they are safely stowed we get under way again, and someone tosses a hand-grenade into the boat to sink her so that she will not drift about and become a hazard to other shipping. There will be some moaning and groaning from her passengers when they find out they are not going home to England.

No sooner has the thought struck me than a very irate colonel is blowing his top on the bridge, demanding to be taken to Dover. He is unshaven, dirty and battleweary, in no mood to have his authority challenged by an underling like Martingale. I shut my ears to the tirade and hold my course, subconsciously preparing to put the wheel over once Martingale accepts that he cannot buck the system.

I could wait forever for that to happen. The colonel grows more apoplectic as his demands are bluntly refused, and the compass-needle remains firmly on south by south-west, aimed at the English Channel, while the French coast gets ever closer to port.

Fortunately the French captain interrupts to defuse the situation, attacking the colonel with a few choice words of his own. The two angry men carry their argument outside and we shut the door on them.

The bedlam of battle abates when we leave the main stream of cross channel traffic astern. For the first time I can hear the softer sounds of the sea on our hull and the steady pulse of our engine. The sun warms the sheltered parts of the ship, and the French stretch out in every corner, sleeping their weariness away. Maybe we will be ignored as the Germans seek out bigger, more important targets in the crowded waters nearer Dunkirk.

Someone bangs on the door and I relax when I recognise Borroughs as he slides it open and peers inside. 'Looks like we have picked up a couple of extra hands, sir,' he tells Martingale, looking down at a slip of paper in his hand. 'A civvy named Henry Wicks. He's a doctor, and the owner of the cabin cruiser we've just destroyed. He ain't very pleased, but he says he can help with the wounded. The other bloke is one of those emergency reservists, and his name, believe it or not, is Septimus Maundy.'

The ship swings five degrees off-course as I lose concentration. 'Who did you say?'

He chuckles. 'I know, chief. That's what I thought, but that is his name all right – Septimus Maundy – poor sod.'

There cannot be two people with that name. 'Where did you put him?'

'I sent him below for some grub. He looks like he's been through the mill. The doctor says he found him walking about aimlessly on the beach muttering to himself. Says he recovered quickly enough when he was asked to help with the cruiser. Reckons that if it hadn't been for him they wouldn't have got the boat off the sand. They had to fight back a mob who was gonna swamp the boat. Maundy fought them off single-handed.'

'Maundy did?'

'That's what the doc says.'

'The Maundy I know couldn't fight his way out of a paper bag.'

'Oh, well it's not this one; he's a tough bastard.' He dodges out again, slamming the door on us.

I hear Martingale clear his throat noisily, too polite to tell me I am making a mess of the steering. I straighten her up and pass the wheel over to Chopper before asking permission to go below. A nasty suspicion is welling up inside me. I believe in coincidence all right, but there is a bloody limit.

All the cabins are occupied by wounded soldiers, but we have kept the mess for our own lads, and the men we rescued from the cruiser. I find them seated at the small table with steaming mugs in their hands. As I enter I come face to face with the startled features of Jack Royal.

He recovers quickly, lowering his mug to stare up into my eyes like a boxer looking for an opening. He is dirty and stubbled like the rest of us, and his eyes red-rimmed with fatigue, but that same insolent expression is there, and he looks as guilty as hell. My mind jumps back to the shattered remains under the blanket in that Dover church hall where the stench of cooked meat sickened my guts. The initial shock has gone and a smirk transforms his face.

'Surprise, surprise!' he sneers.

'What happened to Maundy?' I ask straight out.

The smirk dies a little. 'The poor sod is dead, chief. Burned to a frazzle when that bomb hit the *Brigand*.' His mouth curves into a wide grin. 'I suppose you are wondering why I swopped identities.'

'That doesn't take much figuring,' I state. 'The police are after you, Royal. They say you are wanted for murder. You've got things well worked out, haven't you? First find a man with no relatives back home to care about whether he lives or dies, then steal his identity and jump ship. You can always get back amongst the shambles when the heat dies down. It's all too bloody pat by a long chalk.'

'What do you mean by that?' His tone has a dangerous edge to it.

I turn to the others. They are looking completely baffled, and not a little alarmed. 'Leave us for a minute,' I ask them quietly. 'Go up top and watch for aircraft – you can take your mugs with you.'

After they have gone I slide the door shut and face him squarely. 'It's all too neat, Royal. You are a calculating bastard, and my guess is that it is no accident Maundy died so conveniently for you. It lets you off the hook nicely, doesn't it?' I lean into him, bringing my face close to his; yet he doesn't budge. I throw the words at him. 'The police say you are a killer, Royal, and a man who kills once can do so again; especially if it is to save his own skin. How do I know the corpse I saw in Dover was Maundy? How do I know he isn't lying somewhere with a knife in his back? That dead man could have been anyone. All you needed was a corpse to hang your dog-tags on.'

There is no smile now, just an evil leer as the silence hangs between us for a moment. The outside sounds of the sea washing against the hull add a mysterious quality to the small tabloid. There is no backing down with this man. He doesn't bat an eyelid as he stares me out without flinching. The contemptuous leer is back.

'So you think you have it all worked out, do you, Chief

bloody Petty Officer Grant. You are a suspicious bastard right enough!' He rises from his chair to bring his face level with mine. The ship takes a slight roll and the seams creak in protest. 'What if I was to tell you I have not killed anyone. The man the police accuse me of killing was the drunken old soak in the *Sister Ruth*. I have already explained what happened. Believe what you like.'

'I would need a lot of convincing,' I accuse. 'The police don't make charges of murder without some cause, and you're asking me to believe the word of a man who has no scruples about stealing another man's name.'

His face gets vicious. 'You can go to hell, chief. You and the police. I don't have to prove anything to anyone. The Germans killed Maundy: I just made use of his corpse. Let's face it, he was no bloody use to anyone alive, so I made use of him dead. What do you intend to do about it?'

I lean away from him shaking with rage, but what the hell is there to be done? We have nowhere to lock him away, and no one to spare for a sentry. The only other man in the wheelhouse has listened to all that's been said, but I doubt whether he can grasp half of the implications. It is between Royal and me. I am the only one who can spoil his deception and soon we will be in the midst of the battle again. I will need to watch the sod every minute in case he decides to eliminate me. I doubt if one more corpse will make any difference to him. The first priority is to make sure other people know about it, then he will have to carry out wholesale slaughter to silence us all. In the meantime I am still carrying the revolver Martingale gave me, so I am one up on Royal as long as I hold on to it. He should be locked away, but we have no place to put him. Therefore, it is up to me to keep him under control.

'We are going up to the wheelhouse.' I tell him. 'You will take the helm, and if I see so much as one finger leave the spokes I'll blow your bloody head off. What's more, I am going to make sure the others know the full story, and I'm sure Martingale will be interested to find out that the body I went to identify in Dover is alive and well in his ship. If you've got any sense at all you will go back and face the court. They don't hang innocent men.'

'Ah, but you see, I'm not innocent. In the eyes of the police and those bilge-rats who called themselves sailors I left the skipper trussed-up in his cabin while the ship sank. Now I will be accused of Maundy's murder too if they think the same as you. I am a loser whichever way I go.'

'I have no more time to argue – get moving!'

He goes to the wheelhouse meekly enough even though he must know that this is his last oportunity to make certain his identity is kept secret. Up top we find that darkness is closing in fast. I would have liked to report the situation to Martingale immediately, but he is busy with the navigation, and I can see the colonel hovering in the background, waiting to have another go at him, so I decide not to add to his problems.

'You are relieved, Chopper,' I say quietly. 'Go find the yeoman and bring him back here with you. I have something to tell you both.'

I try to bury my prejudices and explain everything to Borroughs and Chopper as fairly as I can. Somehow it doesn't sound quite so sinister when it is told slowly, without emotion. They hear me out without so much as a glance at Royal. Seamen have respect for other seamen, and when shorebased officialdom interferes with their shipmates, sympathy centres on their own kind.

'Do you want to put him under guard?' asks Chopper reluctantly.

'No. I will take care of him. He isn't going to run very far from this old bucket, and now that he knows you are in the picture he won't be stupid enough to try anything. One thing I can say about our friend here is that he is a crafty sod who will need watching all the time.'

They look everywhere but at Royal as he stands in the background, listening to every word, and I can sense their embarrassment. Borroughs slides out of the wheelhouse without a word and Chopper takes his place in one corner as relief helmsman. I stand behind Royal, watching while he gets the feel of the ship. Once again I am impressed by his expertise, and try to ignore a growing professional respect for a fellow seaman. He could not have assumed the identity of a man with a more contrasting personality than Maundy, for the little OD was one of those weak men who stay in the shadows, always last to volunteer, never the chosen one when someone reliable is required for a special job. He would have gone through life on the backs of other people, offering no more a pair of extra hands, and then only if the task could be explained simply, so that his slothful brain could absorb it. There is always plenty of room for men like him in the service, for they allow others like Royal to climb the promotional ladder. They are small-fry in a big pond, an afterthought in the minds of busy senior ratings, just there to add weight when a rope has to be hauled or an oar to be pulled. Handy to have around, but no one wants to be bothered with them. I imagine that the most significant thing Maundy ever did was to give his name to another man.

I shake my head to clear away these thoughts. The ship is moving out into the channel with the French coastline showing through the gloom to port, while England fades astern. Here and there the glow of distant gunfire lights the eastern sky, and we hear the muffled thump of shells, but out here we are sailing across a gun-metal surface and the real menace grows from within the hull. I feel its icy grip and shiver at the sudden chill. We are tired and numbed by the continuous strain, but I feel no urge to sleep. My brain is too busy with its confused thoughts. Maybe I lose a few moments now and again and slip into a semi-coma, waking up startled after a short time to wonder how long I've been out. Annoyed that I have allowed my vigilance to falter, and amazed that I can sleep standing up. A squaddie told me that he and two of his mates actually worked out a system while they were trying to reach the coast, whereby two men held the other upright between them while he slept on the march. I can believe them now. For most of us it is an endless ordeal to be endured until someone in authority decides it is time to shout 'Halt!'

A last sliver of sulphurous light sits on the western horizon for a brief moment as the sun takes a dive. The thirtieth day of May dissolves into black night and tomorrow is too far away to think about.

IV

The door slides open to admit a much subdued colonel. In the deep gloom his face looks purple, and heavy shadows emphasize the lines and eye-sockets to give him a spectral appearance. 'I have discussed the situation with Captain de Carteret, lieutenant, and I can now see that there is a need for your ship south of the Somme, in case our own troops have to evacuate. Therefore, I suggest that you land the French at St Valéry, then stand by to embark our men if necessary.' His face becomes even more glum. 'There's no point in mincing words; it is quite obvious that France could fall if things deteriorate much further.'

I can almost hear Martingale's inward sigh of relief as one more burden is lifted from his shoulders and an unexpected sanction comes from a senior officer. A good word from such an influential man might mollify those who will sit in judgement when Martingale has to explain why he neglected to follow his orders. 'That suits me, sir. Which St Valéry is it to be, sur-Somme or en-Caux?'

'St Valéry-en-Caux of course,' sneers the Frenchman with an ironic twist to his mouth. 'The Boche are holding most of the Somme and the British are interested only in getting back to their beds.'

'That's damn slander and you know it!' blares the colonel, shaking with fury. 'Dunkirk is part of a strategic withdrawal. What use would be served if all those men were captured or killed in their hopeless position? Elsewhere our men are fighting alongside yours, and I will remind you, sir, that your troops have not got an unblemished record by any means. There has been desertion and wholesale surrender amongst your men.

Even a welcome for the enemy in some places. Throwing men away senselessly in hopeless gestures went out in 1918. The trouble with you French is that you have trench warfare mentality!'

Martingale steps in quickly to stop them coming to blows. 'Gentlemen! There is no point in fighting amongst ourselves. St Valéry-en-Caux is no good unless we catch the tide exactly right. We will have to go on to Dieppe.'

'Very well,' agrees the Frenchman, swallowing his outrage. 'That is only a few miles away.'

'Humph!' snorts the colonel grudgingly. 'You will have to be very careful, lieutenant. I happen to know that Dieppe has been ruled out as an evacuation port because there are magnetic mines in the approaches. You might do better to go on to Le Havre.'

'Le Havre!' explodes de Carteret. 'How much further do you want to take us away from the front line? It seems that once an army starts to run it doesn't know where to stop. The Germans will be knocking on the doors of Paris if we do not stop them on the Somme.'

'I'm tired of your blasted impertinence!' roars the colonel. 'I have a mind to make you answer for your words, sir!'

De Carteret bristles, pushing his red face at the colonel. 'Choose your time, sir. I will be delighted to oblige.'

'Gentlemen – please!' Martingale places himself between them. 'There is nothing to be gained by all this. Allow me five minutes to study my charts and I'll come back with an answer.'

They back down and go off huffing to each side of the bridge while he has a final word with me before disappearing below. 'The Somme' I think to myself, when they have left me alone with Chopper and Royal. That name is synonomous with war. Men are dying in the old battlefields, and the older inhabitants of the villages and towns must sigh heavily when they see it all happening again. A repetitive madness brought about by those we elect into office to look after our welfare. Mons, Cambrai,

Ypres; they are only fifty miles or so to port. The gods of war must be chortling their heads off.

'Silence!'

I start guiltily as though someone has read my thoughts. But it is a relayed message running through the ship in both languages to suppress the hum of voices and still the shuffle of restless bodies. We are wallowing along with just the soft sigh of the ocean washing past the hull. I see the skipper climb back up to the wheelhouse and stare out of the open doorway as Borroughs points an extended arm into the darkness beyond the starboard bow. I jolt myself away from the bulkhead. My body is stiff and sore where it has rested against the hard steel. I might even have slept for a moment and I look up to see Royal grinning white teeth at me over his shoulder, as though he has caught me out.

I snap out of my stupor and tune my ears. I can hear the sound now. A throaty grumble of high-powered engines idling somewhere to starboard. Sounding like the low growl of a beast as it lies in wait in the darkness. Only one type of craft makes that sound, and I have already seen what they can do when they attack larger ships. The noise drives into my bones as I tense with the others with every nerve stretched taut. Another quiet order reduces our speed to cut down the noise of the engine and reduce the phosphorescence of our wake. Like a defenceless mammal trying to slip past marauding carnivores we creep by, praying to remain unobserved.

'Borroughs!' Martingale's heavy whisper sounds like a thunderclap.

'Sir?'

'Do you know the challenge?'

'Only until midnight, sir. It changes then.'

'I can't imagine German E-boats managing to squeeze through the Straits, especially when they have such rich pickings to the north.' He is talking mostly to himself. 'Hold your lamp ready, but don't use it unless I tell you to. We might creep past unnoticed if we go steady. Those chaps will be as jumpy as we are, so we don't want any identity mix-ups. Even friends will be inclined to shoot first and ask questions later on a night like this.'

I can hear the gurgle of exhausts as the outlets slop into the water, while the over-riding growl stays deep and full of menace. The French are peering over the rail with their rifles poised. Their heads and shoulders silhouetted against the purple background of the night. One nervous finger could spell disaster. The tension is almost tangible, and I can smell fear in the taut atmosphere.

I can hardly credit the evidence of my own ears when the noise changes its tone and begins to decrease in volume. We are leaving them astern. My breathing becomes easier and I no longer hear my heart thumping in my chest. The nervous sweat grows cold on my spine. Someone close by expels his breath with a heavy sigh, magnified out of proportion.

'Easy!' I warn in a harsh whisper. 'We are not clear yet.'

My sharp order triggers off a sudden bellow of noise as three dazzling, iridescent flares explode with soft 'plops' high above our heads to turn night into day as they slowly descend on their parachutes. I have no time to study their brilliance before the rattle of quick-firing snarls out of the darkness, and lethal streams of tracer lances in towards us.

'Full ahead – port ten!' yells Martingale.

'Full ahead!' That's a laugh. The most this tramp can do flat out is about seven knots, and then she is likely to burst a blood vessel. We lumber along like a sea-cow as the murdering bastards roar in towards us with their big, powerful engines blasting the air with full-throated roars. They have us to rights as they circle like wolves, waiting to close in on their prey. It is sheer bloody slaughter.

'Switch on the steaming-lights! Switch on everything!' screams Martingale, and I fumble with the latch on the wooden door of the cabinet where the switches are.'

'Cease fire – cease fire! Come on, chief, for God's sake!'

French commands are echoing his orders to stop the firing as I locate the switches and flick them down.

The nightmare goes on for several moments. I hear shells slamming into our sides and whanging off the metal to ricochet into the crouching *poilus*. There are wild screams and yells coming from the waist as the bullets find soft targets. Three more rockets soar into the sky and explode into blatant orbs of white light. I dive to the deck along with everyone else and hug the cortecine as the timbered bulkheads splinter and erupt in the merciless fusillade.

Abruptly the insane racket stops. We are left in suspense with the inearthly glow of those fires exposing our pale faces as we ease up onto our elbows to stare about stupidly. I expect to see bodies strewn about in a welter of carnage with blood and guts everywhere. Miraculously other shapes are rising too, like a slow-motion film of rugby players lifting out of a collapsed scrum. The jade glow of the starboard steaming-light fights against the blanching glare of the flares. I hear the chatter of Borroughs's Aldis flashing a response to the signal from the nearest boat. The vague shape moves in closer and a metallic voice fills the void.

'Who are you?' it asks in an unmistakably English voice.

'*Merde*!' spits de Carteret. 'Who needs enemies!'

Martingale goes out onto the starboard wing and cups his hands over his mouth. 'We are British, you stupid oaf! You've fired on a friendly ship!'

There is an empty silence. The gun-boats separate, one coming in towards us, while the other moves out in a wide circle with her gunners switching their attention to the black wastes beyond the reach of the flares. The nearest boat is close now. No need to use the loud-hailer any more. 'We have been watching you for some time, captain.' The voice is refined and emotionless. 'I gave ample time for you to make your challenge. Our tanks are full of high-octane fuel. I cannot afford to take chances. We are looking out for captured merchant ships ferrying enemy troops south. I'm afraid everyone is firing at shadows tonight. All I can do is apologise profoundly and offer to escort you to your destination.'

'We're going no place!' growls Finney in a voice loud

enough for everyone to hear as he comes up from below to
stand beside me. He is shaking with emotion. 'The stupid
sods 'ave killed me mate. They've punched bloody great
'oles in the bilges and we're takin' water in dahn below. I've
got the pump going full aht and it's not enough ter keep us
afloat fer long.'

'How long?'

'Abaht an hour I'd say, maybe less.'

Martingale ponders for a moment. 'Captain!' he calls to
the Frenchman. 'I need some of your men to form a
bucket-chain. Finney will tell you where, and we can find
you plenty of buckets.' He swings to face outboard,
shouting down to the gunboat. 'Have you got our exact
position, captain?'

The response comes back subdued. 'We are abreast of
Cayeux. The nearest port is St Valéry-sur-Somme. That's
the red glow you can see in the sky over there, but I'm
afraid the Germans are holding it. There is a sort of
no-man's-land between the Somme and the Bresle.'

I can see his face now, pale in the glaring light of the
flares. There is an embarrassed catch in his voice when he
adds. 'You have no choice but to run her up on the beach,
captain. There are long stretches of shingle and sand
along the shore. I dare not follow you in because of the
sandbanks; they're all over the place, and always on the
move. If you wish I'll lay off-shore. We have room for half
a dozen of your crew if you row out in the dinghy after
you've beached her, and the French shouldn't have too
much difficulty finding the Allies if they go south.'

There is a stony silence. The flares hit the water and
fizzle out. I switch off the steaming-lights to leave us
wallowing in an eerie pool of violet light. We are already
steering in towards the coast with the glow of St
Valéry-sur-Somme off our port quarter. The gunboat is a
vague shadow as she putters alongside. Her exhausts emit
a guttural sound while her bilges slop glutinously in the
slow swell.

'No thank you.' returns Martingale impassively. 'If there

is a no-man's-land to the south we can walk to Dieppe.'

There is a note of regret in the other man's voice. 'I'm sorry, captain. You will need to work hard with your buckets, I'm afraid. But if you land somewhere away from the enemy you will have only about eight miles to go before you find our own troops. One warning though. If you do run into a patrol it will almost certainly be German, so keep your heads down and don't move until you are sure. I wish you luck, sir. God bless you all.'

The big Merlins erupt with a blast of sound that hurts the ears. The MGB leaps ahead with a surge of phosphorescence spreading from her tail. She is quickly swallowed up in the night, and we are left alone, with only the clanking of the bucket-brigade and the muted mumble of our own engine to keep us company. Finney has got the French organised with a sort of pidgin-French that they seem to understand, and they are ranged down through the engineroom hatch and ladder into the bilge, laughing at his antics as he dives in and out of his machinery like a demented demon. Eventually he emerges in triumph with the top plate of his false teeth held high for all to see. They drip with a gooey mess of oil and water, and he wipes them with a wad of cotton waste before ramming them into place.

I turn back to Royal. He was given a course to take us into the beach, but it is a matter of pure luck whether we end up on a sandbank or an outcrop of rock, not to mention amongst a crowd of aggressive Nazis. Every man has been issued with a lifejacket, and the bucket-chain, in tandem with the bilge-pump will hopefully keep us afloat until we reach the shallows. The rest is up to the gods. I study Royal's brooding shape draped over the wheel. He looks like a gorilla in the deep gloom: powerful and malevolent, but crafty too. A dangerous combination.

'When we beach,' I warn him, 'you will stick close to me. I intend taking you back to England for a trial even if I have to carry you. Stray more than a couple of yards away and I'll shoot you in the leg.'

He doesn't flinch, but I sense his cynical leer as he concentrates on the compass, fingering the spokes like the expert he is. The bastard! He knows he has me worried. He can afford to relax, while I must stay alert every second. Nor can I rely on Chopper or Borroughs, for they are fully occupied with their own affairs. I should tell Martingale, and there's no doubt that he should know what is going on in his ship, but the couple of occasions when I start to explain are interrupted almost before I can get the first words out. Things are happening all the time now, and I don't want to ruin his concentration under these conditions.

The French are getting restless in the waist as they realise we are drawing close to the shore. There is a lot of metallic clickings as they ease their rifle bolts and test weapons. NCOs move amongst them, issuing orders in harsh whispers. We might be approaching their homeland, but it is a hostile shore, and every shadow could conceal an enemy. Any second the whole coastline could spew tracer at us, and hidden artillery could open up with a lethal crossfire, blasting swathes through our crowded deck.

I can hear the surf, and there is a hardening in the gloom ahead as the solid shape of the shoreline takes form against the purple sky. the last few yards are eaten up and the TRV runs up onto the beach with hardly a bump. She lifts once, takes a surge forward, holds, then with a final lunge, buries her bow into the shingle and sticks, resting on an even keel.

For a moment we hold our breath and peer anxiously out into the night. Lady Luck smiles on us and the night stays firm and unbroken, a solid wall of blackness surrounding the quiet little oasis in the midst of a wilderness of violence. Chopper goes forrard with a spare dan-buoy spar from the stack that's lashed across the after end of the poop-deck. He uses it to probe the bottom beneath the bow, checking to see if it is solid enough for the men to walk ashore when we disembark.

We rig boarding nets and a couple of ladders over the side of the fo'c'sle, and when all is ready, stand back to take a last look at our surroundings before giving the order to disembark. The war-sounds are louder now. We can sort out the heavier thumps of individual bombs and shells; even feel their vibrations through the soles of our feet when they carry through the steel hull from the shingle beneath her. We have been lucky. I can make out the loom of houses along the coast to the south, but we seem to have picked an uninhabited stretch, isolated from the fighting going on about us. It is a weird feeling standing there waiting with our cargo of Frenchmen, half expecting a sudden barrage to erupt from hidden walls and hedgerows.

'Your men will disembark first,' Martingale tells de Carteret. 'Take it quietly as you go and try not to get your feet tangled up in the mesh.'

Hoarse whispers of command set the *poilus* astir, and our men feed them over the side, helping them with their clumsy equipment as they search for footholds. Despite my warning many of them get into difficulties as they scramble down, but soon a procession of wading men is snaking ashore through the shallows, and apart from a few duckings, they all successfully reach dry land, to wait the next series of orders. I cringe at the babble of chatter that comes from the fo'c'sle as men sort themselves out, but still we are left alone to get on with it, and the war stays in the background.

Doctor Wicks and the squaddies rescued from the cabin cruiser go next. All except the colonel who insists on staying behind with Martingale until everyone else is safely ashore, much to our disgust. Before we go Finney wrecks the engine and opens up the sea-cocks, then uses a maul to smash the wheelvalves, making a noise that threatens to bring the whole German army down on us.

'For God's sake!' explodes the colonel.

'Easy, Finney!' warns Martingale; but the stoker PO is done anyway, and clambers up out of his hatch to join us as we climb over the side.

Somewhere close by a dog barks. Shadows move with us as we sort ourselves out. I locate Royal in the darkness and bring him close to me as Borroughs moves in to give me a hand. The merchant seaman accepts it all with a derisive chuckle, content to allow us to play our silly game.

'Now what?' blurts the colonel in a heavy whisper when we are all assembled.

'I will send one of my men to the houses to see if he can find out what is happening here,' says de Carteret firmly. 'The rest of us can take cover until he returns.'

For a moment it looks as though the colonel is about to object, but he relents, realising that we cannot move far until we know our position, and the best people to question the locals must be their own kind. The captain sends one of his NCOs scampering off before ordering his troops off the beach to take cover beneath a long, low wall running alongside the road just clear of the shingle. The British find a spot where a ditch runs inland to give natural protection from all sides, and we all settle to wait for de Carteret's man to return with his report.

A low mist is forming. Waist-high, it hugs the ground like a grey mantle, so that our bodies swim in it, and its dankness seeps into our clothes. I slump down with the rest and mould my flesh into the shape of the ground. The full measure of my exhaustion suddenly weighs down on me so that I have to fight to stay awake. Every muscle and bone cries out for rest, and the earth makes a luxurious bed.

My senses jerk back into gear when I hear the soft crunch of boots returning along the verge. A muffled conference takes place over on the French side, and after a few minutes de Carteret is with us, whispering earnestly to the colonel and Martingale while I strain my ears to listen.

It appears that the villagers are sticking it out while they wait the outcome of the fighting going on about them. Living in cellars. Not daring to venture outside for anything. Twice they have seen German motorcycles roar through the village as though they owned the place, and there has been fighting from time to time, mostly at night, and the villagers cringe inside their homes, hoping it will all go away. We have come ashore somewhere between Cayeux and Ault with the Germans only a couple of miles or so up the road, while at Le Tréport, just three miles to the south, the British troops are standing with their backs to the River Bresle.

The French captain ends his report and there is an interval while everyone ponders on the implications before the colonel declares, 'our duty is straightforward. We must push on south and join up with our own people.'

'*Non!*' The word is like a gunshot from the Frenchman. 'You go wherever you wish. My men and I intend to go east and join up with our colleagues. The man who spoke to my sergeant is an old soldier. He says the Allies are building up for a new counter-attack to drive the Germans away from their bridgeheads on the Somme. If I take my *poilus* south we will end up with the British.'

'May I remind you that I am senior officer here,' protests the colonel. 'If you go wandering about in no-man's-land like that you will surely be fired upon by either or both sides. I repeat, captain. We must go south.'

The Frenchman bristles. 'Wander about! My men are trained infantry, sir. They do not "wander about".'

Martingale jumps in quickly to prevent another confrontation. 'We must move quickly, gentlemen. It is important to get away from here while it is still dark.' As he speaks there is a sudden rattle of small-arms fire and the French leap into action, flinging themselves to the ground as they prepare to face the new threat.

'Come on – let's scarper!' shouts Finney's rough voice as we all dive into a shallow ditch under the hedge.

'Perhaps we should help the French,' suggests Chopper doubtfully.

'You speak for yourself, mate,' declares Finney. 'As far as I'm concerned I'm a bloody matelot, not a fuckin' pongo. Unarmed, untrained, and totally fuckin' useless when it comes ter scrappin' wiv Germans.'

'He's right,' says the Frenchman. 'This is soldiers' work. It is most likely a patrol, but it could bring stronger forces into the area, so I do not want to be burdened with you.'

A fresh burst of automatic fire puts urgency into his tone. 'Leave this to me, colonel. Get away while you can.' He doesn't stop for an argument, but moves off quickly to join his men who are spreading out along a broad front to engage the enemy.

There is only one way left for us to go. 'Come on!' urges Finney, always the expert when it comes to getting away from trouble.

This time it is the only thing to do, so we take to our heels and run down towards the south, stumbling along in the darkness past the blacked-out houses and on into the countryside beyond, while the crackle of gunfire increases behind us. Any guilt I feel for leaving the French to cover my retreat is submerged by the common-sense thought that they wouldn't want to be burdened with a lot of amateurish matelots at a time like this; not to mention the doctor and an ill-assortment of exhausted squaddies.

We keep going until we are well clear of the village before finding a convenient gulley that makes an entrance to a large drainpipe running under the road to carry flood water away to the sea when the rains come. It has the effect of cutting out some of the sound, as though the low mist that creeps over us is filtering out the noise. I lie there relishing the feel of the soft earth as it soaks the tiredness from my body. It is a moment of sheer bliss that disappears abruptly when a sudden thought hits me.

'Royal!'

'I'm here.'

His laconic response comes from a couple of yards away, and I slump back again, expelling the air from my lungs as I relax. Perhaps it is time we had a roll-call. Maybe the sound of my voice will hide the crackle of gunfire and we can forget the Frenchmen who are facing a grey enemy behind us.

'Chopper!'

'Here!'

'Finney!'

'Yep!'

'Yeo'!'

No response. I try again. 'Borroughs?'

The night stays dark and empty round us, and Martingale takes up my call. 'Anyone see what happened to the yeoman?' he asks when we get no response.

'I'll go back for him,' I volunteer grudgingly after a few seconds. 'Keep an eye on our friend here, Chopper. I shouldn't be gone long – I hope.'

I tackle the job with complete lack of enthusiasm, keeping well into the side of the road with my revolver drawn and cocked, listening for every sound as I go. The muted popping changes to a sharper stutter as I approach the firing. It seems to come from a wide front on my right, and I can imagine the *poilus* crouching in their positions, peering out at their unseen enemy, straining their eyes for targets. The last thing I want is to get too near that lot. Shadows close in on me from either side. Vague gateposts turn into human figures standing watching as I creep past, and every black corner hides a potential foe. My heart pumps with a noise like a steam-hammer.

'Borroughs!' I call in a tight-throated whisper, praying his voice will answer from behind me, for the way back is getting longer with every faltering step, and I am getting close enough to hear the French voices shouting orders. Much too close for my peace of mind.

I locate the ditch where we hid when we first came ashore before I find him, and then I wish I hadn't, for he is stretched out on his back, staring empty-eyed at the stars. The way his head is twisted tells me his neck is broken. It could have been an accident of course, but I know damnwell that it wasn't. I retrace my steps with the awful truth gnawing at me. I forget the sounds I am leaving astern and concentrate on the menace ahead. Any doubts I had about Royal are gone. Only Borroughs, Finney and I know the facts, and with the yeoman gone that leaves only two of us.

'Where is he?' asks Martingale when I slump down beside him. I explain as briefly as I can. 'How on earth did that happen?' he asks.

'I don't think it was accidental, sir. I believe someone did it for him.'

'Oh!'

A huge explosion prevents me from telling him more. It is followed by another and another as shells shriek in to crash into the ground, making a pattern that creeps along the coast road between us and the village. It is a concentrated bombardment. A methodical, well-ranged salvo that stops short of the cluster of buildings. It must have been carefully calculated during daylight hours to be this accurate.

'Those are our guns!' exclaims the colonel, as though it makes a difference. 'Twelve inch, mark four howitzers if I'm not mistaken. It means that they have given up any idea of using the road for themselves, and emphasizes the need for us to get away from here as quickly as we can.'

'That makes me feel a whole lot better,' snorts Finney derisively. 'Jesus!' he shouts as another series of explosions shatters the night.

'They are breaking up the road before morning,' the colonel says evenly. He is a mine of useless informatioin tonight. 'I think we had better get off the road and into the fields.'

This time I grab Royal's belt before the scramble begins, and shove my pistol into his back. 'One false move is all I need to make me squeeze the trigger, you bastard!' I grate before we follow the others over the hedge.

He says nothing, and we run across broken turf, bent double as the night reverberates about our ears. We must have covered three or four fields before Martingale orders us to take cover again. This time we are all accounted for, though the doctor staggers in astern of everyone else and slumps down without a word. He is no chicken, and these antics are taking it out of him. He lies in an untidy heap, wheezing breath into his straining lungs. The bombardment ceases as abruptly as it began, leaving a void that gradually fills with smaller sounds.

'Your men are not used to this sort of exercise, lieutenant,' criticises the colonel. 'The doctor cannot go on like this. I suggest that you remain here and rest with your naval contingent while I press on with my soldiers to find our people. They cannot be too far away, and it will be less hazardous if we go on alone.'

'I think we could all do with a few moments rest, sir,' stresses Martingale evenly. 'I'm sure we will keep up with you after that.'

'No, lieutenant. It would be better if you remain here until daybreak. It seems that the Germans are consolidated along the Somme. We don't want a lot of sailors wandering about aimlessly in no-man's-land; they could wreck everything. We will wait ten minutes then leave you here and locate our own forces. The Navy has never been noted for its cross-country expertise.'

'Ah, well, that's where you're wrong, sir, beggin' yer pardon,' says Finney in an aggrieved tone. 'I exercise every day in the gym'.'

'You have a gymnasium?'

'Every submarine 'as one, sir. It's in between the library and the swimmin' pool.'

'Don't be so bloody impertinent.'

'Yes, sir.'

The colonel is in a loquacious mood however, with an axe to grind. 'Can't think how you chaps can carry out your functions without proper exercise,' he muses, as though we are sitting on a park bench somewhere in England. 'I have always taken a keen interest in sport, and find it character-building. I believe it is indispensable if one is to face the challenge of life.' This is obviously his pet subject.

'Well I reckon it's just a con' put abaht by people with more muscle than brain, meself,' says Finney, intending to close the subject, but the colonel is unwilling to let it go.

'That's a damn stupid observation.'

''Ave it yer own way. Like the bloke said, whenever I get the urge for violent exercise I lie dahn 'til the feelin' goes away.'

'The person responsible for that imbecile remark was a degenerate,' protests the colonel. 'Competitive sport leads to competitive thinking, and breeds leaders.'

'And for every winner there has to be twenty losers – what about them?' Royal startles us all when he chips in. 'What becomes of all the middle-of-the-road blokes who come between the bright-boys and the super athletes?'

'In every chess-game there have to be pawns,' declares the colonel, profoundly. 'We cannot all be leaders.'

'I see,' sneers Royal. 'So Beethoven, Dickens, Edison and the rest were all top class athletes, were they?' He has little regard for the colonel's rank.'

'No wonder I ain't an admiral,' snorts Finney.

'It is time we were on our way,' the colonel states firmly. 'I refuse to be drawn into an argument with morons.'

'There is one sort of acrobatics I'm good at.'

'Finney!' I bark.

'What?'

'Shut up!'

The army contingent moves out, buckling on their equipment as they go. They are a very mixed lot, and I don't think they are any more fitted for this sort of warfare than we are, for they are cooks, clerks and non-combatants. However, they are wearing the right coloured uniforms as far as the colonel is concerned, so off they go, and I have to admit that I'm happy to see the last of him. By the look of Martingale he is just as pleased as me. The bombastic officer had been a thorn in his side for long enough. Before he follows his party he has one more parting shot to deliver, however.

'I must ask you for your revolver, Grant.'

'Not bloody likely!' I exclaim.

'We will have more use for it than you. Give it to me.'

I don't bother to reply. He isn't going to get it, no matter what. It is the only thing that gives me an edge over Royal.

Luckily Martingale steps in to save the situation and persuades the colonel that we require some sort of protection. Our total armoury consists of two .38 Wembleys and a French rifle that Chopper 'acquired' from somewhere. I doubt that we represent any sort of threat to the Germans, but it boosts our morale.

Muttering innuendoes about insubordinate sailors with no sense of discipline the colonel goes off after his men. As soon as they have been swallowed up in the murk Martingale orders us to get some rest. I make up a rota for sentries and we settle down. Finney knows only half of the story as far as Royal is concerned so Chopper takes him to one side to explain it all. I doubt if the stoker PO is more than half interested for he has a natural aversion to becoming involved in the intrigues of his fellows. His life is uncomplicated, and centres around booze and sex for the most part. If we tell him that Royal is a man who needs to be watched he will take it for granted, and not bother about the reasons why.

'I'll castrate the bastard if he steps aht of line,' he growls forcefully, then settles his rolled-up jacket under his head and goes to sleep.

I am struggling to keep my eyes open now, for they are weighed down with fatigue, and my bones are aching with unfamiliar exercise. I concentrate on trying to analyse the sounds going on about me for a while, then give it up. It would take an experienced man to decipher some of the weird noises we hear. The mist seeps into our hiding place to hang like a moist shroud. Despite its clammy grip I must have dozed off for a while, for I wake with a start, staring wildly about for a moment, knowing something is wrong. I look towards Royal and find him relaxed in one corner, though it is hard to tell if he is sleeping or not. With Finney there can be no doubt, his sonorous snores fill the hollow. What then has wakened me so abruptly? I shiver and sit bolt upright, listening intently. I hear it almost immediately, a kind of metallic clanking from beyond the hedge-row. I ease up onto my knees and peer over the bank.

'It is coming from across the next field,' Chopper says quietly. He is crouched close beside me.

'What's going on?' Martingale is with us, pulling branches aside to stare across the misty field. The three of us straining our ears to decipher the sound. A breeze has sprung up to drive the mist inland like ectoplasm, holding the contours of the ground and filling the gulleys. There it is again, like a sheet of metal swinging against something solid. It could be anything from a piece of farm machinery to a tank.

'Chopper, take one man and creep over there carefully; see if you can find out what it is.'

'I'll go with him, sir,' I offer.

'No. I want you here with me.' Martingale shakes the nearest man by the shoulder. 'You go with Chopper. Keep low and go quietly.'

They are halfway across the field before I realise that Royal is the other man. I dare not shout, and I scramble up quickly with the intention of going after them. A heavy hand grabs me and pulls me down. 'I told you, I need you here.' growls Martingale.

'But, sir. You don't understand.'

'Keep silence!' he barks. 'What the hell do you think you're doing.' He is holding me firm as I struggle urgently. 'Are you out of your mind, for Christ's sake!'

'Sir!' I plead desperately. 'There is something I've been trying to tell you; we can't trust Royal alone with Chopper.'

'Why not?'

How to explain quickly? I suck in my breath, formulating my words carefully, but before I can utter a word there is an almighty explosion from the other side of the field.

We exchange looks and I'm up and running before the echo has died. My feet fly over the uneven turf, stumbling and picking myself up as I go in a wild rush towards a growing flame soaring above the opposite hedge. By the time we reach it the whole area is lit up by the glare of a fierce fire. I crash through the hedge and emerge unto a road where a truck is blazing and two figures are silhouetted against the flames.

When I reach them I recognise Royal standing up and dragging the other man away. A man with a twisted, screaming mask of a face and a shattered leg. Chopper's screams drive into my head as I try to help drag him clear. Between us we haul him to the side of the road and lay him on the soft grass.

'The doctor!' I'm babbling as I straighten out the struggling limbs and try to hold him down.

'I'm here.' More hands are pushing mine away as Wicks bends to examine poor Chopper.

Looking up I can see that the burning truck is a square-nosed Bedford. The canvas canopy is already stripped away from the skeletal remains of the frame, and now the flames are eating away at the bodywork. There is an acrid stench of burning rubber, and thick smoke pours out to merge with the mist.

'It must have been booby-trapped.' I turn to find Royal at my side, contemplating the wreckage with a bland face that looks demonic in the lurid glow. 'Chopper swung open the driver's door before I could stop him and the whole bloody lot went up. It was the swinging tailboard that we could hear clanking against the body. I warned Chopper to watch out; he should have had more sense, a leading hand like him.' He looks at me with a smug look on his face and the firelight turning his skin orange.

'I'll bet you tried hard to hold him back, Royal. First Burroughs, and now Chopper. You're getting rid of witnesses fast, aren't you?'

His face twists into a sneer. 'You've got all the answers, haven't you, Grant. Just remember one thing, though. It is your word against mine that my name is Royal. Finney lives in a little world of his own; I doubt if he knows what day it is.'

'What's going on?' Martingale calls from the verge. 'Come on you two, we have to get away from here before those flames attract the enemy.'

'Sir,'I persist. 'I have to tell you about Royal.'

'Not now, Grant. See me later.' He turns away, leaving me wallowing while he goes to stand over the doctor. Chopper's screams are subsiding as morphine is pumped into him. He is slipping in and out of consciousness. I can recognise his face now, but despite the dressing Doc has put on his leg it still looks a bloody mess.

'I've eased the pain for a while,' Wicks mutters as he straightens, 'but he needs to be taken into hospital quickly. We will have to carry him gently on some sort of stretcher, and I want his leg raised if at all possible.'

'A stretcher! Where the hell are we going to find a stretcher?' I ask bitterly.

'When I was in the scouts we made stretchers by buttoning up coats round a couple of poles,' suggests Finney, arriving late and blurry-eyed.

'That won't do,' says the doctor. 'We want something solid.'

'There's an old barn or something over there.' Royal points towards some ramshackle buildings on the other side of the road. 'We should find a door amongst that lot.'

'A door would be perfect.'

I go with Royal, and sure enough, we find a door hanging on one hinge. It is old and cracked, but solid enough to take Chopper, so we ease him onto it, trying to ignore his moans, and the way his eyes flicker open to stare at us with no sign of recognition. We strap him down as securely as we can, but he looks deathly pale, so that even I can see that unless we get him to a hospital soon he won't survive. Doc has tied a tourniquet high on Chopper's thigh with a length of stick twisted into the knot.

'I'll look after that,' he tells Martingale, 'but if anything happens to me make sure it is eased off from time to time to allow the blood to flow.'

Martingale nods. 'We must get away from here. That fire could bring the whole German army down on us. I want two volunteers for the stretcher, then we will take it in hourly spells.'

'You can take the head, Royal,' I order with relish. 'No need to relieve you, is there, a big strapping feller, like you? Finney and I will take the other end between us, then there will be no need to keep swopping over.'

Martingale is staring at me with a strange look on his face, but Royal places himself ready to lift the door without comment. For a second or two Martingale seems about to speak, then he thinks better of it, and just grunts an order to get moving. 'If you get tired, Royal, I will give you a spell.'

'That's okay, sir. I'd like to do my bit.'

'Good man! Let's get cracking. We will use the road, but be ready to dive into the hedge if I give the word.'

We move on past deserted buildings where the road is littered with abandoned vehicles and pockmarked with shell and bomb craters. The dull light of a new dawn is turning the mist a lighter shade of grey, and there should be bird song wakening with it. I look at my watch – four-thirty. There will be no dawn chorus today. The obscene stench of war leaves nature impotent. It is Friday, and *Scavenger* is due out of dock over the weekend. She will most likely sail Tuesday or Wednesday to swing and calibrate compasses. There will be no need for a period of working-up, for it has been a short refit, and her crew is already primed and schooled in her ways. I am part of that company, and the way things are going here I will miss her sailing. Other men might relish the chance to miss a patrol, but not me. She is my boat, and her ship's company are my lads.

We walk in silence and even the war-sounds are muted, like the rumble of a distant storm. The whole countryside is loath to wake to this foul new day, and only a lone, strident cockerel has the audacity to voice his clarion call to herald the rising sun.

Royal sets the pace, carrying the door easily with his broad shoulders square and his head held high. His whole bearing exudes cussedness, and I can feel his threat from here.

Weariness is numbing my senses. I am walking like an automaton with my head bent forward, hardly noticing the weight of Chopper on his door. All of us are desperately tired, pushing one foot in front of the other while our brains fight to stay alert; too exhausted to care much anymore. It is enough that we have to keep awake, let alone watch the roads and fields for the enemy.

Thus it is that we almost stroll nonchalantly into a column of German vehicles parked along the side of the road with their nearside wheels slumped into the soft verge so that they are half hidden beneath the shrubbery. We know they are German because someone is shouting to us as we stand frozen in the centre of the road.

'Don't panic!' grates Martingale in a harsh whisper. 'They can't see who we are in this mist.'

He waves a casual arm at the grey shape as it detaches itself from the shadows to stare at us. The vehicles are armoured cars, well camouflaged to blend in with the foliage with their engines stopped. I thank the Lord that we have come upon them from the north, for if we had come the other way they would be much more wary. Round this area they have it much their own way and are self-assured enough to identify their targets before opening fire.

As yet the soldier is on his own, holding his rifle loose in his hands with the muzzle lowered. 'Leave this to me,' whispers Royal. 'I can speak the language.'

The German has stopped, and we face each other across twenty yards of road with the mist swirling between us, so that we are just vague shapes without substance.

'*Wo ist der nächste Unfallstation?*' Royal shouts without so much as a tremor in his voice.

'*Welche Beschwerden haben Sie?*' The man's head is canted to one side like a curious dog, and he takes a couple more strides towards us. I notice a movement behind him as someone stirs.

'I can't hold it,' warns Royal urgently. 'When I say "go", drop the door and run.'

His sudden shout takes the German off-guard and we have the split second it takes for him to realise he has heard an English voice. The door and Chopper hit the ground as self-preservation takes charge and we hurl our bodies through the hedge into the field beyond. They take time to recover and we are halfway across the field before the first shots come. My feet hardly touch the ground as I race over the turf with bullets singing past my ears, but the mist is on our side today as we weave and dodge all over the place.

I place my hand into the middle of the doctor's back and push him along when he begins to falter. The light is improving all the time, and Royal grabs one arm while I take the other so that between us we bundle him across the remaining few yards to the opposite hedge. Luckily the field on the other side is only half the width of the first, so we reach the next hedge safely and burst through into a narrow lane.

Straight over we go, across a low wall and into a farmyard where a maze of buildings and pig-sties provide cover. With one accord we swing left through a narrow, slurry-filled cart-track. The doctor stumbles along blindly; relying on us completely and wheezing air into his lungs, on the verge of collapse. His legs are like rubber, wobbling all over the place as he allows us to drag him bodily through the maze.

We run out into the open again, but there is a small clump of trees ahead. Tangled tentacles of briar clutch at our legs with thorny talons as we bang into solid trunks and bluster on until we emerge on the other side and find a small, broken-down wooden hut where we slump down, panting. No one has energy to speak. We can only fall into heaps and gulp air into our lungs.

Inevitably it is Royal who recovers first. He peers cautiously round the corner of the hut for a sign of our pursuers. The bastard must have the constitution of a horse, for the rest of us are still recovering breath; especially the poor old doctor who sounds as though he is slowly being strangled. I watch as he rolls over onto his back with his chest heaving, staring up at nothing. It is then that I realise that the mist is clearing fast, and already the sun is burning through.

'I don't think they are following us,' Royal comments quietly, and Martingale goes to stand with him. I go too, and we stare out at the woods. Nothing moves.

'I don't reckon they want to leave their vehicles to chase after us,' suggests Royal calmly. 'They know we are just small-fry and well boxed in. In fact, we're not worth the bother.'

'Yes,' agrees Martingale. 'I'm afraid you're right. We have walked in a bloody great circle, straight into the middle of them. We've got our own little "Dunkirk" here, and no armada of ships waiting to take us off the beach.'

I slump back dejectedly. That is a sobering thought. *Scavanger* is looking more remote than ever. The heat of the strengthening sun has a soporific effect on me in this small haven in the depths of rural France where the war could easily pass us by if we remain perfectly still. It is just a mumbling threat on the horizon at the moment, nothing to do with us. Maybe we can merge into the countryside and mingle with the natives until it is all over. After all, they keep telling us it will be all over by Christmas.

I glance over to where Royal and Martingale hold a conference in the corner of the hut, and suddenly I remember that I have not found an opportunity to tell the lieutenant the full story. The way Royal has been operating lately would lead anyone to believe he is an enterprising, strong, courageous man, and not the sneaky, murderous swine I know him to be. He is always at the forefront, volunteering for anything that comes along, and even taking decisions when the rest of us are procrastinating. Even now, while Finney, the doctor and I stretch out in the sunshine, he is there offering advice to Martingale. A cold thought grips me when I recall that Chopper is gone now. Intentionally or not, Royal has got rid of another witness.

I force my reluctant limbs into action again and stand up with them, determined to tell Martingale the whole truth this time. I may never get another chance.

'Sir. Before we move off again I have to speak to you about Royal.'

'What is this all about, Grant?' he asks in a tetchy voice. 'We ought to be on our way.'

'We cannot afford to hang about,' interposes Royal, staring hard into my eyes.

'It will not wait, sir,' I insist, ignoring the interruption. 'You know that Royal is wanted by the police for murder.'

'What!'

'It's true, sir. When we pulled him off the cabin cruiser he was calling himself Maundy. I happen to know that he stole the identity tags from Maundy's corpse to escape the law. If he had not bumped into me again he might have got away with it.' I wait for Royal to object, but he just stands leering at me; sending a hot surge of anger through my body. 'I believe that he could well have got rid of Borroughs too.'

'What an imagination!' scoffs Royal.

'Do you deny it?' asks Martingale.

Royal shrugs. 'He's got some of it right, but the rest is pure fantasy. I admit that my name is Royal and I am wanted by the Dover police, but it is up to you whether you believe I murdered anyone. Septimus Maundy was an orphan with no living relatives as far as he knew. I found this out when I helped him to fill out his "Next of Kin" form. When I saw him lying dead on *Brigand*'s deck I saw a possible way out, but now I can see how stupid it was. I fully intend to go back and face the music. After all, I know I'm innocent.'

'What about Borroughs?' I persist.

'What about him?'

'You know bloody well what I'm talking about. I don't think you went out of your way to help Chopper either. Getting rid of the witnesses one by one. Who was going to be next: Finney or me?'

Martingale steps in quickly when we shape up to each other. 'That's enough – both of you!' he snaps. 'We have more urgent problems right now. I will be keeping a watchful eye on you, Royal. Whether you are guilty of murder or not is for the courts to decide, but anyone who can cold-bloodedly steal a shipmate's identity needs to be watched. In the meantime we must concentrate on getting out of this mess.'

'I ain't 'appy on shore,' declares Finney out of the blue. 'I say let's go back ter the TRV.'

We stare at him as though he has materialized from space. 'What good will that do?' I ask. 'You put her out of action before you left.'

His eyes swim in all directions as he tries to organise his thoughts. 'There's a dinghy and a carley-raft on board. Nah that there's only five of us we could use one or the other ter get away.'

There is a stunned mixture of surprise and respect in our eye, and Royal puts our thoughts into words. 'Of course we could. I know this coast like the back of my hand. If we could wait until after high tide we will have the flow with us for about seven hours going south. It would push us down towards St Tréport or St Valéry-en-Caux. The Germans are too busy to worry about a fifteen foot dinghy.'

There is a new sense of optimism as we see a way out of our predicament. Tired, hungry and disheartened, it had begun to look as though we were just running from one impossible situation to another. The disreputable stoker PO has restored our confidence with a suggestion that appeals to us all. Even to be back at sea again will give a sense of security.

'You will have to go without me,' the doctor's weary voice quells our enthusiasm. 'I can read the signs and know that I will never make it. I won't even get back to the beach, let alone survive several hours in an open boat.'

'Balls!' snorts Finney. 'We'll give yer a 'and, mate. Carry yer if necessary.'

Wicks shakes his grey head slowly. He looks as old as Methuselah as he looks up at us with his sad eyes. 'I'm afraid not. I was stupid to venture out on this enterprise in the first place. Got carried away, I suppose. Make me comfortable and escape while you can, please.' His eyes are pleading now. 'I can't face any more of this. Every movement is sheer agony.' He grins weakly. 'Can't think what my wife will say – she is expecting me home for breakfast.'

Royal bends to take his arm. 'We may not get you home for breakfast, Doc; but we are not going to leave you here. There are four of us, and we can chair you between us for the short distance we have to go. As regards the open boat, this is May, not December. We will make you warm and snug, so don't let's have any more bloody nonsense.'

I find myself clasping hands with Royal under the doctor's bony buttocks while he leans back into our arms. Prejudices are pushed into the background as we move out once more.

V

'There it goes again!' Martingale's warning sends us crouching even lower into the shallow hollow, straining our ears to pick up the sound. We have covered no more than half a mile along the twisting lane that snakes aimlessly towards the coast. We can hear the beat of the surf and the drag of the undertow on the shingle, but always the lane weaves inland just when we seem about to burst out onto the beach. Now at last we are about to emerge onto the main road; only to halt in our tracks as a new sound comes. A whimpering, half-human noise approaching from the south.

I creep forward stealthily, lifting up so that I can part some bracken and peer through the gap. For a moment I see nothing, then a shambling figure reels into view, staggering out into the centre of the road. The man looks drunk as he wavers unsteadily for a moment, recovers, then sidles back to the verge again. I hardly recognise the colonel, for his hair is matted with filth and his uniform torn and caked with mud. His eyes stare vacantly out of his contorted face, and he is blubbering like a baby.

I go out to meet him, gathering up his body into my arms when it is about to drop. He stares at me without recognition and flinches as though he expects me to hit him. As I lead him gently along big tears roll down his cheeks, leaving white tracks in the grime. His whole body convulses and I realise there are words mixed in with the incoherent blabber.

'How dare they – how dare they!' he repeats over and over.

When I get him back to the others the doctor leans over

and lifts one eyelid. 'He is in shock,' he confirms needlessly, and slaps an open palm sharply across a cheek. 'Colonel!' he urges, 'take a hold of yourself.' The eyes flicker and swivel vaguely, finally coming to settle on the doctor's face.

'Here,' offers Martingale. 'Give him some of this.' He hands a small flask to the doctor.

'What is it?'

'Rum.'

The colonel shudders and chokes on the fiery liquid. Doc forces another sip into his quivering lips and he takes it more easily. We watch and wait while his face relaxes and he stares up at us as though he is unable to believe what he sees. Doc bunches up a jacket and wedges it under the colonel's head. A further sip of rum brings more sanity into his expression.

'My God!' he breathes through his slack mouth, dribbling over the words as he speaks in a hollow voice; staring out into a void as the awful memories come. 'They caught us as we forded a small stream. I – I fell into a clump of reeds and couldn't move, but the others tried to scramble out on the other side.' A spasm runs through his body and his mouth twists. 'They didn't stand a chance. The automatics seemed to fire from right beside my ear. All I could do was watch, half submerged in the filth as they were mown down.'

He stops for a moment, reliving the horror. 'They tried to surrender. Held their arms up above their heads and screamed for mercy, but the swine kept on firing, and I swear that I heard someone laughing.' His face is ghastly white and anguished as the pictures form in his mind.

'All right, colonel,' soothes the doctor. 'It's all over now. Try and get a grip on yourself, there's a good chap.'

For a moment the eyes squeeze shut, then they pop open to stare straight at me, boring into my own as though he wants to transfer his visions to me. 'I stayed deep in the water while the shadows bustled about. They fired one more burst into a man who was trying to climb over the bank. I saw the bullets smash into his spine and he rolled back down into the water, ending up only a yard or so away from me, pouring his blood into the stream. I held my breath as they moved up and down the bank, looking for more victims. It seemed a lifetime before they began to move away. And then —' His voice tails off and his eyes close as though he feels pain. 'I heard someone say in English, "That takes care of that bloody lot".

'We·ought to get moving.'

Royal's matter-of-fact voice penetrates the pause that follows. His tone is as cold as steel and he is already moving out into the road, peering up and down, making sure all is clear. The rest of us exchange glances. No one needs to voice his thoughts; we are all thinking the same. 'This hard-hearted bastard is capable of anything.'

'Christ!' His curse snaps our heads round to see him staring north towards the small clump of houses. 'Bloody refugees!'

Sure enough a straggled column of drab, sad-faced people are shambling towards us, wheeling their few belongings in hand-carts, prams, or draped over the handle-bars of bicycles. It is a pathetic procession; nothing like the endless masses that choke the roads further inland. Just a few inhabitants from the group of houses. Women, kids, weak and old; they've had enough and taken the most painful decision of their lives to leave their homes and trudge south where they might find an end to the continuous nightmare of war. They are an indictment of those who glory in war and proclaim the heroism of its perpetrators. Their lives are ruined, and lifetime occupations, ambitions; the very fabric of their lives are being destroyed. They have held on to the bitter end, steadfastly hoping that the nightmare would pass, but now breaking-point is reached and there is little else one can do but take what can be carried and set out along a road away from the stink and abomination.

I feel a deep sense of shame as I watch them go by with hardly a glance at us. They are not interested in which side we represent. We are military and that's enough to tell them that we are part of what is driving them from their homes, their fields and their fishing gear. They look hard at the treasures stored up over generations, valueless to anyone except themselves. They place a hand on the backs of favourite chairs, or finger soft drapes that turned cold granite into homes that pulsated with life. They swallowed the hard lumps that closed their tight throats and shut their doors behind them, then set off with their friends in silent procession, too choked to look back. The age of battlefields, banners, bugles and such is gone. Now the grey, faceless mechanical tide of war oozes across France like a disease.

Their empty faces are like stone as they pass. The shuffle of their feet can scarcely be heard above the rumble and crackle, and a billowing pillar of black smoke lifts like an admonishing finger behind them, urging them along with its menace. They are dry-eyed for they have no tears left. Speechless because there are no more words. Hopeless for they are leaving one greyness for another.

'Are you coming, Grant?' The call breaks the spell and I follow mutely as we move towards the houses. The sun is high and hot now, baking the surface of the road and burning into my back. The doctor has recovered enough to walk with the support of a helping hand from Finney. Progress is slow but at least he is on his feet. Royal takes charge of the colonel, leading him along still glassy-eyed and dazed, with his shoulders stooped and his head sagging. Shocked and broken he has lost his pomposity and allows himself to be carried along with the rest, muttering inanely as he goes. We make a sorry bunch. I take up the rear while Martingale leads us on towards the TRV, coming into view beyond the corner of the last house.

'Hold it!' Martingale's warning brings us to a staggering halt; bunching up as he holds up an arresting hand. I slide past the others to stare out across his shoulder. 'Germans!' he croaks through a thick gullet, and I see a group of grey-clad soldiers squatting against the sea-wall.

'They're unarmed!' I whisper, and before he can reply we see a French infantryman stroll out from our side of the road with his rifle held across his chest. He is followed by another, and when we edge out of the shadows the whole group of de Carteret's soldiers come into view, standing at ease in the sunshine.

'Bloody hell!' I exclaim. 'The French have taken prisoners!'

There is a snapping of rifle bolts as we approach, and several muzzles aim straight at me, but de Carteret himself strides out from the group and his curt orders eases the situation. He smiles recognition. 'Where do you come from?' he asks, then his smile fades when Martingale explains how the enemy has encircled the area and cut us off from the Allies.

'*Merde!*' he growls, looking back at his men and their prisoners. 'Is it possible that my men have fought for nothing?'

Martingale looks dejected. 'It looks pretty hopeless, captain. My lads and I are going to use the dinghy and raft to go south, but I am afraid there is not room for more than six or seven of your men. If you wish to select a few we would be happy to take them along with us. It's all I can offer.'

I look at the battle-weary *poilus* slumped against the wall with their prisoners staring sullenly from the opposite side of the road. Victories are scarce at this time. Right now the enemy seems invincible as he drives across Europe, crushing all in his path; making people homeless, spreading destruction and death with his aircraft and tanks. Every now and again he gets a bloody nose or a kick up the arse, and these Frenchmen have done that here. Now it seems, their effort will be rewarded by receiving even rougher treatment when the Germans over-run this area and take them prisoner.

'That cannot be right!' I blurt out suddenly. 'There must be something we can do for these blokes!'

Everyone's staring at me; surprised at my sudden

outburst, and my brain is scratching about desperately for a solution. 'Why can't we use the TRV, sir?'

Everyone stares at the abandoned vessel sitting high and dry as though it is to become a permanent fixture on the beach. Water pours out of the sea-cocks and shell holes and she is already sinking her keel deep into the shingle. They all turn to look back at me as though I'm crazy.

'That's impossible!' says Martingale, but there is a note of doubt in his voice.

'Maybe,' I admit, 'but if we could plug the holes and shut the valves when she is drained down she might lift off on the next tide. I know the engine is useless, but what about Royal's theory about the tide? Surely if it can carry the raft and dinghy south it could do the same with the TRV?'

'We would have to get her well clear of the beach and out into the channel,' says Royal doubtfully. 'The wind is right; it is coming off-shore and as long as it stays there we won't drift back in. The main problem is to make sure she will not ground when the tide starts to flow.'

'We could use one of the bower-anchors as a kedge,' I insist eagerly. 'Drop the anchor and unshackle the cable, then we manhandle the dinghy over the top and secure the anchor beneath the keel with a strop. We will do it as set out in the Seamanship Manual: wedge a bracing spar between the gunnels and pass the strop right over the dinghy. The tide will do the rest when it comes in and we can row the whole shebang out to the correct spot and release the hook. Once the TRV lifts off the bottom we can haul her out; even without the winch we have enough spare hands to do that. We can also use the dan-buoy spars to punt her out. It all depends on whether she can be made water-tight.'

We all look to Finney and he glowers back at us from under his thick brows. He sniffs and prods the hard tarmac with his toe as he thinks it out. 'I reckon I can shut the valves even wivaht the wheels,' he mutters cautiously. 'The shell holes are small, and we can use hammocks and bedding ter bung them up, then I'll shore it all up wiv baulks of timber; that should do it. She will still leak a bit, but the French pongoes will 'ave ter bail out as we go.'

'We can do better than that,' I say firmly. 'The manual tells us how to patch things up with collision-mats and canvas, lashed and frapped into position on the outside of the hull. I know we haven't any collision-mats, but we have got the heavy canvas hatch-covers. All the shell holes are concentrated aft and we won't be using the screw, so there will not be any turbulence to disturb the patch once it is in place. If we do the job right water-pressure will mould it to the hull and keep her dry for the time it takes us to reach the Allies.

Martingale is impressed. 'Well done, Grant. All we need is for the wind to stay where it is, and a certain amount of luck.' He turns to de Carteret. 'We can take all your men, captain. With God's help we can drift down to our own lines in a few hours. Despite all that's happening on shore, the Navy still holds the sea in this area.'

'Haven't we forgotten something?' asks Royal caustically.

'What's that?'

'Those German prisoners. Are we going to take them with us?'

Martingale shakes his head after a brief pause. 'No. That would be too risky.' He turns to de Carteret. 'We cannot afford to have them on board. If we run into difficulty we will need all hands for the ship. They could jeopardise our chances.'

De Carteret's mouth tightens. 'Leave them to me, lieutenant.' Something in his tone gives me an uncomfortable feeling, but we have a lot to do and I tell myself that the German prisoners are the concern of the French. It's small consolation.

We set about preparing the TRV for sea. As always in these circumstances we improvise and improve on the original ideas, so that by the time the sea reaches the hull we have the anchor tightly lashed to the dinghy, ready for the tide to lift it clear. We throw overboard everything that is of no further use, then we have a meal of corned beef and hard-tack while we wait.

As soon as there is enough water I join Royal in the dinghy, and with an oar apiece we row steadily out until we reach the pre-ordained spot, where we slash the strop with a 'pusser's dirk' and drop the anchor. We have been careful to attach a dan buoy to the short pennant so that when Martingale and a couple of French *poilus* paddle out with the eye of the hawser we can shackle it on. Now, when the time comes we will slip the pennant and be on our way.

Meanwhile Finney and a couple of *poilus* set about plugging the holes to make her water-tight. There are plenty of willing hands now to help pass the lines to haul the canvas patch into place under the hull, all we need is for the enemy to leave us alone for a few hours.

I cast an anxious glance ashore. I have been too busy to worry about the enemy while we were making our preparations, but now I remember just how vulnerable we are. Any moment a column of trucks or a patrol could come down the coast-road, and all they require to blow all our plans apart are a couple of field-guns. I shake the thought away and watch the *poilus* coming on board in batches.

Finney has his bucket-chain well organised, and they are busy draining the dregs of ocean from the bilges. So far – so good. If you have time to study it carefully you can observe the tide running through the shingle and filling the contours in the small patches of sand near the water's edge. We have become used to the continuous rumble of battle, but now it seems to be closing in. I put it down to my imagination, but I can see other faces staring northwards as it becomes obvious that our small oasis is being swallowed up. It's our own little 'Dunkirk' all right, and when I look out to sea it is desolate and seems to stretch away to infinity.

A sudden rattle of rifle-fire startles me for a moment, and I look towards the shore, half expecting to see squads of enemy troops emerging from the surrounding hedgerows. All I see is a party of de Carteret's troops marching towards us, and I know that Royal's concern over the German prisoners is no longer valid. These Frenchmen are an uncompromising lot; almost as hostile to us as the enemy. I watch them wading out to the TRV, still fully kitted-up. They go about their affairs with a grim, purposeful silence, and I can sense the deep-rooted hatred they feel for their age-old enemy.

I reckon the tide is about the same height as when we hit the beach, and our luck holds good, despite the increased sounds of conflict that seems to come from just beyond the hedges. The main Abbeville to Dieppe road slices diagonally across the countryside to emerge at St Tréport, leaving a triangle of sparsely populated area with only minor roads and small clusters of isolated buildings on the flat, featureless landscape. Maybe that is the reason why we are being by-passed.

I look down at the water creeping slowly up the hull. The TRV sits on an even keel and shows no sign of moving. We have organised the *poilus* so that the hawser is manned and ready to haul us aft the moment she lifts. Others form their bucket-chain into the engineroom, but they have little to do, for Finney's patching is holding the water at bay.

'Here they come!' Royal's warning sends a shiver running down my spine and I follow his outstretched arm to see a moving dust-cloud riding like the smoke of a locomotive over the hedges. 'If that's tanks or artillery we've had it,' he goes on in a steady, unemotional voice.

I swing round to report to Martingale and find him already climbing the short ladder to the fo'c'sle. He shades his eyes and studies the dust-cloud for a moment without speaking.

'Perhaps they will think we are just an abandoned hulk, sir,' I suggest hopefully. 'We've got a fair amount of water between us and the beach already. They may not have the time or inclination to worry about a wreck until they have dealt with the main problem.'

'I wish I shared your optimism, Grant. We can make it less inviting, however, by creating a fire on deck with fuel-oil. It will provide a smoke-screen for any activity on deck and give the impression that this is a smoking hulk, driven up on the beach. We can get the bulk of the Frenchmen out of sight in the hold and try to maintain a low profile.

'They could still miss this small pocket, sir,' says Royal. 'I miscalculated before, but now I can see that we have run ashore to the north of Cayeux. That means that we are almost at the entrance of the Somme, and this isn't the sort of territory for tanks or heavy armour. My guess is that they will have to stick to the roads and stay clear of the twisting little lanes that criss-cross these parts. That dust-cloud is on the St Valéry road, I'd say.'

Martingale purses his lips thoughtfully. 'Nevertheless I think we will organise the smoke-screen and swing out the derrick so that it hangs over the side – anything to make the TRV look like an abandoned wreck.'

'I'll get on with it right away, sir,' I concur grimly. 'That coast-road looks good enough to take armour to me, and somewhere along the shore a pile of dead German prisoners are waiting to be discovered. That'll take some explaining if they capture us. If they put two and two together and bring up a couple of heavy guns they could pound us out of the water; and I don't give much for our chances of being treated gently.'

'You don't need to remind me, Grant.' He looks over the side. 'God, that tide is taking its time!'

'You can't hurry it, sir,' states Royal cheerfully. 'It'll come up in it's own sweet time, but I'm certain now that it will lift us off. Look, you can see the tide-mark on the steep slope of shingle over there, and remember, we were a lot lower in the water when we came in with the bilges flooded. All we need is patience and luck.'

'We are going to need more than that I'm afraid,' I growl. 'There is something solid coming out from where the road bends inland about a mile or so north.' The dark shape is followed by another and another as they track south towards us.

Martingale runs aft to the wheelhouse to return with a pair of binoculars. One glance is enough. 'It's armour all right,' he says tightlipped. 'I don't know one tank from another, but these beauties have biggish looking guns on their turrets. There are a couple of motorcycle outriders ahead of the column, and a scout-car leading the tanks.' He lowers his glasses. 'Get your men below, and tell them to keep their heads low, Captain,' he adds to de Carteret. 'I'll go down and start the fires. Let's give them plenty of smoke and flame to look at.'

Within seconds a cloud of black, oily smoke billows from the waist seawards, with yellow flame licking at it's roots. From shore it must look as though we are a burning hulk, stranded on the beach.

I crouch beneath the height of the break of the fo'c'sle, watching as the convoy creeps down towards us. It stops about a quarter of a mile up the road, and I don't need to be told what they are looking at.

'The arse-end is afloat, sir' Finney comes loping forward with his long arms dangling and his rump stuck up in the air, looking like a gangling anthropoid. 'I reckon she is 'oldin' amidships, but we could 'ave a go at shiftin' 'er.'

'Christ!' swears Martingale. 'Those bloody tanks would have to turn up now!'

They are close enough for us to see faces, and infantrymen are moving up the road ahead of the armour, searching the verges suspiciously as they approach the line of houses. The two motor-cyclists are stopped; waiting for the foot-soldiers to do their job, and I see their goggled eyes peering out in our direction. I hold my breath, but someone must have shouted, for their faces snap round and an arm goes up to wave the tanks on.

Each tank has a small cupola on its turret, with the half-lids flung back and the commander standing waist-deep with earphones clamped on his head. The roar of low-geared engines and the harsh, gritty scrape and

clink of tracks carry to us across the shingle as they come
abreast. They have almost reached the houses. The
motor-cyclists straddling their legs to hold their machines
upright while they study the blank windows and doors.

I feel the TRV move as she comes adrift. If we are to
keep her from drifting out of control we must take up the
slack on the hawser. I see my anxieties reflected on
Martingale's face as he leans back against the hard metal.
The moment one of those tank commanders decide we are
worth a shell or two we might as well pack up. Powerless,
and at point-blank range they could pulverise us with
methodical fire at their leisure, without fear of retaliation,
and after the massacred prisoners they have seen they
would probably enjoy every minute of it.

'We dare not risk moving now,' breathes Martingale
desperately. 'We must wait and hope they will move on. It
would be suicide to work on deck; even under the smoke.'

'A couple of us could go aft if we keep our heads down,
sir.' I suggest. 'We could take in the slack to stop her from
drifting even further up the beach on the incoming tide. If
we don't we might lose her altogether.'

'We are wasting our bloody time!' Royal's strident voice
startles both of us. He makes no attempt to keep his voice
down, nor to hide himself. 'They are too busy to bother
with us at the moment. If we wait they'll finish checking
the houses and turn their attention to us.'

Finney and I move together; leaping on him and
dragging him kicking and struggling to the deck. I clamp a
hand over his mouth to stop his yelling and he sinks his
teeth into it. I hold on in agony, and manage to sit on him
until his struggles subside and he lies still, staring up at us
with his face infused with rage.

'What are you trying to do, you idiot!' I snarl. 'You'll
wreck everything, you bloody fool!'

There is blood oozing from my hand, but at least he has
relaxed his jaw a little. I ease away cautiously, ready to ram
my fist into his mouth if he so much as looks like making a
sound. His eyes blaze with fury, and his body shakes

beneath me. He is like a tightly coiled spring, quaking with suppressed energy. I am convinced that there is something evil about this bloke; it is as though the only emotion he ever feels is rage, and it seems to turn him into a monster. Nothing we have seen or done has affected him at all. He is as cold-blooded as a viper and just as dangerous as far as I'm concerned.

Satisfied that we have him in hand for the moment I glance at Martingale, but before he can say a word there is a thunderous explosion that shakes the ship and sends a wave of concussion through the crowded hold. It is followed by several more; each one louder than the last, and the TRV trembles in the water. I lift my head above the gunnel in time to see the next shell burst inside one of the houses. The whole face of the building bulges, crumbles, then collapses onto the nearest tank spreading rubble and a cloud of dust across the road.

Two more shells thump into the chaos, lifting a tank as though it is a toy and tossing it over on its side. 'Get your men up top, captain!' shouts Martingale, all caution gone. He is on his feet and pushing de Carteret ahead of him as he lurches aft. I scramble up and go with them; running up to the poop-deck where the hawser is fed through the fairleads out to the kedge anchor. Bodies are pouring out of the hatches to lay hold of the hawser, with Martingale and the French captain yelling at them to sweat back on the wire. Finney is beside me, and I take a brief look round for Royal, but there is no time to figure out where he has got to as a new barrage of shells spread a scattered row of craters along the road.

I see another tank reversing desperately away from the devastation. It ploughs through the rubble, crushing stone and timber under its tracks. Climbing a loose-shale ridge to poise uncertainly on the apex for a moment before toppling into the deep crater beyond. Infantrymen scatter like ants falling into any cover they can find, and diving into the craters and ditches to escape the bombardment. I could have enjoyed watching, but already the hawser is stretching taut as the *poilus* keep up their pressure. She is moving off slowly. Fighting the tide and wind and yawing slightly in the eddies. I pray we don't find a sand-bank to ruin it all before she runs clear.

A bullet ricochets off the metal door of the galley with a sound like an angry hornet. Even in the midst of the bombardment dedicated German squaddies are crouching to take pot-shots at us. Someone must have noticed movement on the ship and realised she is not just an innocuous chunk of abandoned scrap metal, but luckily for us nothing bigger than rifle bullets come our way.

She is sliding out nicely, helped by the off-shore breeze that slews her sideways so that we go out crab-fashion. Almost sub-consciously I take a bearing on a couple of landmarks, just to reassure myself that we are actually moving. I place my foot on the hawser and it confirms the evidence of my eyes, for there is little strain on the wire: showing that she is moving under her own weight and the *poilus* are only required to haul in the slack.

We must take care not to allow her to over-run the anchor or she may swing the wrong way. Once we are in position we must contain our impatience and wait for high water, then for the tide to flow. It has to be done precisely, for once we cast off the wire strop that secures her to the anchor we will be at the mercy of the elements. A change of wind or a slight misjudgement of the tide could carry us back into the shallows.

The last few yards of wire come sliding in until the angle is 'up-and-down'. I take some turns on a pair of bollards and allow her to take up on the hawser. With slack water and a small breeze she will hold like this until I am ready to set her free. The shelling has stopped and apart from the occasional ricochet all is peaceful. With the sun warming my body through I am content to squat on a coil of manilla to ease my aching limbs. I get an irrational sensation of well-being as my muscles relax, and I stretch back with my hands clasped behind my head to stare up into the clear blue sky; clear that is, except for a hawk circling high and black against the pale, washed out canopy. The deep grumble of battle drowns out smaller sounds, but staring up at it I know that if the day was quiet I would hear the lazy growl of an aircraft engine, for the 'hawk' is a small spotter-plane, hovering over the distant ridges, and relaying ranges and bearings to hidden guns: the question is, whose guns?

I report it to Martingale and we study it together as it wheels in tight circle. It has the sky to itself today, and it is impossible to tell if it is an Army Lysander or a German Storch.

'It has to be German,' growls Martingale sullenly, 'otherwise the Luftwaffe would have blasted it out of the sky by now. My guess is that it has been whistled-up by those blokes over there to take care of the guns that's knocking out their tanks. We must hope and pray she doesn't bother to investigate the TRV.'

One more prayer to add to a steady collection today. Prayers for wind, prayers for tide, prayers for a squadron of Spitfires or a nice big destroyer. Sitting out here wide open to attack all we can do is pray. The sea is like glass, and even the wind is taking a rest as the tide reaches its zenith, so that we are held in a circle of limpid water, baking in the heat of the sun, watching the antics of that tiny aircraft.

The minutes tick by. Tension increases, and all eyes are on that hostile bird. There is no longer any doubting its nationality for we can feel its menace, even though it ignores us. What riles us is that it remains unscathed. Not one single burst of anti-aircraft fire blemishes its area of blue sky. It soars happily, without a care in the world over St Valéry-sur-Somme; utterly indifferent to the turmoil going on below; immune and untroubled by any potential aggressor. It depresses us for it emphasizes the truth, and we know that we are impotent against the awesome power it represents.

I shake my head to clear away these thoughts. 'I think I'll go below and check on the colonel, sir. It will be

another hour or so before the tide begins to run our way
and I'll go nuts if I have to stand here watching that stupid
little plane much longer.'

Martingale nods agreement and I leave him to go aft,
climbing down the ladder leading to the living- quarters.
Except for the main cabin they are unoccupied, and I
stand for a moment in the passage, listening to the water
swilling about in the bilges beneath the deckboards. There
is nothing to worry about there. Finney's makeshift repairs
are holding out well.

I turn my attention to the door of the main mess, and as
I look I hear the muffled sound of men's voices. I assume
the doctor is there tending to the colonel and I take a step
towards the opening, then freeze when I hear a sharp
retort followed by sounds of sobbing. Sidling forward
stealthily I peer round the edge of the door.

'All that public school rubbish won't do you much good
now, will it?' Royal is sneering. 'Look at you, you cringing,
gutless bastard! God, how I detest you supercilious,
upper-class sods!'

Slamming the door back against the bulkhead I launch
my body through as a gurgling cry comes from the
colonel. Royal looms over him, looking as if he is about to
strike, and the colonel is cringing into a corner with his
hands across his head. Blood oozes from his nose and
there is bruising on his face.

I grab Royal's arm. 'What the hell do you think you're
doing?'

He reels back, never taking his eyes away from his
cowering victim. 'I am trying to stop this stupid old idiot
from injuring himself.' He swings on me with a twisted
grin. 'Not that I expect you to believe me. It's the truth
nevertheless.'

I square up to him, ready to hit out if he tries to have a
go at me. 'Too right I don't believe you, Royal.' I snarl.
'Get the hell out of here before I do something I'll regret.'

His face holds its derisive leer but he knows enough to
keep from lashing out at me. Instead he growls, 'That's

right, look after the stupid bastard. God knows he needs wet-nursing! I'm telling you though, all I did was tell him he was required up top and he went into hysterics, thrashing about all over the place and banging his head against the bulkheads.' He smirks. 'I might have lost my temper in the process and shoved him back roughly, but nothing more than that.'

The colonel's face is a mess. 'Christ!' I exclaim. 'You are going to pay for this, Royal. Hitting a colonel on top of everything else – you must be insane!'

'I didn't bloody well hit him!' he protests wildly, but slumps back and shrugs resignedly. 'Ah what's the use? Believe what you like. You might as well know that I can't stand these ex-public-school types, with their plummy voices and toffee-nosed attitudes.' His face is full of contempt. 'I could have had a command of my own if it were not for the likes of his sort. Instead I've had to play second fiddle to an incompetent sin-bosun with a quarter of my sea-going experience. You must know the score, Grant. The system stinks as much in your mob as in the Merchant Service, doesn't it? To get anywhere you must know the right hand-signals. That's one thing Hitler's lot have got going for them: They hate "The Brotherhood" almost as much as they hate the Jews.' He is shaking with emotion, clutching and unclutching his hands.

'I'm not concerned with your hangups,' I snap. 'If you think I'm too stupid to see what is going on here you need your head examining. There's blood all over the place, and on your clothes. Look at your knuckles, for Christ sake!' I point to his bruised hands.

'I was trying to control him,' he persists. 'He would have killed himself if I had let him.'

'Piss off!' I bark, turning my back on him and bending to look at the colonel. 'Where's the doctor?'

'How the hell do I know?'

I straighten up and push my face close to his. 'Find him; and bring him back here. Maybe he can repair some of the damage you've done, you murdering bastard!'

His mouth works as he stares at me. For a moment he is poised to hit me, and I'm relishing the prospect, but the colonel groans, taking the heat out of the situation. Royal backs off, turns, and goes crashing out through the door.

It takes a second or so to get my own emotions under control, then I carefully hoist the blubbering colonel onto a bench-seat. For the first time I realise how old he is. His hair is steel-grey and his eyes lined with age. He had hidden it well beneath a façade of pomposity, but now the pretence is gone and I am looking at an old fraud who was hauled out of retirement to do an officer's job and couldn't resist the temptation to act the warrior again. In the safe chintzy environment of a country village he must have relived old military exploits with his hoary old comrades, and when war was declared he rushed off to 'do his bit'. He had forgotten the full horror of battle. He was completely unprepared for the harrowing devastation of Dunkirk, and the mind-bending, unrelenting violence and noise everywhere. That, along with a sustained period of tension and sleeplessness, coupled with the slaughter of his small party of soldiers has broken his spirit.

I leave him lying on his back, staring at the deckhead, glassy-eyed. At least he is quiet now, but he looks desperately ill, with a face the colour of clay. On deck blatant sunlight lances into my eyes as I go out onto the poop. I find everyone staring up at the sky, and when I follow their gaze I see a pair of Hurricanes sweeping in from the west towards the little Storch. Like avenging angels they home in on it, and in seconds it is spiralling down with a plume of smoke pouring from its tail. The French equivalent of a cheer goes up as the two aircraft reform and zoom off to seek out more imposing targets. I feel like joining in the cheers, taking back all the nasty things I said about the RAF. The German aircraft was a sitting duck, and I doubt the British pilots know that we exist, but as far as we are concerned they were sent especially for us, if only to prove that this war is not totally one-sided.

Looking fore and aft I can see no sign of the doctor or Royal, so I turn my attention to the hawser. There is a definite pull on it now, and the TRV is swinging her bow slowly clockwise to point towards the south. The tide is flowing fast enough to eddy past the rudder with a soft swirl, and I decide it is time to cast off. I get a wild surge of elation when I knock off the pelican-hook. The strop leaps back through the fairleads and splashes into the sea and we are free.

At first there is no sense of movement at all. Only when I study the landmarks carefully for some time is it possible to detect a shift in our position. Moving with the tide we lose the small eddy that surged round the rudder so that there is no sensation of motion. I watch the landmarks again and again to reassure myself that we are drifting southwards. Eventually I can see that there is no doubt, and we are making progress; albeit at the pace of a very slow snail.

There is nothing more that I can do, other than try to contain my impatience and leave things to the wind and tide. I am aware that the rifle fire has ceased as those on shore find more important matters to attend to than a drifting hulk with a few tattered survivors on board. I go to the wheelhouse looking for Martingale, but find instead a small knot of anxious men bending over an inert body in one corner. Pressing closer I look over Finney's shoulder, and he straightens to say glumly, 'Came up from below lookin' like death and gaspin' fer fresh air.'

I push in closer. The doctor is fighting for air with his hand tugging at his collar. His face is puce and his lips purple while the useless crowd stares down at him. His bulging eyes plead for help, but he is the only one who knows what should be done, and he cannot speak.

A French soldier cradles his head and is opening his shirt, but beyond that we can only watch him writhe in agony, struggling to fill his lungs as his wheezing becomes more strangled. He coughs a couple of times, and a weak arm clutches at the Frenchman's sleeve for a moment. He half-lifts himself from the deck and we see his eyes plead frantically for a moment before they glaze over. He sighs a long, rattling breath as he falls back, and I do not need to test his pulse to know that he has gone. When I turn to go out I come face to face with Royal's sneering face.

'You gonna blame me for this one too?' he asks as I brush him aside.

VI

It is impossible to relax as the TRV drifts along the coast. soldiers with small knowledge of the sea move about restlessly, and agitate when they see how slowly we move. To them it is like standing still as they swelter in the heat of the sun and stare out at a never-changing shoreline. Others look up into the sky, unwilling to believe our luck will hold, and expecting to see the evil, black shapes of diving Stukas hurtling down on them. This drifting, impotent hulk is an open invitation to enemy aircraft: A sitting target with no power to manoeuvre or guns to retaliate.

To those of us familiar with the ways of the ocean the worries are different. Each minute that passes, and every yard gained is treasured. We test the wind over and over again, praying that it will stay where it is. We know that its natural tendency is to blow from the south-west in this area, and that would deposit us right back on the shingle, in the enemy's lap.

I know how Nelson's seamen learned the skills of close-hauled sailing when they beat against the prevailing winds on this part of the coast while they blockaded its harbours for months on end. There must have been times when they wallowed with slack canvas while the tide took charge, and men had to sweat at the oars of boats to drag their ships out of danger.

Unlike them, we have nothing to influence our progress. At one time I had considered rigging a hatch-cover from the mast-head to the derrick as a sail, but it would have been a futile gesture, for by the time we could manage to get it working, and trained people to man the guys and topping-lift the wind would probably change and ruin our efforts. Therefore, we must put our faith in the vagaries of wind, tide and Lady Luck.

Martingale takes frequent running fixes and reckons our drift to be something like one and a half knots as long as the wind remains where it is. Assuming the worst we could take anything up to ten hours to reach a position where we can be sure that we are clear of enemy-held territory. I have prepared two of the biggest, cleanest white ensigns I can find to hoist up to the mast and on our stern, for the last thing we want is some trigger-happy Allied gunner mistaking us for the enemy.

'There are a couple of fishing boats approaching from shore,' says Martingale in a calm voice, and I follow his gaze to watch the two small vessels puttering towards us. It looks as though they have come out especially to investigate the TRV by the way they hold on to their course, heading straight for us until the very last minute before swinging out in a big sweep to prowl round in wide circles while they make certain that we are harmless. Only then does one move in to run alongside while its mate lies off, and I recognise an officer standing on deck wearing khaki battledress and a naval cap. Several armed matelots watch us as the French fishermen prepare to pass lines across.

The officer climbs on board and comes directly to the wheelhouse. He salutes Martingale. 'Good morning, sir. I am Sub-Lieutenant Barratt. I expect you will be requiring a tow into St Tréport, but I'm afraid we have to beach you this side of the East Pier because the tides are wrong to make an entrance into the harbour. Sorry we took so long to locate you; it was difficult to persuade the fishermen to put to sea. Indeed, had it not been for the fact that you have French soldiers on board, I don't think they would have come at all.'

'You knew about us?' asks Martingale, incredulously.

'Oh yes. The Army has an observation post in a church spire somewhere near to where you ran aground, and they had spotted you while they were targeting their howitzers. They have to set different charges for different ranges you know. In fact, I believe they probably saved you from a nasty predicament.'

I leave them to their conversation and go forward with Finney and Royal to prepare the tow. The trawler which brought out the subby remains alongside, and we reinforce her mooring ropes so that we can use her to give a certain amount of steerage. The other one will take the headrope and do most of the pulling. Now at last there is an easing of tension as we begin to move through the water at a recognisable speed, with the chuckle of a small bow-wave building under the stem.

It is amazing how quickly the men cheer up when they can actually see the shore sliding by, and the rising cliffs of St Tréport taking shape ahead of us. A journey that only a short while ago seemed interminable is now just a short sea-side cruise as the features of the harbour already show clear on our port bow. The stumpy east pier and the over-lapping west breakwater reach out beyond the shingle where we intend beaching the TRV, and the town itself is catching the late afternoon sun in the windows of waterside buildings.

In less than an hour we reach the point where we must cast off the lead trawler and turn towards the shore. Her mate pushes us gently in towards the shelving beach, and once again we ground with hardly a bump. Within minutes the first French troops are wading ashore to form up in four ranks on the pier. At Martingale's request they carry the doctor's corpse with them, leaving Finney and me to go below for the colonel.

We find him seated at the table with his head cradled in his arms, staring vacantly at the scrubbed surface. Taking hold of an arm apiece we drag him towards the door. It is a bit like trying to manipulate a tailor's dummy, and we have to lift him bodily up the short ladder and out into the sunlight, where he stands dejected with hardly enough energy to blink against the glare. He just slumps between us like a sack of spuds, completely oblivious to all that goes on about him, even when Martingale helps us to lower him down to the beach. Royal stands well apart, making no effort to hide his impatience at our clumsy progress over the loose pebbles.

Barrett fusses about like a blue-arsed fly, dividing his time between us and a small contingent of medical personnel who are standing by with an ambulance and a thirty hundredweight truck. I have my foot on the tailboard of the truck when a sharp command rings out. The *poilus* snap to attention and turn right, ready to march away. They look dirty and worn out, but there is a pride in their bearing that brings a lump to my throat.

De Carteret stands aside, stiff-backed and proud, waiting for them to settle and stop swaying about before he gives the order to march off. I can sense the emotion lying beneath his blank façade. Deep down he knows France is facing the biggest tragedy of her history, yet he believes the Germans could have been held by a concerted effort. Like many of his countrymen he is incensed at the sight of British troops running back to Dunkirk while the fighting continues in the south. He shuts his mind to the thought of how close the Germans are to Paris, but his heart must be in his boots as he watches his *poilus* march off with their heads held high.

I wonder how I would face up to things if the Germans were advancing through the Kent hop-fields, and setting up their forward positions within shooting distance of London and my home. To know that a whole way of life is coming to an end and there is nothing to be done to stop it must be like facing death.

'Come on, Grant!' Martingale's voice jars the thought away, and someone reaches out a hand to help me.

Medics place the doctor's corpse in the ambulance, but they refuse to accept the colonel. It seems they have to be choosy at the moment, and anyone who is warm and can still walk must look after himself. Barratt tells us that there is a hospital ship at Dieppe waiting to transfer the wounded back home, and with any luck we might be allowed to travel with it. Watching the ambulance lumbering away I think of the doctor who spent his last few hours on this earth trying to make his small contribution to the war effort. On official records no one can say he was wounded in action. After all, a man could suffer a heart-attack running for a bus. Nevertheless, in my book he died fighting, and that's as close to a hero's death as makes no difference. He is going home to be buried; unlike the colonel, who has to face up to life in the close society of his conservative community; swallow his broken pride, and admit that the battlefield is an arena for younger men.

Our small pick-up waddles out over the uneven surface towards the ugly sprawl of the industrial sector of the port alongside the inner basin. This area is in direct contrast to the more elegant houses of the town that nestle beneath the shadow of the high cliffs. The pier leads out onto an outer port and a set of lock-gates that bottles up the inner basin. As we drive by we look out of the rear of the truck to a scene of dejection, with discarded pieces of military hardware waiting to be claimed. The rusting black flank of a small merchant ship comes into view alongside the wharf.

'Hey!' exclaims Royal suddenly. 'That's the *Sister Sarai*!' He is leaning past me, staring up at the high flank.

'Siddown!' I growl, pushing him back inside. But he ignores me, thumping on the deck with his boot and yelling for the driver to stop.

We jolt to a halt, and Martingale appears at the opening, breathing fire. 'What's wrong now?' he roars.

'That ship, sir. She is the *Sister Sarai*, one of my company's colliers. I could get us back to England on her, if you allow me to contact her captain.'

Barratt comes running back to jig from one foot to the other as he frets alongside Martingale. 'My orders are to take you to Dieppe, sir,' he insists urgently. 'This ship is out of bounds. We have tried to reason with her captain, but he refused to do anything without the authority of the owners. He went ashore two days ago to try to contact them and still hasn't returned. The first mate went off after him, as did several other members of the crew. We haven't seen hide nor hair of any of them since. I doubt there is more than one third of her crew on board, so we have washed our hands of her.'

'That settles it,' asserts Martingale. 'Get back inside, Royal. It's your party, Barratt. Let's get on with it.'

'Aye aye, sir.' He climbs back into the cab of the ambulance and we set off once more, heading towards the main Anneville/Dieppe road.

That's as far as we get before grinding to a halt again as two helmeted despatch-riders loom out of the growing dusk holding their arms up for us to stop. Beyond them a long convoy of Bren-gun-carriers and other types of army vehicles lumber northwards. A sergeant comes to lean into the driver's window.

'Where do you think you're orf, laddy?' he demands in a gravelly voice, then jumps back to attention when Martingale leaps out the other side and comes round the bonnet to confront him. The sergeant snaps a smart salute as Barratt runs up to join in the fray.

'We are going to Dieppe,' the subby says cheerfully. 'If you can just allow us out into the road, we'll be on our way.'

The sergeant's face hardens. 'Can't do that, sir.'

'Why on earth not?'

'My orders are ter keep this road clear.' He stares past Barratt's shoulder and speaks like an Army manual. 'There's a big push goin' on at Anneville and this convoy has priority.'

Martingale intervenes. 'We are joining a hospital ship there, sergeant. Trying to get back to England with our wounded.'

The sergeant's face softens, and emotion shows for the first time as his voice drops. 'Not in the *Maid of Kent* you're not, sir. Jerry's bombed 'er and set 'er on fire. By now I reckon she must be a gonner. Dieppe's not bein' used much for evacuation neither – there's too many mines ahtside the 'arbour.' His tone drops even more. 'Look, sir, even if I was ter let you out on the road you won't get more than 'alf a mile before they push you inter a ditch. If you take my advice you'll turn and go back to St Tréport.'

'I told you we should have used the *Sister Sarai*,' says Royal with a self-satisfied smirk. 'We need a full tide to get her out of the harbour, so the longer we piddle about the less our chances of getting away tonight.'

'Be quiet, Royal!' Martingale barks. 'When I want your advice I'll ask for it.'

'I'm afraid he's right, sir,' interposes Barratt reluctantly. 'It's more than a week since I was in Dieppe, and I have no doubt that everything the sergeant has told us is right.'

The sergeant barks an order at the other despatch-rider, sending him back to the junction. 'I must go now, sir. We can't afford any 'old-ups.' He salutes. 'Best of luck, sir,' and then he is gone.

No one makes any comment as we turn the vehicles about and drive back to the basin. It is a solemn procession as we wend our way through the drab waterfront and judder to a stop in the shadow of the ship's side.

Royal doesn't wait for orders as he slips over the tailboard and goes towards the steep gangplank. Before he reaches it a gruff voice shouts down from the upper-deck. 'Who are you – what do you want?' The head and shoulders of a powerful man are silhouetted against the night sky as he glowers at us.

'Melody!'

'Who's that?'

'Jack Royal!'

Silence for a moment or two while other shapes take form beside the burly man. 'Royal! What the hell are you doin' here?'

Royal chuckles to himself. 'Never mind that, you big ape. We want a passage back home. What about it?'

Melody comes to the gangway, and now I can see what a

massive frame he has. Set on two stumpy legs he reminds
me of a Clydesdale draught horse. When he reaches the
dock he is shoulder high to me, but in all other respects he
makes me look a midget. 'That ain't so easy, Jack. The
skipper's gone ashore to find Eli Spring, because the
froggies won't work the cargo. We are loaded with Welsh
anthracite that no one wants to pay for. The Navy has told
us to take it back to Barry, but the skipper has refused to
do anything until he's talked to Eli.'

'What's Eli doing here?'

'What he is always doing; trying to turn a profit. He
came over with us, and went off to negotiate with the local
agent.' He sighs heavily. 'That was almost three days ago.
When the Navy began to make noises the skipper went
ashore, followed by the mate and the second, leaving me in
charge. The engineer's pissed out of his mind in his cabin,
and several of the crew got windy when they heard the
fighting getting near. We are down to what you see here.
Two firemen. The donkeyman, and a couple of ABs.
Christ knows what's goin' on ashore.'

'Who is your skipper?'

'Methuselah.'

'I see,' grunts Royal drily.

Melody's grins at the tone of Royal's response. 'Yeah,
you've guessed it. Him and Eli would sell their mothers
for a price. Eli reckons France is about to pack up, and
then Britain will have to make a pact with Germany. So he
wants to stay here until the fuss has died down, and sell to
the highest bidder. Patriotic bloke is old Eli. Him and
Methuselah can always convince themselves that whatever
they get up to is sanctioned by God.'

Martingale steps forward. 'Am I to understand that
there is no one on board authorised to take this ship to
sea?'

'This ain't Navy business,' asserts Melody in a surly
voice.

'Never mind that,' says Royal. 'We have to know.'

'The only officer on board is the engineer, and he's lying

on his bunk, surrounded by empty whisky bottles,' Melody replies grudgingly. 'I'm the bosun, and I'm in charge at the moment. That is all you need to know.'

He is glowering at Martingale from beneath heavy black brows, but he has chosen the wrong man to brow-beat this time. Martingale steps right up close to him and glares straight into his eyes. 'This ship is sailing on the next tide with or without your skipper. Naturally we would like your co-operation, but we can do without it if necessary.'

The bosun takes a menacing half-step, but Royal's arm stops him. 'When is the skipper due back?' he asks, mainly to take the steam out of the situation.

'Gawd knows!'

Royal turns to Martingale. There is an authoritative expression on his face. 'I'll take her out if Methuselah doesn't come back in time. How is the tide, Melody?'

'About half past two – we could sail at midnight.'

'Right, then that is what we will do. We'll give the skipper until then. Meanwhile, we will raise steam. Finney, you had better go below and take a look at the engine, if we can't sober up the engineer, you might have to take her out. Know anything about coal-burners?'

Finney snorts and spits into the black water of the basin. 'I done me time in a bloody old steam-kettle that masqueraded as a boom-defence vessel, and a spell on a trawler. So I can probably sort this one aht.'

Royal turns back to Martingale. 'That's settled then. I am resigning from His Majesty's service and I'll be obliged if you will afford me the courtesy due to a ship's master, sir.'

For a second I think Martingale is going to explode, but he gets his feelings under control enough to mouth through clenched teeth, 'Just remember, Royal. You might be running the ship, but she is under my control until we reach England. In the meantime I suggest we prepare her for sea, and hope that the captain returns in time.'

'Bloody hell! Ain't 'ad none – don't want none – ain't

gonna get none!' Finney is pointing towards a corner of a building where three nuns stand like black ravens watching us. One of them comes forward with her hands clasped on a large wooden crucifix and an anxious look on her oval face. We are struck dumb by these outlandish figures in the midst of the industrial waste, and can only stare transfixed while she looks from one to another until her eyes settle on me.

'Excuse me, sir.' She picks her words carefully, speaking without any trace of an accent. 'The children have no fathers or mothers and we wish to take them to England.'

'Orphans,' I say needlessly. 'We call them orphans.'

She smiles gratefully. 'Thank you, sir. We have walked all the way from Moyenneville.'

Martingale steps forward to take over from me. 'Perhaps you should go to the authorities, sister. This ship is not suitable for passengers; it could be dangerous.'

She nods, smiling. 'We know this, sir. But we cannot find our authorities, and our school is in the fighting. The children have walked too far already. The roads are choked and we have nowhere else to go.'

'How many children are there?' asks Barratt with a catch in his voice.

'Forty-two. They are aged from five to thirteen, boys and girls.'

'Blimey!' Finney exclaims, echoing my thoughts.

For some reason she has decided that I am the one to talk to, and I can sense a hidden strength beneath her soft voice. She is pleading with me, yet she never loses her dignity, and when I glance towards her two mates they are watching me anxiously, as though I hold the key to their future. It would be easy to give in to them, but there is a cruel stretch of water out there waiting for us.

'You will all be much safer here,' I say gently but firmly. 'The Germans will not harm children.'

The smile fades. 'Sir, the children have lived through too much fighting already. Our school is gone and we have nowhere to go. Will you turn us away?'

There is a long, embarrassed silence while everyone tries to ignore his conscience and try to find words to explain how impossible it is to grant her request.

Royal saves us the trouble. 'Sister,' he states in a cold voice. 'We do not carry passengers, especially women and children.' He is an uncompromising bastard as he lays down the rules. He is full of himself, with no time for sentiment nor compassion. 'You must go elsewhere with your children.'

'That is not your decision!' snaps Martingale, then turns to the nun. 'Should you not stay in France, sister?'

She sighs heavily and looks down at the ground. 'France is much too busy for us. The fighting is everywhere, and we must find peace until the madness is over.'

Martingale swallows hard. 'Come on, Grant. We will go and take a look at the ship.' He looks into the nun's face. 'I can promise you nothing, sister. We do not know what this ship is really like, but I will see what can be done.'

Whoever designed her knew how to cut corners. She is a standard, two-island coaster with a tall, thin funnel stuck on her after deck-house and a scruffy, square bridge amidships. She is basic, with cold, hard-flanged steel upperworks. Even where the builder has been forced to relent and introduce timber on the wheelhouse it is plain, tongue and grooved planking without even a strip of beading to relieve the austerity.

The ship breeds filth. Every seam and corner is hidden under layer upon layer of paint so that it blisters and cakes and falls away at the touch of a hand. The deck hides under a carpet of coal-dust with 'drifts' up to a foot deep in places. The tackle on her derricks and davits is stiff, ungreased and brittle through lack of care. Every length of hawser and rope slumps in loose coils amongst the winches and bollards. Royal is right: this is no place for kids.

The disgust on our faces amuses Royal. He chortles as we try to pick our way through the soot-caked obstacles. 'Not a pretty sight, is she, sir?' he scoffs. 'The sort of money

Eli pays don't buy the services of prime seamen. His bunch of no-hopers are the riff-raff from dockside boozers and police cells. They don't take too kindly to spit and polish. I wouldn't trust the ship's cat alone with them.' His voice is jovial and the *Sarai*'s crew snigger in response. Like he says, they are an unsavoury lot, and I have no doubt Melody requires his brawn from time to time when keeping them in order.

'Beggars can't be choosers,' Martingale says quietly, wiping away Royal's grin. 'Even this old bucket must have a saloon and a few cabins that are habitable. We will put the children in there.' He ignores the rumble of protest from the disconsolate men and leans over the bulwarks to shout down to Barratt. 'She will do, sub. If you can get the nuns to bring the children we'll get them on board.'

'But, sir!' protests Royal. 'She is not fit for cattle!'

Martingale studies him for a second or two. 'If it was a herd of cows and we could prevent them from falling into enemy hands I would use this barge, Royal. A little dirt and discomfort never killed anyone, and it is my experience that youngsters are more resilient than we credit. Most young lads will wallow quite happily in dirt, so they should enjoy this disgraceful hulk to the full. As for the enemy: you say the tide will not be right before midnight. Therefore it will be dark when we sail, and if all goes well we should be inside British waters with air-cover before dawn. I think it is worth the risk.'

He takes a breath before going on. 'Get steam up as quickly as you can. I will go ashore with Grant and arrange for our passengers to come aboard. If any of those wretches come within five yards of the nuns or the children I will personally heave him overboard.'

Leaving Royal staring after us Martingale leads me down the ladder to the dockside where the nun is waiting for us with a contented smile on her face. 'God has touched your heart, sir,' she tells Martingale, and he blushes bright red.

Clearing his throat he looks away. 'Where are the children, sister?'

She nods across at the other nuns and they hurry round the corner of the building. In a moment a crocodile of uniformed children troop into view, walking hand in hand, paired off in sizes so that two tiny tots lead out with each following pair growing in height until two five-footers take up the rear. Each one carries a small bag and a school satchel. They march through the slummy dockside clutter with only the soft shuffle of their shoes to mark their progress while the reverberation of war thumps and bangs across the roof-tops behind them. My heart bleeds as I watch them. 'Some day the bastards will pay for this,' I promise under my breath.

They line up in two ranks, facing the blank wall of the ship's side, with their small, serious faces firmly set, as though they are determined not to cry. They have walked something like thirty kilometres with the harsh sounds of battle dogging their heels every step of the way; sleeping in barns and village halls. Their clothes are creased and dirty; yet they wait with infinite patience and trust as we prepare to take them on board. I would like to have a couple of politicians here to look into those innocent eyes and explain to them the reason we go to war.

We form a chain to help them climb the steep gangway to the upper-deck and look into the strange world of harsh steel. Even the villainous crew can only look on in mute compassion as the children file across the open deck to where Martingale ushers them through a door into the island. When the last one has passed through the English-speaking nun nods her thanks before following them, leaving a strange, empty silence on the upper-deck.

Martingale comes back and we stay silent, listening to the scrape of shovels echoing from the stoke-hold, and the deep rumbling thunder from the north. An explosion, more violent than the rest, drags our eyes to where a yellow glow fills a sector of the sky and a revolving ball of fire soars high above it. There are smaller pulsation flushes of flame all along the broken horizon, reflected on the underside of nightclouds.

'We should take the opportunity to get some rest, Grant,' he says. 'We will need all our faculties when we sail. Sub-Lieutenant Barratt is arranging for the lock-gates to be opened at midnight. High water is about oh-two-three-oh and I think it is tempting providence to try and get out at midnight with a full cargo of coal, despite what Royal says. We will slip an hour before high tide. I do not want to risk running aground for the sake of an hour. Otherwise Royal seems to have things in order, so we can take advantage of a spell of rest before it all begins again.'

'I suppose it is all right to trust him with it, sir?' I ask doubtfully.

'We have little alternative, Grant. After all, there isn't much he can do to sabotage things, if that is what you're thinking. Those merchant seamen are just as eager as we are to get back home; if only to get their wages. As soon as we get to sea I intend to radio ahead and inform the authorities that we have him on board. After that it will be up to the police.'

'What about you, sir?'

'Me?'

'You will have problems of your own when we get back.'

He heaves a sigh. 'I am trying to avoid thinking about that. I must admit that I had hoped the colonel might speak up for me, but there is small chance of that now. I have lost a TRV, damaged a destroyer and disobeyed Admiralty instructions. I reckon they'll lock me in the Tower and throw away the key.' He shrugs despondently. 'Come on, there is no sense brooding about what might happen. Let us get some shut-eye, and see what tomorrow brings; after all, it is the first day of flaming June.'

The crew seem quite happy to allow us to run things and we sort out a duty rota wih Royal and Finney. By mutual consent we bed down in the wheelhouse. All the best cabins are occupied by the children and the nuns, and one look at the fo'c'sle is enough to discourage any idea of using the bunks in there. It is a rat-infested place, dark and thick with the stench of sweaty bodies and stale food, mixed with the acrid stink of rancid wine and spirits.

It is a fitful slumber, for the sounds of conflict are emphasized when we lie down on the deck. Every now and again a stronger explosion shakes the ship and I have to force myself to lie still. The time drags by as night takes over completely, although the wheelhouse is illuminated by dancing reflections of distant fires. I am quite relieved when Finney comes to tell me it is time for Martingale and myself to take over the watch, and when we go on deck the ship shimmers with warmth as the stokers build up a full head of steam.

Looking aross the dock gates I can see that the outer harbour is flooded as the incoming tide fills every corner, turning the whole area into a placid lake. I go to the starboard rail and peer out at the fighting. The whole sky flickers with light to the north, making the cranes and dockside buildings stand out starkly against the glare. On the point of turning away to go in search of Martingale a sudden movement catches my eye. I look again, squinting to stare into the shadows as two figures emerge and move out into the pool of semi-darkness that swamps the dockside.

As they get closer I recognise the stocky shape of a British squaddy with his helmet tipped back on his head and his battledress blouse unbuttoned to his waist. He wears his webbing loose and lop-sided as he prods a long bayonet into the spine of a tall German officer, who keeps his hands high and darts nervous glances over his shoulder at his belligerent little captor. The contrast between them is incongruous. The Nazi wears an immaculate uniform with a high-crowned cap set squarely on his arrogant head, and even from this distance I can see the skull and crossbones of his SS badge glinting in the light of flares.

'Sir!' I call to Martingale, who comes running to stare down with me at the weird twosome. Without speaking we climb down to the waist and over the gangway to confront the little squaddy and his prisoner. The pugnacious features of the Englishman are squeezed up into an expression of hate and he doesn't take his eyes away from the SS man for one second.

'What have we here?' asks Martingale jovially.

The little man has no time for small talk, and there is not the slightest hint of amusement in his face. He is as suspicious of us as he is of his prisoner. At any other time he would make a comic figure, with his oversized rifle and bayonet poised ready to pierce the expensive cloth of the officer's jacket. Now he can find nothing to laugh at, and there is a ferocious expression of blind hate in his eyes. Martingale's tone alters to one of deadly earnestness as he persists.

'What's this all about, soldier?'

'I ain't 'andin' 'im over to no one, sir.' His red-rimmed eyes never falter and the Nazi is scared. He tries to hide it, but it shows in his eyes, and his mouth is twitching nervously, plain to see even in the vague light.

'This sod is gonna pay for what 'e's done and there ain't no mealy-mouthed bastard gonna go soft on 'im.' The squaddy's words are bitter and heavy with threat.

'Come on, mate,' I coax quietly. 'We are all on the same side. How can we help you if you won't tell us what it's all about?'

At last his eyes swivel towards me. 'All I want is a trip back to Blighty. If anyone tries to take 'im from me I'll shoot 'im: I'm warnin' you.' He is shuddering with emotion, close to tears. ' 'E's gonna get 'is dues. I don't know 'ow, but 'e's gonna pay good and proper, and no one's gonna soft-soap me.'

'All right, mate,' I say consolingly. 'We are not going to take him away from you; but he is an officer, and a prisoner-of-war. So he is entitled to certain rights.'

'*NO!*' His shout startles us and causes the German to utter an involuntary cry, cringing into his high collar as he feels the prick of the bayonet in his back.

'You're all the fuckin' same!' screams the squaddy. 'You'll put 'im in a posh officers' camp and let 'im live aht

the war like a gent, after what 'e's done! I'll kill 'im first: If
I never kill another German I'll kill this bastard!'

'What has he done, for Christ sake?'

His breathing becomes laboured as he tries to assemble
the words. 'What's 'e done? I'll tell you what 'e's done. I'll
tell you what the slimy sod done to me mates.' He draws a
deep breath before going on. 'Marched 'em dahn a quiet
lane and locked 'em in a shed, then 'ad a little game of
slingin' 'and-grenades through the winder. When a couple
of the lads staggered out still alive this sod shot 'em 'imself,
the cold-blooded sod!' He rounds on his prisoner.
'Thought I was dead, didn't you?' he hisses through
clenched teeth. 'I followed you, mate. I didn't give a shit if
I got caught neiver. I waited till you walked away from
your mate and then I gotcha.'

He turns to me as he goes on. 'I 'it 'im on the swede wiv
me rifle butt and dragged 'im away.' His mouth breaks
into a devilish grin. 'That ain't the only place I 'it you
neiver, was it, Fritz? You must 'ave bollocks like cocernuts
now.'

Martingale tries to calm him down. 'I know how you
must feel, but there are rules for prisoners on both sides.
If we don't behave properly how can we expect our own
men to be fairly treated when they are captured?'

'I knows all about that.' The bayonet digs harder into
the German's spine. 'If 'e was an ordinary squaddy I'd look
arter 'im proper, but this one's a murderin' rat 'an
deserves nuffin.' His voice takes on a plaintive quality as he
turns to Martingale. 'Me mates tried to surrender. They
knew they'd 'ad it, sir. Put their 'ands up in the air and
pleaded for mercy.' He swung back to his prisoner,
spitting out his words. 'Didn't make no odds to you
though, did it? You killed the poor bastards anyway, didn't
you? Geordie, 'arry, the sergeant: you spread them all over
the walls.'

'All right, soldier.' Martingale's voice is taut, with a
brittle edge to it. 'Calm down and think clearly about what
you are doing. Your first duty must be to report back to

your unit. If you don't, you can be posted missing or even charged with desertion.'

'I cain't. I got cut orf from them after Jerry crossed the Oise. We couldn't stop the sods. All we 'ad was Froggie one-pounders mounted on 'andcarts against bloody great tanks. The shells just bounced orf 'em.' His voice almost cuts out as his memory paints pictures inside his head. 'They ploughed right through us. Me and me mates ran like 'ell for the Somme, but the sods were everywhere; in front an' behind. In the end this bastard and 'is mates caught up with us.' His voice tails off and we are left with a strained silence.

'What's your name?' I ask, in an effort to break the tension.

'Fred.'

'Well, Fred,' I say when I realise we are not going to get any more from this small artilleryman. 'None of us can run the war to suit ourselves. Your first duty is to the Army.'

His mouth tightens, and his rifle moves towards the German's shoulder-blades. 'This is as far as we go, mate. I've walked too far with this bastard already. Me mob's gorn norf, and I've met nuffin but froggie pongoes ever since I left the Somme. If you won't take us wiv you, 'ere we stay.'

I look at Martingale, and he shrugs back at me. 'You win, Fred,' I relent. 'Get your prisoner on board and we'll find you a place to put him so that you can relax a bit. In the meantime, ease off on that trigger before you kill someone, and take him up the gangway.'

He prods his prisoner in the back and the German looks over at Martingale for support. 'Surely!' his expression says, 'you are not going to allow this peasant to treat a fellow officer like this?' but Martingale's face is dead-pan as he nods to the little squaddy. The tall Nazi is in all kinds of trouble when he tries to climb the steep gangway with his hands held high, but Fred makes no concession, and each time the German looks like dropping his hands to grab the hand-rails he receives a sharp reminder from his small tormentor.

'You will need somewhere safe to stow him,' I say as I follow then over the side. 'A place where you can keep him secure. You will have to watch over him all the time, I can't spare any of my own blokes.'

He looks suspicious. 'I ain't lettin' 'im out of me sight.'

'All right – all right!' I reassure him quickly. 'No one is going to pinch him from you, I promise.' I look towards the fo'c'sle. There are two doors beneath the break; one leading into the crew's quarters, and I guess the other must be some kind of store. Moving across I take off the clips and open it up to reveal a small paint-locker. It is about three feet square; just big enough for a six-footer to stand semi-upright amongst a mess of paint-pots and brushes. The German's chin drops in dismay as he peers into the claustrophobic cell, with its rank, acrid stench of white-spirit, linseed oil and old paint.

An evil smile brightens Fred's face. 'Lovely!' he breathes sadistically.

I have a slight twinge of conscience as the rifle slams into the German's stomach, causing him to double-up in agony and gasp for air. Fred places a hob-nailed boot into his backside and pushes him into the smelly locker. Even with the door shut and the clips rammed home we can hear the Nazi wheezing and groaning. He will have to remain upright in the narrow compartment amongst the piled clutter of sticky pots and brushes.

'You will have to open up now and again to give him some air.' I warn Fred. 'There isn't much ventilation in there, and a man could choke on the poisonous fumes.'

He looks at the door for a moment, listening to the muffled sounds of distress. 'I'll try to remember,' he replies without conviction.

I place a friendly hand on his shoulder and feel him tense up. 'Look, mate. Don't get yourself into serious trouble for the sake of that bastard. We all know what he deserves, but if you do something stupid it could reflect on all of us. Sods like him will get what's coming to them when the time is right. If you wanted revenge you should have taken it when you first got hold of him. Something must have made you hold back and think; so don't go back on it now.'

He drops his rifle butt onto the iron deck and allows his body to slump for a moment as he looks up at me with pain-filled eyes. 'I almost did. I almost rammed my bayonet right up to the 'ilt in 'is guts. I should 'ave enjoyed doin' it too. Just to see 'im squirmin' wiv all that steel in 'is belly would 'ave done me a power of good. I couldn't care less abaht being fahnd doing it neiver. Right then I would 'ave bin 'appy to die wiv me mates, as long as I took 'im wiv me. The point of me bayonet was an inch from 'is belly, and I could smell 'im sweatin' wiv fear. Shit scared 'e was.' He is gloating now. 'One lunge and a nice slow twist and 'e would scream like a stuck pig. Jesus! I wanted to do that more than I ever wanted anything before.'

He thinks hard for a moment, his eyes wandering away from me to search the hidden corners of the ship. 'It would 'ave bin too quick though, and I knew that there 'ad to be more to it than that. No cold-blooded, murderin' bastard can murder a bunch of my mates and get a soldier's death.'

He screws his face up as if he is trying to analyse his own motives. 'I don't know 'ow, but 'e 'as got to pay for what 'e's done, and why 'e's being punished. Gawd almighty! I don't think 'e even knows 'e's done wrong, and 'e would never 'ave known if I had stuck me bayonet in 'im there and then. I don't want 'im sittin' in no bloody rest-camp neiver: I'll think of somethin'.'

He looks at me, looking for sympathy; but I can only stare back helplessly. The pleading expression is replaced with a sudden, hard determination, as though he realises he is on his own. 'My own private Nazi, that's what 'e is. I could go right through the war and never see the blokes I'm arsked to kill. Me mates and me 'ave bin shot at, bombed and chased from arsehole ter breakfast-time by these bastards, and it's as though they come from another planet. Well, arfter this I won't be scared of them anymore; not when I've made this sod scream for bloody mercy; just like me mates.'

He looks down. Embarrassed at the way he has unveiled his inner thoughts. I study his crumpled features, sensing the torment he suffers. He is a tough little man who has found no one to hate before. Where he comes from men do not kill other men for no good reason. Up to now he has never drummed up enough hate to want to kill anyone in cold blood, but he owes it to his mates to see that their murderer is punished, and he knows he can't trust the authorities to do it the way he wants. I leave him there, slumped over his rifle with the muffled sound of his German to comfort him.

On the bridge everyone is awake and moving about. The ship is seething with life, and there is a steady plume of smoke pouring from the funnel, drifting across the dingy dockside. Finney reports that we have enough steam to get under way, and Martingale looks into the face of the chronometer on the after bulkhead, hesitates for a moment, then states firmly, 'We will wait another thirty minutes, Grant.'

'Aye aye, sir,' I respond automatically. 'I suggest we pass a warp across to the bollards on the opposite side of the basin to haul our bows in line with the lock-gate.'

'You took the words right out of my mouth,' interjects Royal, who has been listening to every word. 'Once we get through the gate we must take her over to port and keep her there as we go out. That will keep us clear of the shallows.'

'Thank you,' Martingale says drily, 'I will value your advice when it is asked for. Otherwise I will tolerate no interference. Is that understood?'

I leave them facing up to each other and go forward to prepare the warp. Fred is hunched into himself, with his rifle clamped between his knees, looking sad in the gloom.

VII

On the fo'c'sle the night breeze chills our bones as we strip the painted canvas cover from the drum and reel off the hawser. Two crewmen have come forward to help us, and they handle the wire so that Royal and I can cross over to the wharf. We take the eye from them and walk it round the end of the basin, across the lockgates, to the bollards on the other side. With that done the crewmen can haul in the slack on the long bight.

Slipping the eye over the bollard seems to have a therapeutic effect on me. My tense muscles relax as I watch the wire straighten and hold firm. Once it is secured we make our way round the far end of the basin, looking into the glutinous pond of impenetrable water to ensure no floating debris will foul the propeller when we get under way.

I sense Royal dogging my footsteps. We have to trust him, for he is the only one capable of guiding us out into the Channel. The local pilots refuse to leave their families while the town is threatened by the advancing Germans. These quiet, unassuming, seafaring folk are waiting in their homes, feeling menaced from all sides. Even the stream of Allied armour grinding up the main road must constitute a threat to their peaceful existence. We are surrounded by a continuous babble of noise from beyond the clustered buildings and hidden streets, but here, in this quiet pool of isolation beneath the brooding jibs of cranes it is like an oasis of sanity.

Coming round the high stern of the ship we see a covered truck rumbling slowly towards the gangway, and when it jolts to a stop de Carteret steps down from the cab, stands reeling for a moment, before turning towards the rear of the truck. Inside, seated facing each other across a pile of boxes and chests, half a dozen *poilus* wait for orders, their rifles between their knees.

Royal and I drop the tailboard, then stand back while they clamber out. Two of them take station with their rifles poised, while their mates haul the chests over the stern and stack them on the ground. They behave as though their goods are sacred and refuse any help from us. So we stay well back, respecting their wishes, and watching them struggle up the steep gangway with their treasured possessions. Once it is all stowed safely inside a locker under the poop de Carteret posts a sentry at the door and the others settle into any corner they can find. Then he moves amongst them with a quiet word for each man. There is a great sadness about the way they respond to his gentle voice; a solemn camaraderie that sets them apart from us. When he has checked them all de Carteret allows Martingale to lead him away to the wheelhouse and the leather bunk in the captain's sea-cabin.

I find myself standing with Royal at the head of the gangway, waiting for Martingale's order to single-up the moorings. The time is ripe, and we are impatient to get under way. The moon breaks through the cloud to send ribbons of light across the wharf, painting hard shadows of the rigging on the quay and filling the basin with an unearthly glow that gives the water a metallic sheen.

Now there are men moving on the piers, calling to each other quietly. Slowly, ponderously, with a skirl of disturbed water, the lock-gates swing open. The turbulence stirs up bubbles that sparkle like jewels as they catch the light. The mumble of traffic and the heavier crump of distant artillery throb in the soft air as we try to contain our impatience.

A flurry of new sound drags our attention to three figures who detach themselves from the shadows and come along the dockside. As they draw closer they enter a shaft of bright moonlight with the familiar figure of

Barratt leading them out. The other two are civilians, and strangers.

'Jesus Christ!' blurts out Royal. 'Eli Spring and Methuselah!'

I can tell which is which without being told, for one is a tall, blunt-featured man with a seaman's gait and broad shoulders. He wears a dark, battered, peaked cap slumped over one ear, and a reefer jacket with four faded gold stripes on his sleeve. He looms over his frail, crowlike companion scurrying along beside him. A gaunt, lantern-faced, funereal individual with hollow eyes staring out from beneath the narrow brim of a bowler. He has to take two steps to one of the other man; tottering along stiff-legged, with his boney shoulders rocking from side to side like a puppet.

They follow Barratt up the gangway to stand in the waist while we crowd round them. Methuselah pushes his way past Eli to confront Royal.

'What the hell are you doing here, Royal?' he demands in a booming voice.

Martingale thrusts Royal aside, inserting himself between the two men. 'What's this all about, Barratt?'

'This is Mr Spring, sir. He owns the *Sister Sarai*. This is her skipper, Captain Tardeval.' He turns half sideways. 'Lieutenant Martingale, gentlemen.'

'I repeat: what is that man doing on my ship?' Tardeval points an accusing finger at Royal.

Before anyone can give him an answer Eli intervenes in a complaining tone. 'Will someone kindly show me to my quarters? Or do I have to stand here all day while you argue amongst yourselves?' He looks at no one as he speaks, preferring to gaze out over the rail with a pained expression. He is the epitome of the ill-used, magnanimous employer, ignored by his ungrateful underlings.

'Donkeyman!' growls Methuselah. 'Show Mr Spring to my cabin. I will use the first mate's for this trip.'

'Aye, sir.'

'I am afraid that will not be possible, sir,' states Martingale firmly. 'All the 'midship quarters are occupied.'

The melancholy eyes look up slowly. 'Occupied – by whom?' The hollow voice has a steel edge now; belying the benign expression on the long face. Only the eyes are in tune with the palsied drawl.

'We have taken on board a party of orphans and their teachers. I believe they are sleeping now, and I would not wish to disturb them.'

'God's teeth!' roars Methuselah. 'You've got a blasted nerve, lieutenant. This is my ship, and I will decide who sleeps where in her.' He swings on the donkeyman. 'Take a couple of men and clear out my quarters.'

'Stand fast!' barks Martingale, moving to stand in front of the captain. 'I have already told you; these kids have had a tough time. They must not be disturbed.'

'The hell they won't! This ship is not a kindergarten, lieutenant. They must be taken ashore at once.'

'Hold!' Eli's hand is raised like a preacher's as he faces his small audience. 'We must be charitable.' His thin lips twist into a frosty smile. 'Suffer the little children, Tardeval. We must do what is best for them.' He turns to Martingale, still simpering. 'Do you think it right to take them away from their home-land like this, lieutenant? Could this not be a hasty decision that will leave them stranded in a foreign country where no one even speaks their language?' He lifts his hand to stop Martingale's protest and looks up towards the heavens. 'I will take a moment to ask for guidance.' We stand aside like a lot of idiots while he moves into a remote corner and places his hands together to pray silently.

'With Christians like him who needs Satan?' growls Royal.

I can see Eli's lips moving. His eyes gleam in their deep hollows and the deep lines of his face look as though they have been etched with charcoal. At last he seems satisfied and returns with his hands clasped, wearing a soulful look.

His sloping shoulders droop even more as he formulates each word with great care. 'We are doing an evil thing, lieutenant. We are compounding an ungodly act by taking these children into a wilderness of uncertainty.'

Royal steps forward with suspicion written all over his face. 'Why are you so keen to get rid of these kids, Eli? For all you know there may be money in it when the war accounts are settled.'

The ship-owner scowls, but before he can reply Methuselah growls, 'Enough of this bloody nonsense! They are going ashore, and there's an end to it!'

He moves to give his orders, but finds Martingale blocking his way. 'This ship is under Admiralty orders, Tardeval. I say who stays and who goes on this trip.' He turns to Eli. 'As for your ethics, Mr Spring; these children come from the war zone where their home is in the midst of the fighting. Since then they have been wandering like nomads and have nowhere safe to go on this side of the Channel. We are not going to leave them here in this madness. When sanity returns they can come back; until then they must be left in peace.'

'I feel bound to make a formal complaint, lieutenant,' warns Eli. 'You are exceeding your authority.'

'Leave this to me, sir,' thunders Methuselah, taking a menacing step towards Martingale, but finding himself confronted by Royal's stocky figure. 'I'm warning you, Royal. Get out of my way before I heave you over the side.'

I make a quick grab at Royal's arm as he launches a blow at the captain, too late to prevent it landing on Methuselah's jaw. He goes down like a log with blood spurting from a split lip. Everyone crowds in to restrain Royal before he can move in to finish the job, but it is Eli's screech that prevents further bloodshed.

'This is my ship!' he screams, his sallow features contorted with fury. 'I say these children and their idolatrous guardians have no place in a Christian ship. We do not wish to carry their papist hypocrisy across the Channel. The time is come for Europe to scourge itself of this evil. The Lord moves in mysterious ways. Sometimes he will use one evil to stamp out another. These things are ordained by a greater authority than your Ministry of Shipping.' The outburst has left him breathless, tottering on his spindly legs.

Methuselah hoists himself to his feet, wiping the blood from his mouth with the back of his hand. He squares up to Barratt. 'You had better tell these people where their duties lie.'

Barratt looks embarrassed. 'I'm afraid he is right, sir,' he tells Martingale. 'We have no authority regarding the children. So long as the crew agree to take the ship where directed their internal affairs have nothing to do with us. They can refuse to take the children if they wish.'

Martingale wrestles with his conscience. Twice already he has disregarded orders, and he faces sanction when he gets back to England. Now he has a chance to redeem himself if he plays it right and suppresses his feelings.

'There is no more time to lose,' he delares, staring directly into Methuselah's eyes. 'We will miss the tide if we do not sail at once. The children will remain on board. Get moving, Grant. Prepare for warping out.' He turns to Barratt. 'If you value your career, sub, you will get ashore before it is too late. I am in no mood to abandon my principles for this pair of self-centred villains.'

Barratt backs away and goes to the top of the gangway, hesitates undecidedly, before turning to retrace his steps. 'I have nowhere to go. I have been ordered to see that this ship and her cargo do not fall into the hands of the enemy. How can I be certain of that if I do not come with you?'

'That is entirely up to you. Just so long as you realise what you are getting yourself into,' says Martingale curtly. 'Now, Captain Tardeval. What is it going to be?'

'It's up to the owner.'

Eli scowls at us, his dark eyes searching our faces as he gropes for a way out. 'I am God's servant. He has shown me the way; if you defy Him it must be on your own conscience.'

'You have your God, old man – we have our rifles!' Everyone turns to see de Carteret standing at the top of the bridge-ladder with his *poilus* formed up in a line beneath him; weapons held across their chests. 'I am charged with getting those documents to England, and if we do not sail now we will miss the tide, so get on with it!'

That settles it, and his uncompromising stance makes it easier for Methuselah and Eli to back down under pressure without losing face. The donkeyman shrugs and goes forward of his own accord to set the winch turning on the fo'c'sle. He is a thin, miserable-looking man, who resents us, but goes out of his way to anticipate our orders so that he is not placed in the invidious position of being told what to do. Like many of his kind he has small regard for the senior service, and makes little effort to hide his feelings.

I join him on the fo'c'sle, taking a couple of turns on the drum to hold the slack on the warp. The wire slips easily on the damp metal when I ease off and allow the winch to hold the weight. Royal is there too, standing in brooding silence right up in the bow, looking down at the jetty. The whole ship is seething with expectancy as the time ticks away, with an underlying excitement at the thought of going out into the black ocean once more. The double ring of the telegraph shows how things are moving on the bridge. The brass arrow on the dial has moved to 'Stand by', and Finney is poised to experiment with his engine.

There is no point in relying on the ship's engineer for help. He made one brief appearance on the well-deck a while ago, staggered all over the place raving about seeing three angels of death and a multitude of cherubs, all come to take him off to eternity. He finally ended up face down on one of the fo'c'sle bunks, still holding a half-bottle of whisky and confessing a lifetime catalogue of crimes to make the devil's hair curl.

Only one person in the ship seems at a loss for something to do. The colonel has found the after island the least occupied part of the ship. A place where he can remain unobtrusive with his terrible thoughts and contemplate a sad future without fear of interruption. There is also a warm seat on the engineroom skylight, even though the opaque windows with their metal safety bars are covered with canvas to hold in the light. In total darkness he sat there, totally ignored by everyone, and oblivious to the shadowy figures coming in and out through the doors in the deckhouse, or the amorphous shapes that mutter amongst themselves as they single-up the after mooring-lines.

Now he has come forward into the well-deck. A dejected, solitary figure, surrounded by aliens who have neither time nor respect for him. I watch him scrambling along with scraping shoes on the port side, feeling a surge of compassion for the poor old devil. He needs someone to confide in, but he has isolated himself from ordinary men with his pompous arrogance. The only man on board with a background remotely similar to his is Barratt, who is much too young and proud to become involved with a shambling has-been. The youngster has worked on the class-levelling decks of small ships where brusque, experienced NCOs treated him with deference while he learned the intricacies of seamanship.

Martingale has come up through the hawsepipe without the public-school advantages, or the homespun privileges afforded the colonel. He has overcome prejudice and social barriers to attain his commission. Small wonder that he has little sympathy for the broken old colonel. De Carteret too is a professional soldier; intolerant of anyone who wears the uniform of an officer and behaves as the colonel has behaved in the past few days.

However, despite that they contain their feelings and choose to ignore him for the most part. Not so Royal. Now that he has assumed a new status, second only to Methuselah in the pecking order of the *Sarai*'s crew he shows open contempt for the colonel. The thought makes me look forward to where he stands right up in the fore-peak, a dark, bulky shape with shoulders hunched as he looks down at the jetty. I take an extra turn on the drum and secure the wire so that it cannot run out, then go to stand with him. I detest the bloke, yet I am unable to bury my curiosity about him.

'Where does the name "Methuselah" come from?' I ask by way of an opener.

He remains staring down at the lockgates. 'That's Eli's fault. Methuselah is his senior captain; been with him since he was a wet-eared third mate. He believes he owes everything to Eli, but in fact his debts have been repaid with interest, for he has rescued the crafty old ship-owner from many a legal scrape during their time together. When other captains make noises about the state of their ships or the rabble they have to work with Methuselah comes along to nose about the hull, sniffing into every corner and muttering about the days when he first went to sea, and how lucky they are to sail in such luxury. I have seen fo'c'sle scum chortling behind their hands when their skippers are made to look like incompetent idiots in front of them when they objected to the running of things and their dubious cargoes.

'The kind of officers Eli employs know that they have small chance of obtaining another berth so they back down easily, and if anyone asks why Methuselah always talks them round the answer is always "Captain Tardeval has the experience."

'There came a day when one of the more aggressive skippers refused to take his ship to sea because it had sprung-plates and an engine that was living on borrowed time. Methuselah made his usual inspection, proclaimed the ship seaworthy and derided the captain for being over-cautious, but this time the skipper was not easily put off. He and the ship's carpenter had listed the defects and set them out in a report which they both signed. They threatened to place it in the hands of higher authorities if Eli didn't back down.

'Methuselah leered at them. Led them out into the waist where a group of seamen stood waiting for the outcome.

He stood on the hatch and looked down at them. 'You had better pack your sea-bags and draw your pay, then go see if you can find other berths.' With that he got down and strode over to the gangway as though that was an end to it. They were stunned for a moment, before someone had guts enough to pipe up an objection.

' "Blame yur worthy captain," he told them. "He has written evidence to prove this ship is unfit for sea. It appears my long experience and expert knowledge have no weight here. Far be it for me to send you out onto a perilous ocean under such circumstances. Better you find other ships."

'He had underestimated them, however. One man stepped forward and stood squarely in front of Tardeval. "We knows the truth of it," he declared. "We knows Eli and you are a pair of crooks and this ship is the worst of a fleet of floating deathtraps. If we takes her out we should get a bonus on our pay."

'There is nothing in this world more certain to bring Tardeval's blood to the boil than the prospect of paying over the odds for anything. He turned purple and threw the report into the harbour, bellowing at them, "I have more experience than all of you put together and I tell you this ship is seaworthy. Any man who thinks different can go ashore right now." '

Royal chuckles bitterly. 'No one did, of course, and their skipper was forced to choke back his protest and accept a promise of an early refit. The whole thing died a natural death, but not before some wag reckoned up the combined seatime of the crew and proclaimed that Tardeval would have to live as long as Methuselah to acquire that much experience. From that day Tardeval became Methuselah.'

This is the longest conversation we have had until now. Royal seems in the mood for talk, even with me. So I encourage him. 'Isn't it about time you eased up on the colonel. He is a harmless old codger; a bit eccentric, that's all.'

'Rubbish!' His mood changes abruptly as he rounds on me. 'He is a bloody nuisance to everyone. A throwback from the Empire builders who used men like puppets and lived on the backs of competent artisans like parasites. I'll bet he is on the local council at home in his cosy little village. One of the vicar's men, patronising the peasantry and organising the Saturday cricket match. Now his bombast has blown itself out and he knows that he has grown old, scared and useless. He has pulled rank over others with more ability and led his last crusade.

'I was there remember. I saw him brush aside advice from the Navy, the arrogant swine! That is why you came to find us adrift like that. If it had not been for your colonel we would have been taken on board a destroyer, or at least followed a convoy of other small boats to Dover. That wasn't good enough for him. He needed to prove that he was not just a desk-bound has-been. Consequently we almost lost our lives, and the doctor suffered his heart attack. I would heave the stupid old sod overboard if it was left to me.' He goes silent and turns away to stare out to sea.

I go back to my hawser to wait out the final few minutes before we slip. I can see the dull pewter glint of water showing between the open lockgates. I glance aft to the bridge where the blank windows stare back at me and the vague shapes of two men move out onto the wing to look fore and aft along the quay.

'You ain't got nuffink ter be ashamed of, sir.' Fred's disembodied voice drifts up from below. 'I've bin nuffin but scared ever since I came to France.'

'That's different,' says the colonel's solemn voice. 'I am an officer.'

'You're a man too, sir. You got feelin's same as me. Not like that killin' machine I've got locked in there.'

'What do you mean?' I sense a quickening interest in the colonel's tone.

' 'Im! The fuckin' Nazi! 'E ain't got any feelin's. 'E would murder 'is gran'mother if the Führer told 'im to.'

'I – I'm afraid I'm not with you. Are you saying that you have a prisoner in there?'

'O' course. That's what I'm doin' 'ere wiv me rifle between me legs. I got me own, personal Nazi.'

'Can I see?'

'Only if you promises not to try and take 'im away from me, sir.' Fred's voice is anxious.

'I'll do no such thing. I am not in the habit of making promises to rankers. Open that door at once!'

I hear the click of Fred's rifle bolt. 'Don't you try nuffin, sir. I'm warnin' you.'

I shout to the only man available. 'Royal! The colonel is getting out of hand. You had better get him away from Fred before someone is shot!'

'I take no orders from you!'

'All right, then take this from me and I'll go down myself.'

He spits over the side. 'Leave it to me. I'll get rid of the bastard.'

'Take it easy. Remember, he is an old man.'

He goes by me without comment and I hear him remonstrating with the old fool. 'Come away from there. Get aft where you belong or I'll lock you up in the spud-locker.'

I cringe. There is no room for diplomacy where Royal's concerned. I shut my mind to the scuffling and the colonel's plaintive protests as he is dragged aft. After a few moments Royal climbs back up the ladder and resumes his stance right up in the bow.

The night closes in as a cloud crosses the moon. For a moment we are in total darkness before it rides clear to give us light. Royal's arm lifts to wave response to someone's signal from the bridge. He snaps curt orders and I hear the soft splash of the breast-rope and know that we are free. I tighten the turns on the drum to bring the hawser taut; not putting too much strain on it though, as I wait for the bow to ease out. Gruff voices mouth orders quietly aft where the sternlines are being taken in and stowed. Already vibrations come from the first slow turns of her big propeller. The rudder will be hard over to swing the stern out to line up with the gate.

The beat of her propeller increases as we move ghostlike towards the narrow exit. We are a spectral shape sliding almost soundlessly along with the moon slanting the long shadows of the masts and superstructure across the wharf. I watch them slither in and out of crevices and undulations like liquid. Soon the walls close in and bloodless faces peer up at us as we go by.

In the outer basin we move over to the port side, feeling the first breath of sea wind tugging at our clothes. Royal has gone aft to the bridge where he can keep an eye on Eli and Methuselah, for no one trusts them, and he has the experience to know if they do something suspicious. We are clearing the breakwater; lifting as we cross the bar and feel the open sea. She judders slightly, as though she knows she is shaking off the land. The telegraph jangles again, and the vibration hammers against the soles of my feet. She is pushing her blunt nose into the channel, building a bow-wave as we come round to our course. I help stow the hawser away and square up the fo'c'sle before going aft to the bridge.

The harbour is losing its form in the deep gloom astern. There is a halo round the moon as it drifts across a big gap in the cloud. By the time I reach the wheelhouse it has been swallowed up by another heavy bank of cumulus, turning the night black and silent. The *Sister Sarai* rolls gently; long, slow, even rolls, with the weight of her cargo regulating her movements. She picks up a cupful of spray and hurls it inboard to keep us awake. She is an old lady who has been treated badly, and has worked her knuckles bare, but when she is at sea she retains her dignity. She never asks for favours, and always earns her bread.

On paper she is owned by that evil old hypocrite with the screechy voice, but in reality she belongs to no one. Those who man her have to serve her and nurture her in her old age. Their greed makes them slaves to her demands, and keeps her from the scrapyard. It is their sweat that keeps her alive beyond her natural span. They abused her when she was in her prime, and prostituted her for their own ends. Now it costs them money and toil to chip away the flaking crust of age and slap thick coats of paint to close her seams. Every rope, every block, every piece of her machinery has to be greased, repaired, watched over constantly if they want the last ounce of work from her. She knows she is a rotting corpse, held together with paint and grime.

Her joints are brittle. Her muscles tired and weak, but when they take her out into her own element she confounds them all with her quiet dignity and unhurried pace. Her crew rant and rage at her lethargy. They grow impatient and take it out on each other, cursing the tides they miss and the water she ships. They struggle to restore badly trimmed cargoes, for she makes no compromise to slack seamanship. She noses into remote Cornish harbours where the rattle of her winches echo back from green hills. She sidles into Liverpool beneath the shadows of greater ships, and her drunken crewmen have disgorged their stomachs on the quays at Rotterdam and Hamburg, yet the steady pulse of her engine has hardly altered from the day she was launched.

I feel the rough, scored wooden capping beneath my hands and know she is unloved. Those who designed and built her thought her to be no more than a work machine, but I know different, for I am one of a band of fortunate men who can read into the soul of a ship and know that she has a heart. Not like the brightly-lit fancy ocean-going aristocrats that carry multitudes of loud people on aimless journeys, nor the glittering toys that seem to run on gin and sex, but a special breed, with working derricks and winches, and a bellyful of cargo. I always feel out of place and uncomfortable when taking passage on a ferry or a passenger ship. Unable to settle, restless amongst the chatter and unseamanlike clutter about me. It is entirely different when you live in a ship and become part of her.

You get to learn her secrets when she is your home twenty-four hours a day, month in and month out, with just a few hours on shore at intervals to shake free of her clinging skirts.

That is the one thing the Navy has in common with these work-horses: we take our world with us wherever we go. The scenery may change as we move from port to port, from Hong Kong to Malta, or Narvik to Capetown, but the ship remains the same, and after a run ashore we are always glad to be back on board.

'So there you are!' Martingale comes out of the gloom. 'I think we must have a little get-together with Sub-Lieutenant Barratt, de Carteret, and possibly the colonel, if he's up to it. There are certain issues which must be sorted out regarding Tardeval and Mr Spring. Then there is the problem of Fred and his German. We can't just allow it to run on like this.'

'What about Royal, sir. Since he is our liaison with the crew he ought to be taken into our confidence.'

'Hm!' He leans on the rail and contemplates the wash. 'I don't really know what to say about him. He is a strange bird.'

The radio-room is where we meet amongst a jumble of antiquated wireless equipment. It is a tight squeeze in there with de Carteret, Barratt, Martingale, and Melody, who has come in place of Royal.

'Give me a call if I am required,' Royal told me when I invited him along. 'I do not wish to leave the bridge. Anything you want to know about the ship, ask Melody.' He grinned knowingly. 'Nothing very complicated about him, Grant. His loyalty to the ship is total. Whatever happens you can rely on him to bust a gut to get her into port.

'What about the colonel?' I ask when we are assembled, and everyone looks the other way.

Martingale acts as though he hasn't heard me. 'It is mainly a case of allocating responsibilities,' he says. 'The running of the ship can be left to her officers and crew while they behave themselves.'

It is a short meeting, mainly to establish co-ordination. For the moment Fred will be left to his own devices in the hope that with time he will come to his senses. Barratt will try to get the radio working with more will than knowledge, although Melody reckons that Methuselah has some idea about wavelengths and Merchant Navy frequencies, so might be persuaded to help to send a signal to drum up support for the last phase of our journey.

De Carteret remains on the fringe, totally committed to his own affairs, and when the meeting breaks up he returns to his *poilus* without comment. Melody and I are given the task of inspecting the upper-deck, with special attention to life-boats and rafts, plus anything else we can use in an emergency to keep people afloat. Martingale stations himself with Royal on the bridge where they can keep their eyes on Eli and his colleague.

All in all it seems to be falling into place when we slide out into mid-channel, leaving the conflict fading away to starboard. There should be an air of quiet optimism, but I have a persistent, irrational, niggling feeling of trepidation inside me that refuses to be shaken off. On the face of it most of our troubles are over as we sail into the final leg of our journey, and I keep telling myself that my fears are unfounded, yet when I look at the humped figures of Eli and Methuselah the nagging doubts persist.

Melody assures me that the two life-boats were tested three months ago when Board of Trade officials came on board for a routine inspection, but you wouldn't know it to look at them. Their keels are wedged into the chucks with a welding of old paint and dirt. Their falls are hairy and brittle with age and non-use, while their pulleys look as though they are rusted solid. Each boat is designed to accommodate twelve adults, and when I lift the edge of their canvas covers I see that they are cracked and dry with neglect, used as a convenient deposit for all manner of garbage thrown in by passers-by. Why anyone should go to the effort of lifting the corner of the canvas to shove in half-eaten sandwiches or empty beer bottles when a casual flip of the wrist would send it overboard is beyond me.

The bilges are awash with stagnant water to keep the seams tight. Mottled with a mess of floating rubbish and butt-ends. Everything is gritty and black-rimmed with coal-dust, while the jagged edges of broken bottom-boards sprout beneath. We strip away the canvas to take a closer look, and cringe at what we find.

Melody is full of self-reproach when he stares at the mess. As bosun this is his resonsibility, and he catches the condemnation in my eyes. 'I guessed what we would find. I have been telling the mate for some time about these bloody boats, but it is like talking to a brick wall. That's the only excuse I can offer.' He slams a heavy hand at the boat. 'This ain't the only coaster with boats like this, and I ain't the only bosun who has to argue for them to be made seaworthy. Even in good company ships you will find neglect. When I was in Southampton I saw a cross-channel packet with lifeboats almost as bad as this. Money is tight, and we ain't got the hands to spare for jobs like this. Providing they are made ready for routine inspections when the time comes they can be left to rot in between times.'

I open the stowage compartment in the sternsheets of the port boat and pull out the emergency ration container. It is half empty, and what remains is not fit to be used, so I heave it overboard. There is a supply of flares in a watertight tin though, and they seem to be in good order. Melody routs out a couple of ABs who turn to and replenish the food and water with supplies from the galley. With that done we leave them to grease the blocks and make certain the boats are free to be hoisted out.

We pull out the stoppers and allow the stagnant water to drain from the bilges before cleaning out the rubbish. The seams won't dry out and open in the time it takes for us to reach port, so we leave the bilges empty and throw out the broken timber. Beyond that there is not much more we can do to make them fit for use.

We should be able to squeeze fifteen children into each

boat, with a competent seaman to take charge. That leaves twelve others and the three nuns before we can begin to think of the crew and ourselves. In addition to the two boats there is a raft lashed to the deck-house just abaft the funnel. It looks like a couple of orange-boxes clamped together with metal buoyancy-tanks inside the wooden battens. If the weather stays quiet we might be able to get the nuns and the remainder of the children on that. The rest will have to fend for themselves.

'Let's hope that we do not run into any real trouble,' I say with feeling.

Melody nods. 'If it comes to taking to the boats we'll need those French rifles to control the mob. If I know anything about that lot in the fo'c'sle there will be one almighty stampede if we have to abandon ship in a hurry. Every man for himself and sod the hindmost.'

We stand back to survey our handiwork. The two ABs are tidying up while we ponder over what more can be done. Looking along the upper-deck there seems little that can be used to make rafts. The hatches must remain battened down and there is no other timber about.

'There are a few oildrums about the ship. We could empty those and lash them together,' suggests Melody, and I nod agreement. It isn't much, but everything helps, and maybe we are worrying about nothing. After all, the English coast will be in sight when the sun comes up in a few hours, and we should be safely tucked up in harbour by noon.

'I'll go and rout out some more hands from the fo'c'sle,' he says. 'Who knows, if I put it to them they might even have some ideas of their own.' He goes off, leaving me to stare after him with that ever-present sense of foreboding.

That is when I hear the knocking. A persistent rat-a-tat with short intervals, as though someone is listening for a response. I follow the sound round the afterdeck-house until I am stood right aft among the clutter of coiled hawsers, the winch, and the big emergency steering-wheel on her tiny stern. The sound leads me to a steel door at the rear of the superstructure. Three clips are firmly secured and as I press my ear to the clammy metal another staccato rattles out.

Whoever rammed those clips home meant business for it requires a hefty bang with the detachable handle from the steam valve on the winch to knock them off. As the last one flies back the door bursts open and I am faced with an apoplectic colonel who rounds on me like a raging bull. Gone is all the remorse and despair. He seethes with pent-up anger; unable to find words adequate to cope with what burns inside him. He blusters and snorts, with a dangerous purple hue infusing his puffed cheeks. All I can do is stand there and hope he doesn't explode.

'My God!' he manages to blurt out at last. 'Heads will roll for this! I'll see you all stripped of your rank and reduced to the lowest form of service life.' He lifts a hand to point at my chest and I shudder when I see the state of it. It must have been crushed in the doorway when he was thrust inside the small bosun's store for it is a mess of mangled flesh and broken skin. He must be in agony, but his anger is greater than the pain. He stinks of wet rope and pitch and his face is grimed with layers of rust and dirt.

'Try to calm down, sir,' I urge lamely.

'Don't be such a damned impertinent idiot!' he shouts, beating his good fist against the side of his trousers. 'And don't stand gaping like a bloody goldfish. Take me to your officer at once!'

He blusters along behind me as I lead him along the port side and up the short ladder to the wheelhouse. Everyone is struck speechless by his wild appearance. He fills the doorway with his dishevelled frame, looking from one to the other until he homes in on Royal. His arm snaps up to point a wrecked fore-finger accusingly. 'I want that man put under arrest. I want him charged with assaulting an officer, even attempted murder! I – I could have suffocated in that steel coffin, and – and look what he did to my hand.' He spreads his emaciated claw for everyone to wince at.

Royal just stares back at him with a sneer on his face, waiting calmly for the colonel's tirade to die down. 'I warned you to keep your hand clear. I put you in the bosun's locker for your own safety as well as ours. You were not thinking straight, and you were a bloody menace to everybody.'

'All right, Royal,' snaps Martingale. 'Leave it to me.'

'Get that maniac outside!' thunders Methuselah. 'I will not put up with your petty squabbles on my bridge!'

'Petty squabbles!' chokes the colonel. 'Petty squabbles!' He struggles to retain his outrage. 'I refuse to be treated like this. You will afford me the respect due to my rank and status!'

'Get him out of here before I heave him bodily off my bridge,' warns Methuselah.

'I think you had better come with me, sir,' persuades Martingale. 'We can discuss it all in private, and with some dignity.' He places himself between the blustering colonel and Royal, gently easing him back towards the open doorway. The protests fade as they descend the ladder until we are left with only the sound of the sea and the creak of the hull.

One of the *Sarai*'s seamen is on the helm and I glance over his shoulder at the compass. It shows we are heading north-north-west, give or take a degree or two. I watch it for a moment with an uneasing feeling that I cannot explain. After all, it is no concern of mine, and Royal is there to ensure that they follow our instructions. He says he knows this area like the back of his hand and I can think of no logical reason for me to worry, yet I cannot shake it off even when I go down to find Melody, so that we can continue our inspection of the upper-deck.

We gather everything that floats into piles at various vantage points, but it doesn't add up to much, although we do find extra life-jackets stowed in a remote locker and a few wooden crates that might keep men afloat for a while. We make a final sortie, working aft from the fo'c'sle. He takes the starboard side while I search along the port side, just to satisfy ourselves that we have done all possible to ensure the children have a chance if the ship is attacked.

It is when I reach the lifeboat that the reason for my apprehension becomes clear. It is turned out ready for lowering so I have to clamber over the davit and swing out on the falls to get across to the gunn'l. Beneath me the wash surges past the hull as I straddle the black void for one anxious moment, and I try to shut out the vision of a big, bronze, churning propeller waiting to slice me up into small chunks if I should slip. One extra lunge and I fall into the boat, struggling amongst the hard timber thwarts and bottom-boards. The whole thing sways as I launch myself aft and reach into the sternsheets to pull out the small brass-bound compass. I set it upright and shine my handtorch into the face. The lubber's point is stuck on west; a cardinal point, with no room for doubt.

'What are you doing there?'

I look down into Melody's serious face. 'Any idea what the magnetic variation is round here?'

'Gawd knows! The skipper always sets it on the compass before we sail. About seven degrees west I'd guess. All I can tell you is that our course from St Trepórt to Southampton is always about nor-west-by-west till we pick up · Nab Tower. It depends on the tide of course; sometimes we go up through Spithead, sometimes round the Needles.'

'Why should this compass show due west and the one in the wheelhouse nor-nor-west?'

He purses his lips. 'Well it's only a boat's compass. You wouldn't expect it to be as accurate as the one in the binicle. There's deviation to think of too.'

'Not forty-five degrees worth there isn't. ' I scramble down to him, still holding the compass. 'Let's see what the other one says.'

It shows the same, and to confirm our suspicions all we do is look at the tattered old ensign fluttering at the staff. There is hardly any movement with the following wind, but enough to show that we have it on the port quarter. If the wind hasn't changed in the past hour we should be feeling it coming in from the starboard side.

'What do you reckon?' he asks.

'Can you think of any reason why Eli and Methuselah would not wish to go to England with this cargo?'

'There is only one motive for anything they do together – money. You can bet your pension they've got it all worked out between them. I know that Eli is convinced Britain will make a pact with Germany when France is out of the way. He believes the Germans will pay over the odds for anthracite when they start to re-establish industry.' He looks away. 'There could be other reasons too.'

I see he is reluctant to go further, so I urge him along a bit. 'You can tell me what's on your mind, Melody. Remember, we have the lives of those young kids to think of.'

He looks back at me, deadly serious. 'It's only guesswork based on a lot of rumour, but I think there's something in it. It concerns Royal and the *Sister Ruth*. There has been a lot of loose talk about why she ran ashore in broad daylight in a place most of her crew knew like their own back yards. It's incredible that they would stray out of the fairway even if Royal had to leave the bridge for a moment.'

'You mean she was deliberately run onto the rocks: an insurance fiddle. Were these ships heavily insured then?'

He chuckles bitterly. 'Not the ship, Ben. Insurance for the cargo I'm talking about. My guess is that it is well over-insured and Eli would stand to make a packet. Everyone knows that he was on his uppers when the war broke out. Every ship is overdue for refits – major refits that would cost more than their true value. I think he has had a gutful, but doesn't want to cut his losses without a fight. Some of the *Sister Ruth*'s crew were far too keen to shop Royal in my opinion. Oh I know they hated the way he made them sweat for their money, but they're used to hard-nosed mates. Two of them actually swore out affidavits accusing him of deliberately causing the captain's death. That doesn't ring true, Ben. Those buggers go out of their way to avoid the law, not chase after it like a lot of avenging angels. In any case, they detested the skipper even more than Royal. No, there must be something more to it than plain cussedness.'

'I'll have a word with Royal and Martingale. Keep this under your hat for now, Bose.'

He nods. 'I'll wait here. Let me know how you get on.'

Martingale is on the bridge again, and not to make things too obvious I ask about the colonel. 'I've settled him in the galley with a note-pad and pencil busily making a complete list of all his complaints in writing while they are still fresh in his mind. Seems we are all going to suffer for our crimes, Grant. In fact, if he has his way we'll be drummed out of the service. I have never seen such a change in a man. One minute he is consumed with guilt, and the next he's Colonel Blimp, rampaging about the place like a wild boar. The sooner we get him ashore the better. Fortunately I have managed to persuade him that it is in his own interest to allow us to get on with the job of getting the ship back to England.'

I notice Eli and Methuselah listening in the background. 'I don't want to distract the helmsman, sir, but I'd like to make a full report of the life-saving equipment if you have a moment.'

'Any report of that kind should be made to me,' orders Methuselah aggressively.

I face up to him. 'Melody will do that, sir. We agreed that is the best way to do it.'

For a moment I think he is going to object. His eyes squint suspiciously as he tries to decide whether or not we are trying to hide something from him. Finally he nods reluctantly. 'Remember, Martingale. I will not tolerate interference with the running of the ship.'

'I'll send Melody up here to you, sir,' I state bluntly.

VIII

We invade Barratt's small sanctuary once more, to find him in shirtsleeves tinkering with knobs and producing a mixture of squeals and groans from a background of static. Just to get the antique radio working at all is an achievement, but now it is driving him potty when it refuses to pick up a coherent message. He welcomes the diversion when Martingale and I squeeze in with him, and both officers listen intently while I explain about the compasses.

'I knew something like this was going on,' grumbles Martingale. 'Why the hell didn't Royal tumble to it?'

'Why should he?' I stress. 'The compass in the wheelhouse is showing the correct course and it is too dark to see the coastline. Even when the sun comes up we will have the coast of Normandy dead ahead. It will take some time before anyone notices that it is not the Isle of Wight.'

'We must do something immediately,' says Barratt anxiously. 'Every minute we hold on to this course makes it more difficult.'

'No need to flap, sub. It isn't that drastic. We are steering due west instead of north-west that's all. That is easy to rectify. The real question is how we go about doing it. I do not want to turn the ship into two camps, if I can avoid it.'

Before anyone can answer the door swings open and Royal stands there looking at us. 'I thought you ought to know there is something weird going on up top. Eli and Methuselah sent Melody forward to rout out the engineer and try to sober him up. I know Eli of old. When he is being devious he is like a bloody old vulture.'

He shows no surprise when Martingale tells him about the compasses; just gives vent to a couple of choice expletives as he listens. 'I should have my bloody head examined,' he growls. 'All they had to do was open the small door in the binnacle and fiddle with the innards. I must be losing my touch.'

'Well there's no point in self-recrimination,' grunts Martingale impatiently. 'What do we do now?'

'There is only one way to treat a crafty old sod like Eli. Throw it all straight into his face. Plain facts always confuse that twisting bastard.'

'All right,' agrees Martingale. 'Sooner the better; so let's get on with it.'

'Hold on a minute,' cautions Royal. 'Have you got that radio working, Barratt?'

Royal's familiarity takes Barratt aback for a moment, but he chokes back his indignation and shrugs despondently, 'All I can get is static and interference I'm afraid.'

'It would put us one up on those bastards if you can get it working.' He leans over Barratt's shoulder to study the equipment for a moment, then his mouth widens into a knowing grin. 'You would do better if you connect up to the aerial.' He reaches up to plug a lead into a connector high on the bulkhead. Immediately a stream of morse bleeps out. Barratt twiddles his tuner until he settles on a frequency. 'Wish I could read fast enough to understand that,' he complains.

Royal's arms swoops in again to click over a large switch. The bleeps change to a babble of discordant human noises. He rotates the control and the static clears. Suddenly the well-modulated Oxford accent of a BBC announcer informs us that a cold front is moving in from mid-Atlantic. 'Play with that for a while,' suggests Royal. 'Perhaps we'll find out what's happening to the war.'

'I would like to send a signal,' says Martingale.

'One thing at a time, sir. Let's sort out Eli and Methuselah first, then I'll see what I can do.' He steps out across the coaming, leaving us to stare after him.

'Do you get the feeling that Royal is taking over?' asks Barratt plaintively.

Martingale mutters something unintelligible before sliding out to follow. When I start to go after him he turns to me. 'No need for you to come, Grant. I'd like you to go below and put Finney in the picture. I do not want the ship's engineer to take over down there. When you've done that keep an eye on things on deck.'

'Aye aye, sir.' I watch him go, then clamber down into the steamy heat of the engine-room where Finney lurks like Dante in his inferno. Despite its age the engine is not noisy. The big, pendulous pistons rotate in oily viscosity with a rhythmic beat amid the hiss of leaking steam. It is a comforting sound, like the beating of a heart in the body of the ship.

The stoker PO accepts all I tell him with his usual laconic preoccupation, so that I'm left wondering if he has taken it all in. However, I have known him long enough to trust his judgement. If the engineer turns up I have no doubt they will eye each other up with mutual, alcoholic distrust, and it won't be Finney who backs down. He has cultivated the art of convincing others that he is subservient while doing exactly what he has a mind to do. So I can leave him in his simmering jungle and go back to my own environment without any qualms.

I stare aft at the wake to find it stretching out as straight as an arrow until it is lost in the gloom, so I assume the argument goes on in the wheelhouse and we are still plodding westward. Well, that's their concern. My first task is to find Melody. His loyalties may be divided when it comes to personalities, but as far as the ship is concerned we are in tune and I know we can work together. Also, I desperately need an ally that I can trust.

Going past the galley I glance in to see the huddled shape of the colonel slumped over the worktop with his back to me. I had not intended to stop, but something in his attitude makes me hesitate and take a step backwards to look through the open door. He sits in the deep gloom, perched on a high stool, staring at nothing. He must have been in the dark for some time, for someone would have yelled if he had switched on the shaded light above his head. I move in closer, until I can see him breathing and hear a kind of shallow muttering. I am almost touching him, yet he makes no sign of having heard me.

'You all right, sir?'

I have to wait a while before his back stiffens and he leans back to turn his grey head towards me, crinkling up his eyes as though he is trying to recognise me. The change in him is staggering. Gone is the arrogant bombast. Now he is a beseeching old spaniel pleading for someone to understand him.

'They were so young,' he whimpers soulfully. 'They trusted me and I watched them die. De Carteret was right; when it is dark in no-man's-land everyone is an enemy.'

I shuffle with embarrassment. 'You can't blame yourself, sir. You ran out of luck, that's all.'

He looks away. 'I wish I could believe that. The truth is my blundering stubbornness has cost them their lives. Even on the beach I wouldn't listen to those with more knowledge than I. I needed to prove that all that golf-club talk wasn't just hot-air. Now I have to live with my folly for the remainder of my days.'

He lapses into silence and all I want to do is get away from him, for I know he is telling the truth, and that he is a stupid old idiot who wanted to jangle his medals just once more. I cannot condemn him outright, though. Perhaps he is only one more casualty in this bloody farce.

'We all make mistakes, sir. Try not to blame yourself too much.'

That's my exit line, a verbal excuse to back out and leave him to it, for I have neither the will nor the profound insight to offer solace. I go back to my domain where the tang of tarry rope and the sting of salt helps to drive away the disturbing traumas of other men's maladjustments. The steel-hard, unfeeling ambience of the upper-deck is almost an extension of my personality. 'To hell with anyone who tries to humanise it! I want no complications in my life,' I tell myself.

As though that solves it all I push on forward in search of Melody, for he too finds the idiosyncrasies of other human beings of secondary interest to the fundamental demands of keeping the ship alive. I find him checking the hatch-covers; thumping the big wooden wedges into place with satisfying whacks with a large mallet. In the blackness above our heads the derrick-gear creaks and rattles with the swing and vibration of the ship. A dark world of mysterious sound that only a sailor's mind can sort out.

Once again my thoughts turn to *Scavenger*. There is a dull ache inside me when I think of her pushing out into the North Sea without me. Taking with her all my shipmates, and the familiar taste and smell of her that haunts me like the memory of an old friend. For the thousandth time I ask myself how it is possible to become so much a part of a ship; especially a submarine. Perhaps because without me and my companions she would be only a useless piece of metal. We breathe life into her, and in return she gives us an identity.

'Well, that should do it,' grunts Melody, breaking into my thoughts. He slumps down with his backside on the canvas and his feet dangling over the coaming. 'What a bloody mess, eh?'

I place a boot on the hatch beside him and sway against it, feeling the muscles in the back of my thighs tighten satisfactorily. 'How'd you get on with the engineer?'

'Pah!' He spits over the side. 'It'd take an ocean of coffee to swill the booze out of him. He is lying in his own spew, and it smells like he's shit himself, the filthy old sod! We'll get nothing out of him before we dock. He is drinking cheap cognac, about one jump up from kerosene. If anyone lights a match near him he'll go up like a torch. Where Eli manages to find these drop-outs beats me.'

'Royal and Martingale are persuading them to alter course for Southampton.'

'Good luck to them.'

'We might have to take over the running of the ship.' I am testing him out carefully. He spits again and I squat beside him and wait. I want him on my side but I know he will not be pushed. I get a whiff of funnel-smoke and know that we are still on course for Cherbourg. Presumably the argument is dragging on in the wheelhouse; a wordy contest between Martingale's diplomacy, Royal's aggression, and the conspiratorial threats of Eli and Methuselah.

'You're asking me which side I'm on?'

'That's about it. At times like this it's good to know who your friends are.'

'I will make up my mind when the time comes. Whatever happens I am still the bosun, and Methuselah is my skipper. I'm too long in the tooth to go against that easily.'

'Even if it endangers the ship?'

He looks away again. 'Ah, that's where conscience comes into it. You'll have to let me sort that out in my own mind, Ben. Don't push me to give you an answer when I don't even know it myself.'

We lapse into silence for a moment, then he gets to his feet. 'I'm off to check the forward hold – you coming?' He traipses off without waiting for a reply, and I follow him through the covered walkway beneath the port wing of the bridge. Even though I strain my ears I cannot hear any part of the argument going on just above my head, so I follow Melody round the perimeter of the hold as he goes on knocking wedges into place.

Fred still squats in isolated silence beside his paintstore. He is watching us with his eyes shining flintlike in the gloom. His body is tense, and his fingers fiddle constantly on the rifle. I glance at my watch. It is almost two hours since we cleared St Tréport; say fourteen miles, about one third of the way across the Baie de la Seine. 'You all right, Fred?' I ask as I draw near to him.

'Dunno,' he mutters. 'Maybe I am – maybe I ain't.'

'Well, when you've made up your mind let me know,' I chide, hoping to draw him out.

'You think I'm daft, don't you?'

Ah! the ship's swinging at last. I feel her heel slightly, and the wind touches my right cheek for the first time as I face forward. At last she is pointing her blunt snout towards home. 'I don't give a sod either way,' I say sourly. I have had my fill of this bloody nonsense tonight.

There is no stopping him now. He seems as eager as the colonel to unload all his troubles on me. 'It's just that those bastards stick together. Officers, I mean. That poxy colonel, for instance. 'E'd 'ave that bloody Nazi swannin' abaht in one of the cabins if 'e 'ad 'is way. Sometimes I think officers think more of their own kind than the poor lousy squaddies, even if they are the enemy.'

'Depends on the officer,' I grunt, trying to bring the conversation to an end.

'Well they ain't gonna 'ave 'im.' His voice gets angry again.

'You can't hold on to him forever.' I could cut off my tongue for rising to him. I hadn't meant to feed his need to talk.

'No, but I know what I'm gonna do to 'im now.'

'Oh!'

He keeps his head down so I cannot see his face, but I can sense the satisfied smirk as he states determinedly. 'I'm gonna give 'im the chance to swim back 'ome.'

The wind is full on my cheek now, and she is feeling the chops on her flank as she settles to the new course. 'You'll spend the rest of your time in jankers if you do that.'

'I'll say 'e was trying to escape.'

'I know different.'

He looks up to study my face. 'But you'll keep your mouf shut, won't you?'

'Don't bet on it. You are talking about murder, Fred. I will not be party to that.'

His voice goes icy cold. 'That's up to you, mate.'

There's no point in going on with this. I had sympathy for the poor sod at the start, and I could have patted him on the back if he had stuck his bayonet into the Nazi when the hurt and anger was still hot, but the longer it goes on the more calculated and obscene it becomes. He has played cat and mouse with his prisoner for far too long, keeping his hate on the boil until it festers. It is no longer a simple case of giving the German what he deserves, but more to do with a plain uncomplicated bloke like Fred turning into a perverted, self-elected executioner.

There has always been a nagging doubt in my mind about how I would behave if I was caught up in a frenzy of hate. There was a couple of occasions when serving on the China Station when I found myself part of a squad sent on shore to quell riots. The local peasants had revolted against their mandarin, and we found ourselves facing a hostile mob, outnumbered by about five to one. Young, scared, I had needed to charge myself with something close to blood-lust to overcome my fear. I launched into the mob with my yelling, screaming mates, beating about us while the NCOs and officers tried to keep control. Afterwards I experienced a glorious sensation of power when I realised that I hadn't disgraced myself, and kept up with my mates all the way. Later, when I wore badges of rank on my sleeve the memory sickened me.

Fred is treating me like a mate. Assuming that I will not betray his trust and stay loyal to the unwritten law that says no ranker will ever shop another in these circumstances. If he had thought for one second that I would not keep his secret he would never have entrusted me with it. Now, for his own sake, I have to tell Martingale. Somehow Fred has to be stopped before he wrecks his whole future.

Before I can do anything more about it de Carteret comes out of the shadows. 'I saw you examining the lifeboats,' he states accusingly.

'Yes, sir.'

'Is there to be an allocation of places then?'

'The kids and their nuns with one experienced seaman in each,' I tell him bluntly.

'I'm sorry, that is not possible. My men have placed the records in one of the boats, and I have posted sentinels to make sure they are safe.'

I've had enough. 'Fuck your stupid records!' I blast in exasperation. 'I'm talking about children, for Christ's sake!' I am beside myself. The bloody ship is full of cranks. It's like Bedlam with all their conflicting self-motivated ploys.

'Grant!' Martingale is calling down from the bridge. I'm not surprised; the whole ship must have heard me. 'What's all the fuss?' he asks.

I am speechless for the moment, so de Carteret replies for me. 'I have taken over one of the lifeboats, lieutenant. My chests are more important than a few lives, I'm afraid.'

Martingale takes the ladder in two strides. 'Are you mad? What possible value can you place on a few mouldy old records when set against the lives of those kids?'

'You do not understand. They are not just archive material and official records. They also contain lists of organisations and people who will carry on the fight even after France is occupied. More important, they list the names of those who cannot be trusted, or who have openly proclaimed their affiliation to Nazi ideals.' He relaxes, smiling consolingly at Martingale. 'Your fears are groundless, lieutenant. It is very unlikely that we will not reach port safely tomorrow. We will help you in every way that we can, but,' and here his face hardens again, 'there is no room for argument. My men will fire on anyone who attempts to get at the lifeboat.' He turns his back on us and strides away.

'Like Melody said,' I grouch sullenly, 'what a bloody mess!'

'It's what's known as a Gordian Knot, Grant. No sooner do we unravel one tangle than we are faced with another. It is not enough that we must fight the Germans; we have to scrap amongst ourselves.' He pulls himself together. 'I want you on the bridge now. Eli and Methuselah were taken off-guard when Royal stalked into the wheelhouse, opened the binnacle and laid bare their deception. They were unable to do more than look as guilty as hell. We have persuaded them to alter course, but I have no doubt that they will be up to their old tricks as soon as they have recovered. What do you think of the crew? Will they rally to their captain when the chips are down?'

'They will go along with Melody, sir. He's been keeping them in order for so long it is second nature to follow his lead. Remember though, they're only interested in getting their back-pay. It is in their interest to stick with Eli until the ship pays off.'

'Tell them the Navy will see that they get what's coming to them. What about Melody?'

'The bosun is a man who makes up his own mind, sir.'

'I see. Well let's hope it doesn't come to that. So far we have managed to confine the problem to the wheelhouse, and Finney still holds the fort down below. We are thin on the ground though. I will need you on the helm until we find out which way the crew will go. I had counted on de Carteret's men to help us, but now it seems they are busy with their own affairs. We are down to Barratt, Royal, Finney, you and myself. We cannot trust the colonel, and Fred is in a little world of his own.'

'Talking about Fred, sir. I'm afraid that we have another problem there.'

He sighs heavily. 'Don't spare me the details, Grant. What's he up to now?'

'He has decided what to do with his German. He reckons he is going to make him swim back home.'

'Bloody hell!'

'I've told him not to be bloody stupid, sir. The longer he broods, the worse he gets.'

He heaves another hefty sigh. 'Why the hell doesn't he get on with it then? He's like some idiot threatening to jump off a roof and never getting round to it.'

'He's bloody determined.'

'Well we are just going to have to leave him to it, Grant. I have more important things to do. Let's hope he changes his mind.'

'Aye aye, sir. There is one small glimmer of comfort though. I am certain that if de Carteret knew that Eli and

Methuselah are trying to stop the ship getting to England he would come out on our side. He wants to reach Southampton as much as we do.'

I'll bear that in mind.'

We find Royal standing over the two scowling conspirators and a bemused helmsman. They make a strange tableau as he watches over them with stolid self-assurance, wearing his perpetual sneer and not giving one inch. It gives me a moment to study Royal carefully.

Perhaps he is not the villain I have made him out to be. I sniff cynically: It will take more than this to convince me otherwise. I feel almost duty-bound to hold myself aloof from the new image he is trying to cultivate, and remember that beneath it all he is a scheming impersonator with the charge of murder hanging round his neck. Nothing will vindicate that in my eyes, and I intend to make certain he answers to the law when we reach port. In the meantime I will bury my feelings and admit that without him we would be in an even bigger mess.

I relieve the helmsman, who almost trips over himself in his hurry to get down to his mates and spread his gossip throughout the fo'c'sle. Royal watches him go before asking Martingale if he should relieve Barratt and try to get off a signal to the Admiralty with our ETA at Nab Tower. 'I think my morse is up to that,' he suggests.

Martingale nods agreement, then turns to Eli and Methuselah. 'In the meantime, gentlemen, I must ask you to go into the chartroom. I will feel easier in my mind if you are safely tucked away where I can keep an eye on you. When you have made up your minds to co-operate I may let you out.'

I hear a sharp intake of breath from Methuselah, but Eli just glares into space as though he hasn't heard. Royal moves to the rear of the wheelhouse and throws open a door leading into a small charthouse with a spare bunk for the skipper when at sea. 'You can stew in there for a while, until you come to your senses,' he grates.

Neither man utters a word as they pass through the door, but their malevolence is almost tangible. Even when they are shut in behind the locked door the threat is there, and when I take the wheel there are icy fingers playing up and down my spine. I shake off the feeling and try to concentrate on the course, running the polished spokes through my hands and relishing their familiar touch as I feel her buck against the pull of the sea.

Barratt arrives, bringing the musty, electronic tang of the radio-room with him. 'Royal says I am to come up here and leave him to operate the radio, sir.'

'That's right.'

The subby clears his throat nervously. 'Can we trust him to send the right signal, sir?'

'Have you got a better idea? Can you operate the set, or locate the right frequency?'

'No, sir. It just occurs to me that we will never know what message he sends, nor indeed, if he sends one at all.'

'That's right.'

Barratt blusters for a moment, shuffling about as though he cannot come to terms with it.

'I would be obliged if you would stop fidgeting about like a nervous schoolboy, sub,' snaps Martingale angrily. 'We have to take Royal on trust whether we like it or not. I don't think he has anything to gain by not giving our ETA. Now, if you have no other urgent problems I'll leave you in charge here while I go down and have a word with de Carteret. We will need all the friends we can get.'

He stumps out and the wind rattles the starboard door with a gust that shows how it is growing. I can hear the bluster of waves on the hull, and the ship is rolling with long, ponderous swings. It has a healthy feel to it, as though we are shaking off the torpid calm that has held us in its smouldering grip for so long. The weather played its part in the evacuation of Dunkirk by producing a miraculous spell of sustained calm that allowed even the smallest boats to cross the Straits and work in the shallows. Troops could wade up to their necks in the surf without fear of breakers sweeping in to knock them off their feet. For all that, however, it had an oppressive quality to it, and I welcome the freshening wind as it breathes new life and hope into the ship.

The door slams back, jolting me out of my thoughts. It is Melody, filling the wheelhouse with his bulk. 'I would like to speak with the captain,' he says bluntly.

'I – I'll have to ask Lieutenant Martingale,' Barratt blusters.

'It has nothing to do with the Navy. I want a word with my Captain.'

'That you, Melody?' Methuselah's muffled voice comes through the door.

'Yes, sir. We've had a fo'c'sle meeting and I am representing the crew.'

'Good for you. Open the door, Barratt, before I kick the bloody thing down.'

For a moment Barratt searches round desperately while I grit my teeth and try to stay out of it. A hefty crash thunders against the door, threatening to burst it from its hinges. Methuselah is a big bloke and he must have used his shoulder against it. A couple more like that and he will be in here with us. I grip the wheel hard, determined not to interfere.

Barratt still dithers. 'You'll have to open up, sir,' I urge. 'He'll only kick it down if you don't.'

'All right!' shouts Barratt as another crash comes. The mahogany façade is purely cosmetic, and the solid-looking door is merely a frail sham. Barratt lifts the key from its hook and darts across to open it up.

'About time!' thunders Methuselah, towering above the squat figure of Melody, while the crowlike shape of Eli hovers about in the background. 'So, the lads have come to their senses at last! Well it took them long enough.' Methuselah scowls down at the bosun.

'We want to know where you intend taking the *Sister Sarai*, sir.' Melody stands his ground and directs his words straight into his captain's red face.

Methuselah's expression alters a fraction as a brief moment of doubt crosses his mind. Barratt has dodged out through the door and I can visualise him scampering aft to find Martingale.

'I am not in the habit of discussing the running of my ship with foremast hands,' roars Methuselah.

'No, captain,' comes the silky whine of Eli as he peers round the bulk of his protector. 'We must hear what they have to say. It is only fair under the circumstances.' He eases his bony frame past Methuselah. His smile is sickly; as lifeless as the chalky colour of his lantern face. His dark eyes are socketed pools of limpid black. 'We have a valuable cargo in our holds, Melody, contracted to our French agents. We have a duty to deliver it for them. The conflict on shore is coming to an end, and already businessmen and enlightened politicians are preparing to negotiate a peace. After that Britain will have no option but to sign an agreement with Germany. I promise you it will all be settled within the next few days because we just do not have the means to prolong a useless struggle. It will be everyone's duty to restore trade and economic stability as quickly as possible. Therefore, it is pointless to take this cargo to England, only to bring it back again. However,' and here his tone takes on a more subtle note and the cold smile becomes a simpering, inveigling, patronising smirk, 'In view of the extraordinary conditions I am prepared to offer a bonus. A third on top of every man's wages if he will do his duty.'

All eyes are on Melody as he stares back into Eli's hypocritical leer. 'The crew will only take this ship to an English port, sir. Wages don't come into it at all.'

Eli's smile fades and his death-mask becomes even more ghostly. Methuselah steps in front of him, bearing down on the stocky bosun with a furious glare. 'You can get back to that scum and tell them to turn to before I come amongst them, mister. I'll have no more of this bloody nonsense. You'd do well to remember who employs you before coming up here with your mutinous talk.'

'That's enough of that!' Royal's heavy voice comes from the open door. 'All right, Melody. Get down to your men and tell them that the ship is going to Southampton. As for you, Tardeval; you have danced to your master's tune for so long you don't know right from wrong anymore. There's bigger issues at stake here than a few lousy pounds worth of profit. Even those dockyard scrapings forward can see it more plainly than you and your sanctimonious boss. I managed to get a signal off, and we are to rendezvous with a naval escort thirty miles south of St Catherine's Point at oh six double oh. That leaves you with two options, Tardeval. Either you continue to command this ship under the directive of the Navy, or you remain locked in the chartroom with Eli: I know which I would prefer.'

Methuselah's mouth works for a moment without making a sound. His fists are balled up white-knuckled as he stares back at Royal, breathing like a rampant bull. I can almost see his blood-pressure rising. Just before he explodes, however, Eli shatters the atmosphere with a strident squawk. The mean little man screeches a stream of blasphemy at Royal, cursing us all to hell and damnation with a wild string of invective more profane than anything I've heard on the mess-deck. He is dancing like a demented demon on his spindly legs, and for a moment I think he is about to throw a fit, but it is pure, unadulterated rage, and when he splutters to a stop everyone, including Methuselah, is staring at him aghast. His flinty eyes dart from one face to another until he settles on his senior captain and sees the repugnance written there. It is as though he has been struck a physical blow, for he recoils from Methuselah's condemning glare into the safety of the chartroom, closing the door behind him. I reach across and deliberately turn the key.

After that there is no need for further talk. By the time Martingale and Barratt return one of the crew is on the helm and Methuselah stands at the fore-part of the wheelhouse, peering forward across the bow in the age-old stance of shipmasters who have everything in hand. The two naval officers look about them with expressions of bewilderment, unable to accept that all is in order in the quiet calm of the wheelhouse. The compass swings dutifully a point or so either side of the mean course and the helmsman eases the spokes through his fingers as though he has stood there for a lifetime. Royal checks the charts on a table in the background.

That should have been an end to our troubles. The ship under control again, with her bow pointed towards home and everyone working in harmony. Eli is out of sight and mind, locked up with his villainy, while honest sailormen work his ship back to port, and there is a general air of relaxation as we push on northwards. In this euphoric atmosphere no one notices the colonel when he wanders out into the waist, slowly making his way towards Fred and his prisoner.

IX

Someone is singing, using the sea for harmony as he takes us 'South of the border, down Mexico way'. It suits my mood and comforts my soul, so that all of a sudden the war seems a million miles away. From horizon to horizon the night is unblemished. Not the slightest glow of a fire, nor a man-made sound destroys the tranquillity of that vast, soft darkness. I allow my thoughts to tease me with memories of warm flesh. Visions of responsive limbs and animal lust has me reaching down to adjust my clothes to accommodate a growing response to these carnal thoughts. It is becoming almost painful, and I try to push the visions away to concentrate on less disturbing things, without much success. It is not as though it is anyone I know; just a phantom seductress, teasing and titillating with every delightful variation that my over-active mind can conjure up.

Two shots shock me back to reality, and I leap to the front of the wheelhouse to stare down into the waist. At first I can see only the vague shapes of deck-gear, and dark chasms where pools of solid blackness fill remote corners. Then there is a movement of the forward end where the ladder leans against the fo'c'sle-head to form a shadowy space. Someone crouches there, using the flukes of the spare anchor as a prop for his rifle. And I don't need to see his face to know it is Fred, and that he is peering out across his sights towards the portside of the well-deck.

I shift my gaze and study the black gulf running between the hatch-coaming and the bulwark. Foot by foot I examine it until I locate the colonel almost at the forward end. The fore and aft derricks are secured diagonally across the hatch, lodged into their yokes on either side of the deck. The after one goes to port, and the bulk of its heavy pulley-blocks and cargo-hook provides cover for him even when he stands upright. I ease my body through the door and find myself beside Martingale, looking down unto the scene.

'Can you see what's going on, sir?' I ask.

'I heard a shout but I didn't think anything of it. That damned lonesome cowboy wailing about his Mexican floozy didn't help. It looks as if the colonel is up to his old tricks.'

My memory shoots back to the altercation between Fred and the colonel that took place earlier on. After the heart-searchings that went on in the galley I assumed it had all been forgotten, but it seems the colonel blows hot and cold, alternating between periods of self-recrimination and bellicosity. Unable to make any impression on us, he has turned to Fred and his prisoner, hoping for a soft target.

'We had better get down there before someone gets killed,' says Martingale, moving towards the top of the ladder, then leaping back smartly as another bullet whangs off the steel close by his head. 'Bloody hell!' he gasps as he tucks himself in behind the windbreak.

'Let's use the after ladder, sir,' I urge. 'We can creep forward with our heads below the coaming from there.'

He nods briskly, and we creep out together, using infinite caution to slide down the smooth handrails without touching the steps with our feet. Now it is easy to crawl forward, keeping doubled-up, with the solid flank of the coaming well above our heads.

The colonel is holding his service revolver in his right hand, peering through a tangle of falls that separate the two pulley-blocks. The wind is tossing his thin hair about as it skirls around inside the small alcove formed by the high fo'c'sle and the downward curve of the bulwark. It has a couple of old newspapers trapped in the corner, and is teasing them mercilessly with its bluster.

'What the hell are you doing?' demands Martingale in a hoarse whisper.

'Bringing that idiot to his senses, I hope.' The plummy voice is back, and he stands upright, looking dishevelled but arrogant. 'Someone has to restore discipline, lieutenant. This nonsense has gone on too long already.'

'All you will achieve is to get someone shot, sir,' persists Martingale. 'He will not listen to reason.'

The colonel pulls himself up to his full height, bristling with indignatiion. 'Reason with him, sir! I have no intention of doing any such thing. Leave this to me: I know how to deal with these people. They always respond to authority. As long as you allow him to think he can get away with it he will persist with his stupidity. He is a trained soldier, lieutenant. He will recognise military commands when he hears them.' He turns away from us to concentrate on Fred, with his pistol pointed skyward. 'You thar!' he bellows in his best parade-ground manner. 'Put down that rifle and show yourself!'

The next shot ricochets off the metal derrick and snarls out into the night. Martingale joins me in diving to the deck, but the colonel doesn't turn a hair. 'Damn you, man! Come out from there before I am forced to come and fetch you!'

Fred gets off two more shots as fast as he can work the bolt. I count six shots out of a possible ten in his magazine; and then I remember the full ammunition pouches he was wearing and give up any ideas along that line.

'Sir!' I breathe urgently. 'Why don't you let me have a go at talking to him? He thinks I'm one of the lads; perhaps he'll listen to me.'

'Hah! I should say not! If it were not for your blasted soft approach this would have been resolved long ago.' He brings his revolver level, with the muzzle aimed at me. 'I will brook no interference from either of you; nor will I hesitate to shoot anyone who defies me.' His voice drops to a menacing growl. 'Move away from me, and be sure that I shall report your conduct when the time comes.'

We creep back on all-fours until we are kneeling between the hatch-coaming and the bulwark, with about five feet between us and the colonel. He waves his pistol at us for a moment, just to show that he means what he says, then turns back to Fred.

'Soldier! I am counting to three. If you do not comply with my order by then I intend to come and get you.'

'Piss orf!' Fred's voice is a mixture of pleading and defiance as he goes on. 'Leave me alone, fer Gawd's sake!'

'One!' The colonel's voice rings out like a gunshot.

'I've got a 'and-grenade!'

The air about me freezes as Fred's voice takes on a new and dangerous tone. I know he isn't messing about, and a vision of that compact little pineapple clasped in his sweaty hand sends a shiver down my spine. The colonel is standing stock-still; shaken by this new revelation; unable to bring himself to utter the next number.

'If yer don't go away I'll throw this inter the paint-store. Leave me be – I know what I'm doin'!' His voice tails off into a more plaintive note. 'Orl I wants is ter be left alone.'

'Sir!' Martingale's whisper cuts into the silence that follows. 'Come away now. There's nothing to be gained with this.' He lifts his voice. 'Fred! put that grenade away. I promise we will not come near you!'

'Promise be damned!' roars the colonel. 'I'm still counting, soldier. Two!'

'I warned yer!' shrieks Fred. 'I told yer I'd do it!' I cringe down low, waiting for the end as I hear the clips being knocked off the paint-store door. I press my body hard against the cold steel and sweat as Martingale stretches his length beside me. We hear the door swing back, and there is a sustained animal scream before the reverberating crash of the explosion.

With my ears ringing I lift my head in time to see a blinding flash of orange leap from the battered door, followed by a series of smaller explosions as the drums and cans of volatile liquids ignite, burst, and spew their contents in all directions. I stare across the expanse of canvas to see a staggering human torch revolving like some horrific marionette with its arms outstretched, clutching at nothing.

We reach the after end of the well-deck together and crouch down behind the hatch, staring out at the roaring flames and exploding cans. Rivers of fire stream out across the hatch, to cascade in molten cataracts into the passages. The colonel is trapped in his corner with his arms held across his face in an effort to ward off the whirlpool of fire that is being sucked in by the up-draught. We are hypnotised by the sight of the greedy tongues of flame consuming his flesh as he cringes into the corner. We can see his face for a second, and his mouth is a gaping cavern, uttering hoarse croaks as he slumps into a blazing heap.

We stare on, mesmerized by the horror of it all when a new sound wrenches at my insides. Terrible screams of abject terror from inside the fo'c'sle, where some of the crew had been sleeping. The thin steel bulkhead at the back of the paint-store has burst into the living-quarters, and long tentacles of flame has reached into dry bedding and timbered bunks, turning the whole place into an inferno, with trapped men staggering about in wild panic, finding no way out through the barrier of fire that blocks their only exit.

Martingale and I are frozen by the sight. Unable to wrench our eyes away from the dreadful scene as the screams turn to choking cries, and the sharp crackle and snap of burning timber overcomes the other noises.

A heavy object thumps down on the deck beside me, rolling away into the scuppers. 'Come on!' yells Royal's gruff voice from above. 'Get those hoses rigged. Pass them forward and stop the fire from spreading aft!'

I make a grab for the reel, hauling it across to the connector under the fore-part of the superstructure, then throw the hose out across the hatch-cover. The nozzle is clipped into its lodging above the hydrant, and Martingale is already wrenching it clear as more urgent shouts join in the chorus.

More hoses snake out across the canvas, and dark shapes scramble about as I open the valve and listen to the sharp hiss of the water forcing its way through the flat trunk; snapping the kinks straight, to turn it into a writhing serpent for a moment before it goes stiff and solid, ejecting a full-powered stream of water towards the seat of the fire. More jets join in, and Royal is yelling orders from the bridge, directing the hoses to where they are most needed. No one questions his authority as he stands tall and strong, controlling operations.

The fire is spreading; searching for new, combustible material to feed on. Canvas covers and tarry, tinder-dry hatch-boards make ideal fuel for the hungry flames, while livid streams of melting paint, linseed oil, thinners, pitch, flow like lava into the anthracite, fanned by the blustering wind that comes in from starboard. The ship is swinging to bring that wind aft to help keep the fire from spreading, but the intense heat causes the air to rise, creating a vacuum to suck in air like the forced draught of a furnace.

The shapes of toiling men wheel about starkly against the lurid back-ground, and the whole fore-part of the ship is alive with a dancing, incandescence that must be visible for miles around. The eerie glare throws weird patterns onto the face of the bridge superstructure with exaggerated shadows of men providing an animated, spectral tableau. A heavy, black cloud of dense smoke pours over the fo'c'sle and rolls out across the sea as the anthracite begins to burn. A large section of hatch-cover heaves up like a blossoming flower, leaving a black chasm for a second or so before the fire rushes in with a triumphant roar to send men staggering back from its blinding heat.

I stand with Martingale, taking the weight of the hose as he directs the nozzle. The heat forces us back step by step, but other hoses are coming into play now; coupled together in long, winding lengths from her stern, so that a wall of water is building across the hatch, and for a time it looks as though we might contain the fire.

Suddenly a new thought hits me. 'The children!' I yell. 'Christ, the children!'

He stares at me, his face set, warning me to stay calm. 'Away you go then. I'll manage here. Take them aft to the boats and make sure they are wearing lifejackets.' I lose the rest of the words as I race off along the port side.

I reach the door leading into the passage that runs through to the cabins and stop when another thought comes. They won't understand what I am saying and I don't want to start a panic. Ignoring the door I race aft to where de Carteret and his *poilus* are preparing their boats for lowering. 'I need your help, captain!' I shout at him. 'The children; they're still in their cabins!'

'I cannot leave my men,' he replies without looking at me. 'We have our duty to do.'

'Sod your fucking duty!' I throw at him. 'Sod your bloody useless papers! Those kids are going to roast if we don't get them out!'

The soldiers are looking at me, reading the anxiety in my eyes. They have stopped what they were doing, some still holding boxes as they stare from my face to his. He backs away from the boat, his face working with indecision for a moment, then he barks an order and they begin throwing out the chests to empty the boat.

'Come!' he yells at me, and I run after him towards the open door. The nuns are already helping the children into lifejackets; tying the over-sized, clumsy, corkstuffed canvas to their tiny frames. De Carteret issues his orders in a gentle voice, coaxing the children into the passage, where they line up with their hands on the shoulders of the ones in front so that the nuns can lead them out in a long crocodile, past me and on towards the stern. Grinning French soldiers beckon them aft and sit them on the deck beside the boats; their bemused, elfin faces staring wide-eyed at the leaping flames beyond the bridge. The *poilus* stem any lurking tears with soothing words, and the kids settle in two frightened groups.

At last we have them all out of the cabins and in their

abandon-ship stations. Time now to take a breather and size up the situation. The fire-fighters are struggling desperately to keep the flames at bay, but they are coping well enough without me, so I climb up to the bridge where Royal is standing out on the wing, still issuing commands to the men below. Inside the wheelhouse the helmsman concentrates on his job, trying to keep our stern to the wind so that the bulk of the superstructure shelters the fore-part of the ship.

'We have got all the children aft,' I tell him.

He nods brusquely and I look to see who else is on the bridge. 'Where is Captain Tardeval?'

He doesn't look at me. 'Christ knows!'

'I would have thought he would be up here, taking command.'

'Well he isn't. Come that, you're not a lot of use either. Why don't you go down and help in the waist?'

The bastard! I'm still choking on a response when we are interrupted by a hefty explosion that has us both diving for cover. When the dust settles and I pluck up enough courage to peer over the top of the wind-break I see that two-thirds of the fore-hatch has erupted to leave the hold almost totally exposed. Huge fountains of sparks and flame leap mast-high, driving the men back to the after end of the well-deck, and the whole fore-part of the ship is ablaze. The heat blisters the paintwork on the bridge and takes away our breath when we try to stare into it.

I feel we are losing the battle. Soon the fire must reach the island and take hold on the timbered wheelhouse. After that it will feed down into the cabins and there will be no stopping it progressing right through the ship. I clatter down the port ladder to where men are clinging tight to the side of the island in an effort to shelter from the full force of the flames while they try to direct their hoses towards the fire.

No one can work in the waist. The hoses that were coupled to the hydrant have burned through, leaving us

with just the two elongated ones that lead from right aft.
All that we can do is try to buy time. Martingale throws
aside his useless nozzle and yells something at me as he
waves an arm towards the stern. I follow him aft to where
de Carteret's men are watching over the children, who sit
cross-legged, with their trusting eyes looking up at us,
while the nuns check their lifejackets and encourage them
to sit quietly.

'Get them into the boats, captain!' orders Martingale.
'Grant! Tell Finney to come up out of it with his black
gang. We have lost most of the deck crew so it will be up to
some of the firemen to man the boats and look after the
kids when we lower. As for the rest of us; we'll have to rely
on our lifejackets, or whatever we can find that floats.'

We pack them in tightly, tucking them below the
thwarts with their backsides between the legs of their
mates. I had not realised how small some of them were
until now. Tiny fragile bodies that take so little room that
we are able to stow the lot of them, including the nuns,
into the two boats. I select the more able-looking firemen
to man the tillers, and all we've left to do is cast off the
gripes and take turns on the stag-horns for lowering.

This is the trickiest part of the operation. Many lifeboats
have spilled out their occupants when careless seamen
mishandled the falls at this stage. I take hold of the
forward ones, while Martingale handles the after end. He
will give the commands when the time comes, and we take
our time to check that each boat is cleared away properly,
for we trust no one but ourselves with this task.

Someone clears away the lashings on the raft so that it
can be pushed overboard when the time comes. After
that's done we stand back and wait for the ultimate order
from Royal. All is ready for the moment when we must
abandon her, and the man who makes that decision is
silhouetted against the flames on the port side of the
bridge, for Methuselah has not been seen since the fire
broke out, and no one disputes Royal's authority.

The crackle and roar of the fire fills the sky, and if it was

not for the glare we would notice the dull grey light of dawn
spreading across the sea. I take a mental roll-call while I
wait. Besides the children and the nuns I recognise Martingale, Finney, Royal, part of the *Sister Sarai*'s crew, de
Carteret and his men. A baker's dozen. Providing the
weather stays reasonable the raft should keep us afloat,
even though we will have to take turns hanging over the
side. I would expect to be picked up fairly soon if Royal's
radio message got through.

I look up again at the lone, enigmatic figure on the
bridge; his heavy shoulders humped above the wind-break
as he stares down into the fire. He should be moving now if
he is to get us all clear before the whole bridge goes up, yet
he seems reluctant to leave his station. He has shown
himself to be an unshakable leader in this crisis. A reliable
fulcrum round which order was restored when everyone
began to chase about like startled ants. I've no doubt that if
it had not been so Martingale would have taken over, with
me to back him up, but we would have had conflicting
forces to contend with. The ship's crew, reluctant to take
orders from anyone but their own masters, de Carteret and
his *poilus*, who were determined to see their own duty
through to the end, and the nuns, who wouldn't know
whom to obey. One undisputed leader rose above us all,
and I should be grateful that he measured up to the job. Yet
when I look at the familiar shape defying the flames I am
unable to shake off an overwhelming feeling of mistrust.

The midships superstructure appears to be holding back
the fire now. The paint is peeling and the wooden planking
on the fore-part of the wheelhouse is scorched and charred,
but there is ten feet of protective steel between it and the
deck, and a large area of inflammable iron deck with a
cargo-winch and other metallic obstacles for the fire to
overcome before it can run riot through the officers'
quarters. Even the wooden planking is backed with steel.
The two remaining hoses are spraying the island to keep it
well damped-down, and if only there was some means of
tackling the fire in the forward hold we might still beat it.

I see a dark, crouching figure come running out of the smoke, and I recognise Melody. I feel a surge of guilt when I realise that I had forgotten him when I took my roll-call. He is filthy and black like the rest of us, but I can see he has been much closer to the fire, for his clothes are scorched, and even from here I can see that his eyebrows are singed.

'Who's keeping pumps going?' he demands aggressively when he notices Finney and the stokers milling about on deck. 'The pressure is already falling. How the hell are we gonna keep her afloat if we don't keep up the steam-pressure?'

'We were more concerned to get the boats ready for lowering,' I say lamely, for I suspect that we might have panicked a bit. It was right to get the children aft and into the boats, but the ship lives on, and she isn't even down by the head; while, for the moment at any rate, the fire seems confined to the forward waist.

'I'll go below again,' grunts Finney. 'I only came up in the first place 'cause someone told me to.' He looks chagrined as he slopes off to his hatch, and when Melody barks at a couple of the trimmers they follow him below.

'The hoses are only just keeping it in check,' states Martingale. 'It seems to have a hold on the coal, and once it gets past the island we won't stop it. I wouldn't have believed coal could burn like that when it is so tightly packed.'

'It ain't the anthracite. Eli and Methuselah always stow a few extra pieces of cargo under the hatches when the stevadores have finished loading her. With things as they are the Customs ain't bothering too much, and there's all sorts of goods that can be sold at a profit on both sides of the Channel. That's what is burning mostly; if you look you will see that the flames ain't so fierce, and there is a lot more smoke than anything else.' Melody's face has a look of disgust as he explains.

'Why the hell didn't Royal notice all that?' complains Martingale sourly. 'He knows we have been too busy to realise what's going on.'

We all look up again at the figure on the bridge. 'I'm going up there,' declares Martingale determinedly, then turns to de Carteret. 'Captain, I am going to leave the children to you and your men. Barratt and a couple of the crew will be here to help if you have to lower away in a hurry, though I hardly think there is much likelihood of that now. Grant! You and Melody can come with me. I want to see what Royal has in mind.'

It is quite light now. The sun is trying to burn away the mist that hangs funnel-high over the scene. When we reach the bridge I am surprised at how much the heat has diminished. It was like a furnace when I stood here last, but now the hoses seem to be keeping it off the boil. Looking out across the hold I see islands of flames dancing on the black surface of the coal, and the fo'c'sle is a smoking ruin of bare, roasted steel, with writhing skeins of steam issuing from every aperture. It doesn't do to look too hard into the corners where unidentifiable charred remains lie amongst the ashes.

The fire is still very much alive in some places however. The hold runs beneath the bridge superstructure; divided from the after one by a solid cross-frame of steel. It must be glowing red by now, and I have no doubt the heat is trying to penetrate the soft base of the island itself. However, until someone has the guts or the time to go down to investigate I will shut my mind to that.

Royal makes no comment and keeps his features blank as we pour over the top of the ladder onto the bridge. He has a way of taking charge without putting himself into direct conflict with anyone. Always waiting for the other person to make the first move, yet ready with a blunt retort that always seems to leave him on top. Gripping the capping on the after rail and wearing that same damned sneering half-grin he waits for Martingale to take stock of the situation.

'What happened to Captain Tardeval?' asks the lieutenant as though he hopes to take the other man off-guard.

'Dunno. I thought he was with you.'

'I wouldn't be asking if that was the case. He was up here with you when the fire started; you must have seen him leave.'

'Nope!'

Martingale eyes him carefully and shakes his head. 'Well, no matter now. We will get round to that later. The question is, what is to be done here? Do you think we can control the fire?'

'Control yes – extinguish no. It is burning deep down in the hold I reckon, and no amount of water will prevent it from simmering away, giving off gases that could ignite or even explode at any time. We have two hydrants in the cross-passage below the wheelhouse. If those are opened up the water will flood that area and pour down the hatches and ladders to keep the fire from reaching here. Remember though, we are pumping water into her at a fair old rate and we cannot keep doing that forever.'

'How about if we put her astern? Would that not help to keep the fire forward until we make port?'

'It might, but the outcome really depends on what is building up below. If those gases expand in that restricted area and ignite, the explosion could tear the ship apart. She would go down like a stone with her holds full.'

Martingale screws up his eyes. 'You wouldn't like to take a gamble like that?'

Royal grins devilishly. 'For myself, yes. You've got the children to worry about though, haven't you?'

'Open the valves!' orders Martingale without taking his eyes from Royal. 'Grant, you can take the helm. We will try to take her into Portsmouth. With luck that escort will realise we are not going to make the rendezvous and come looking for us.'

'Always supposing the signal was sent,' I insinuate.

'What the hell do you mean?' At last Royal stirs out of his complacency.

'Take it whichever way you want,' I hold my voice level as I face up to him. He is big all right. Powerful and utterly ruthless. But I know how he takes pleasure in making us look like idiots, and that's enough to overcome any misgivings I might have about tackling him. 'It's about time you came clean and gave us some answers. Such as, what happened to Captain Tardeval? How come you did nothing to stop us when we were on the point of abandoning ship when you must have known she was not foundering? And did you really send that signal?'

'I don't have to answer to you, Grant. Think what you damned-well like.'

The shouts of fire-fighters are coming from below the fore-end of the bridge and I can hear them coupling hoses to the hydrants. They are winning then; working their way across the well-deck, with the sharp hiss of water dousing the surface of the anthracite. A plaintive shriek from a flexible voice-pipe clipped to the after bulkhead wrenches Royal's eyes from mine as he grabs the mouthpiece, blows down it, then holds it to his ear.

'Finney says they have a full head of steam,' he announces firmly.

Martingale snatches the tube. 'What are conditions like down there, Finney?' We watch his face break into a wide grin as he listens. 'Never mind the lurid details; just give me a straight report.'

After a short exchange he walks over to the telegraph and moves the handle to 'Full ahead', back to 'Full astern', then settles it on 'Stand by'. The small repeater jerks in response as Finney acknowledges.

'Speed is the answer now,' says Martingale as he stares out across the bow. 'We will pour on coal and work up to full power, then head for the rendezvous as fast as we can drive her.' He turns to Royal. 'I will give you benefit of the doubt, but if the escort is not waiting for us you'd better have some answers ready.'

The sea is green now. Foam-crested and boisterous as the wind rattles the rigging. Shredding the mist to allow the sun to brighten the day. The telegraph jangles again and the vibration of the screw comes through my feet as I put the helm over and watch the bows sweep across the horizon until the compass shows she is heading due north. A touch of port wheel stops the swing and I ease off until she is settled on course. Immediately we can see that the wind has changed to come in from the southwest, throwing the odd cupful of spray inboard. It brings a new worry. If it continues to build and we get another emergency, lowering the boats will be a hazardous business.

I shake away that thought and concentrate on the course. No helm orders are required; if there was a row of street lamps stretching out ahead of me it couldn't be plainer. Even the slant of the incoming coamers tells me which way I must steer, and I can almost smell the green fields of England as we work up to eight knots, with a thick plume of smoke pouring over the stern.

Barratt arrives to report that all is in order down aft. The children are settled on the lee side of the after-deckhouse, with de Carteret's men watching over them. 'I came forward in case you wanted to have another go at the radio, sir,' he says.

'Good idea,' agrees Martingale. 'Melody can take some men forward while we go down and see if we can get the thing working. Even if we can't send a signal, we might find out what's happening in the outside world.'

'You won't,' sneers Royal. 'The aerial is down forward and that set only just about operates at the best of times.'

'That's easily fixed, sir,' says Barratt. 'There is enough wire left dangling from the main-mast to rig a jury aerial. It won't be perfect, but it's enough for what we want. With any luck that escort isn't too far away, and she should be listening out for us. Even on low power she should pick up our signal.'

'I wouldn't bet on the escort,' I'm thinking. Royal is standing right behind me, almost breathing down my neck, just waiting for me to voice that kind of thought; so I keep my mouth shut because I do not wish to hold Martingale back from what he has to do by starting another futile altercation.

They are gone only two minutes before the door slams back and Martingale storms into the wheelhouse. 'We've found Captain Tardeval, Royal. Do you still expect us to believe that you don't know where he is?'

'As I said before – believe what you damn-well like. I'm none the wiser even now.'

Martingale controls his voice with difficulty. 'So you have no idea how he comes to be slumped over the radio with his hand amongst the electronics?'

I hear Royal take a deep breath. 'What has that got to do with me?'

'Are you saying that a man like Captain Tardeval deliberately sticks his hand into the guts of a live radio?'

'I am saying nothing. I haven't left the bridge; nor did I see Captain Tardeval leave. There is no use asking the helmsman because he is Norwegian, with only enough English to obey orders. If you want my opinion that is exactly what happened. The ship was on fire and he wanted to send an emergency signal. He must have noticed something loose in the back of the set and reached in to adjust it. He could easily have been sent sprawling by one of the explosions.'

'Always ready with a glib answer,' I put in sarcastically.

'Can you think of a more logical explanation? What you are suggesting is crazy. Do you honestly think that someone deliberately risked his own neck by physically pushing Methuselah into the set? Whoever tried that stood every chance of being electrocuted himself.'

'Not if he was wearing rubber seaboots like you are,' I snap quickly.

'Jesus Christ!' he exclaims viciously. 'What do I have to do to convince you that I am telling the truth?'

No one answers. Logic or not we are all accusing him now. I can feel him searching our faces, reading the disbelief and feeling like a cornered rat. 'All right,' he snarls. 'Let's try one other thing.' He steps across and drives his boot into the soft panel of the chartroom door.

We hear a muted sound from inside and he kicks again,

shaking the bulkhead with the force of the blow. Yet it brings no real response from within. Royal's boot slams into the panel and splits it from top to bottom. We hear a startled cry as Eli staggers back from the splintered woodwork. Again and again the boot crashes in on the flimsy door, until there is a hole large enough to allow a hand to reach through to withdraw the brass bolt. Royal launches in and grabs at Eli's lapels, hauling him bodily out of the door and shoving him up against the bulkhead with his feet inches off the deck.

The terrified ship-owner croaks as his head is rattled against the bulkhead. Incoherent cries of outrage and fear escape as he is shaken unmercifully with his skull rolling loosely on his thin, boney shoulders, so that he couldn't utter a comprehensible word even if he had a mind to.

'Come on, you slimey toad!' shouts Royal. 'Let's have the truth for once!'

Martingale steps in quickly. 'Easy, Royal. Give him a chance to say his piece.'

Eli slumps down unto his quaking legs when the pressure comes off. His face is blue and his lips are blubbering as he struggles to recover. I can almost hear his dry bones rattling inside his skinny frame when Royal shakes him about. He is a frightened mess; heaving painfully to suck air into his lungs.

'The truth now, you old bastard!' grates Royal. 'Or I'll shake your evil brain right out of your skull.'

Eli shrieks, and a huge fist tightens again, wrenching him upright to bring his petrified face close to Royal's. 'Tardeval has told us most of it, so you might as well tell us the rest.' The grip slackens to allow Eli to speak, but immediately tightens when he looks like losing his fear and recovering some of his old craftiness. His eyes bulge as his air is cut off, and he gasps for mercy.

'Right now,' breathes Royal evenly, needing to hold Eli's weight while he spits each word into his face. 'Tell us about the *Sister Ruth*, and the deal Captain Tardeval made to run her onto the roks.'

For a second Eli hesitates, but an extra twist sets him straight. 'What do you want me to say?' he croaks, pulling in air between every word. 'You know what happened better than I. Are you trying to make me lie? You cannot implicate me in your evil. I am a Christian, for whom the taking of life is a sin.'

'Hah!' Royal's shout sends Eli cringing against the wood-work. 'Cheating, lying and scheming is part of your religion, is it?' He relaxes his grip again. 'We know the *Ruth*'s skipper wasn't in on it, so who was meant to do the job?'

Eli's eyes go cloudy. Every muscle in him has gone slack so that his face sags into a shapeless mask. He struggles hard, but seems unable to bring out the words. Another shake rattles his teeth and brings results.

'You know I was going to wind up the company. It was your idea to go for the insurance; I told you it wouldn't be enough to save the line, even if I was stupid enough to go along with it. You knew that you would be on the beach if I sold out, and you did it to spite me. Nothing you do will make me confess to something I haven't done. I will not bear false witness, no matter what you do to me. Thou art an evil man, Jack Royal. Be sure your sins will find you out and you will rot in hell when you leave this world.'

Royal is shaking. He knows he is beaten, and he releases his grip to allow the ship-owner to fall into a heap at his feet. An awkward silence follows as we all withdraw into ourselves. I clutch the polished spokes to bring her back on course. The gravelly crunch of a wave hitting the ship's side, and the growl of wind through the wheelhouse doors is a condemning chorus when I stare down into the blank face of the compass. The *Sister Sarai* judders, lifts, slumps down and buries her head deep into a trough. The slanting rays of sunlight lance into the wheelhouse to set dust particles alive as they dance in its brilliance, and all the time the steady pulse of her engine drives us on.

The atmosphere is strained and Eli's strangled breathing punctuates the silence when, suddenly, the excited whooping of a destroyer's siren cuts into our thoughts. Within seconds Melody bursts into the wheelhouse. 'The Navy's here!' He shouts grinning all over his face. 'There's a bloody great warship almost alongside; came up through the smoke!'

Eli is forgotten when we rush out to the wing. Her lean shape is cleaving in towards us with fenders dangling over her side and seamen standing by with heaving-lines on her fo'c'sle. Even as we watch, her loud-hailer crackles into life, and the metallic voice spans the shortening distance between us.

The telegraph jangles and the vibrations decrease until we are wallowing in the swell. The destroyer's captain must be a veteran for he brings her alongside so gently she would not have cracked an egg. I join Melody and a bunch of men on deck who are taking in the hawsers and making fast to hold the ships together. Now we can send over the children, passing them into the waiting hands of the seamen while the nuns gather their voluminous skirts and launch themselves across with surprising agility.

De Carteret's men are collecting their chests and refuse to allow anyone to interfere with their precious cargo now that they are relieved of other responsibilities. Martingale and I single out a nucleus of men to stay behind to work the *Sister Sarai* when all the others have gone, and all seems to be coming back to order, when a deep, rumbling explosion sends the ship reeling beneath us. Almost at once she begins to lift her stern and roll to port, grinding her flank into the soft body of the destroyer, and bringing an anxious shout from her bridge. I run to the engineroom hatch and yell down to Finney, but he has anticipated me and is already halfway up the ladder, hard on the heels of his faithful stokers.

'Come on, she's going fast!' Melody is shouting, and I run to the rails where men are leaping the gap and Royal is casting off the hawsers. A brief glance past his shoulders shows the bows already awash as the sea pours into the hold.

'Look alive there!' Martingale is standing on the destroyer's guardrail, reaching out to grab the arms of men as they leap over.

The two ships are drifting apart and I find myself beside Royal. We will be the last two to go. I take a last look round and come face to face with him. 'Come on, Royal. It's the last chance you'll get to save your miserable skin!' I chuck at him.

'Eli!' he gasps. 'Where's Eli?'

We both look towards the bridge. I feel the ship judder again and slump even further over onto her side. Her stern is lifting as she prepares for her last dive. I jump back from the rail. 'Don't be a bloody idiot, Royal. She's going. Can't you feel her?'

He doesn't even hear me. He shakes my hand away and starts running forward towards the bridge, and like the fool I am I go after him. He takes the ladder three rungs at a time with me close on his heels. We burst into the wheelhouse to find Eli on his knees with his arms wrapped round the binnacle. His wide eyes stare up at us and I feel the ship lurch as her stern cants upwards to an impossible angle. Seconds are all that we've got. I can feel the dead weight of her when she poises ready to plunge.

We struggle against the slope, picking Eli up like a bundle of washing. 'You!' he is screaming as he stares at Royal. 'He sent you of all people!'

She is sliding now, lifting her stern high with the echoing crash of loose gear resounding through her hull. We fall together in a tumbling heap of flaying arms and legs to the front of the wheelhouse. I am still grasping a fistful of clothing, dragging them both with me when I roll out through the open door.

We go down in a mad swirl of water with the huge black shape of the ship going down with us. I can feel her suck as the greys and greens turn violet and black. My lungs ache and I am losing consciousness when our lifejackets haul us to the surface, still clutching at each other.

I have hardly time to fill my lungs before the destroyer's

motor-cutter is with us, and strong arms reaching down to heave us clear of the sea. When we reach the ship I am recovered enough to climb unaided on to her steel deck, where I slump down with others. Quite a crowd is gathered there, mostly from the *Sister Sarai*, for the destroyermen are busy hoisting their cutter and getting their ship under way.

Royal has hauled Eli's bedraggled frame inboard with him and sat him down in the scuppers with his back against a stanchion, determined not to allow the moment to go cold. 'This is your last chance to clear your yardarm, Eli. You thought your time had come, didn't you? Hanging on to that binnacle with all your rotten sins before you, you old sinner. I was sent to save you, Eli. To give you one more chance to confess before you are damned forever.'

He is a sodden, black crow, with his sallow, funereal face stone-grey in the harsh sunlight, and his voice is a hoarse croak; full of fear. 'Thou art an evil man, Jack Royal,' he repeats.

'Never mind the biblical jargon,' Royal snarls at him. 'You can blaspheme all you want after you've told us the truth.'

'Truth!' Eli's voice is low, like it no longer belonged to him. 'Oh yes, I will give you the truth. Before my maker I will give you the truth!'

There is no holding him now. He condemns himself with every word. About twenty independent witnesses hear how Methuselah sent the helmsman below for a lifejacket while Royal was busy on the wing of the bridge. The *Sarai*'s captain had finally had enough of his overbearing patron and was going to send a signal that would tell the truth about the *Sister Ruth*.

Eli's eyes are staring into a void. He is communicating with someone only he can see while we stare down at him, soaking in every word. 'Satan drove me to it. I had no will of my own when I followed Tardeval down to the radio-room. I wouldn't have known what to do if he had not guided me. I could see his hand amongst the valves and wires, and his other hand against the steel bulkhead. All I had to do was reach up to the big switch and turn on the current.' He splutters to a stop looking drained, and we drift away, leaving the destroyermen to carry him away to their sick-bay.

The only thing that matters to me is to get back to HMS *Dolphin* and my own kind. Perhaps by some miracle *Scavenger* has been delayed and I can reach her before she sails. I feel no satisfaction for finding out the truth. It was just one more sad little episode to add to the sorry mess that began at Dunkirk.

*

'It is up to you, Grant. Officially you are still *Scavenger*'s coxswain and you can catch her at Harwich, but under the circumstances I can send a relief.' The drafting officer looks up at me from his desk, studying my face and trying to be open-minded.

'I'd like to go to her, sir.'

He smiles back at me. 'I was hoping you would say that. I can organise immediate transport for you. Are you free to travel?'

'Yes, sir. Most of my kit is at Chatham, and I have already drawn replacement kit for what I have lost.'

'Good!' He stands and reaches out his hand. 'You did a great job. I happen to know Lieutenant Martingale quite well. He doesn't waste words and he speaks most highly of you.'

'It didn't go too well for him, sir.'

His forehead creases into a frown. 'That's the way life is at times, Grant. However, if I know anything about him he will bounce back. You can't buck the system and go off on an independent course without offending our lords and masters as he did, but there is room in the Navy for men who are not afraid to think and act for themselves, even though it will take time for the traditionalists to come to terms with it. Don't concern yourself too much. Officers like Martingale are desperately needed now, and those documents you brought back from Abbeville were vital to the war effort, so perhaps that will go some way to redeeming him.'

'Thank you, sir.'

I chop him off a smart salute and go out into the sunshine. The parade-ground bustles with men going about their affairs as I go to collect my railway warrant and stride off towards the jetty and the boat that will convey me to the Harbour Station.

'Oi!'

I look over my shoulder to find Finney loping after me.

'Where yer orf?'

'Back to the boat.'

He stops in his tracks, wide-eyed. 'What the 'ell fer?'

I stare him straight in the eye. 'I've volunteered.'

His mouth gapes open for a moment. 'You are a pillock!'

We stand in the centre of the parade-ground, staring at each other. His eyes revolve one complete turn. 'Yer got five minutes?'

'Yes.'

'Give me time ter get me warrant – I'm comin' wiv yer.'

WELCOME

THIS BOOK REVIEWS THE ISSUES YOU ARE MOST
LIKELY TO FACE WHEN YOU ARE REFURBISHING
OR RELOCATING YOUR OFFICES

THE **BLACK BOOK**

This book reviews the issues you are most likely to face when you are refurbishing or relocating your offices. There are many reasons why any business would need to upgrade its offices or relocate, and they are normally a combination of the following:

- Growth, expansion or contraction of staffing levels
- Your need to increase efficiency
- A desire to enhance your corporate image
- A desire to improve your bottom-line profits
- The need to retain or attract key staff
- To be nearer or further away from your competition
- A rent review or a lease renewal is imminent

Refurbishing or relocating can be extremely beneficial but, if not planned and executed properly, it can prove to be disruptive and costly. It makes sense therefore to select the best company to guide you through the planning and implementation phases of your relocation and fit-out. The risks of getting it wrong can work out catastrophically for your organisation...

...so how can you avoid the traps and pitfalls?

Firstly, you need to spend some time reviewing and contemplating the guidance provided in this book and,

secondly, you need to find a design and build fit-out specialist in whom you can have confidence and trust.

This book covers the complete life cycle of a project. Every company is different and not all aspects will apply to you. The book has therefore been arranged in easy-to-read chapters, so that you can dip in whenever you feel the need of guidance. There is an index at the back.

ISBN No. 978-0-9559734-3-7

office**principles**
total business interiors

CONTENTS

MORE INFORMATION

1 PREPARE BUSINESS FORECASTS

First Principles

- Relocating your business or extending an existing lease are decisions which will affect your business for years to come
- You need to know how your business is performing
- You need to be aware of the long-term company financial and business plan
- You are ready to instruct professional advisers once you have provisional answers to your strategic questions

Relocating your business to a new building or extending the lease on your present building are decisions which will affect your business for years to come.

Before making any premises decisions, you therefore need to have a strategic plan as to where your business is going. What are your forecasts?

- What is the ideal location, taking a balance between

  - where your present and target customer-base is centred
  - where your key staff live
  - accessibility by road/rail/air, and
  - the locations of your suppliers?

- What are your growth plans? What turnover is forecast for 5 years, for 10 years, etc?

- What does this imply in terms of staff numbers?

- Does the building provide for the needs of the staff, and will it attract the quality of personnel your organisation needs when recruiting?

- How many staff will need a personal office? How many will need a desk in an open plan area? How many will need just occasional use of a desk?

- How important will the image of your building be? How often will clients visit your premises?

- How many meeting rooms will you need? And what size?

Once you have provisional answers to such strategic questions, you are ready to instruct professional advisers.

Jargon Buster

Human Resources	HR, dealing with all aspects of your staff
Talent management	The latest way of describing HR

2 THE SPACE AUDIT

First Principles

A workplace audit can include:

- Your existing and projected space requirements
- The evaluation of your working practices
- Storage analysis
- Circulation space
- Amenity space
- Meeting rooms, conference and break-out areas

Before deciding what size of building you need for the future, you should commission your fit-out specialist to develop a workplace audit. This is a key document which carefully scrutinises your current operation, including use of space and working practices. The workplace audit will provide clear and concise calculations that will appraise you of the efficiency of the space you occupy.

It will look at your staff and the various teams set up to tackle your organisation's workloads, your storage requirements, and any special elements necessary for your business.

Your workplace audit will also evaluate your future requirements, allowing you to make more informed decisions when it comes to acquiring new premises. See *Chapter 43*.

It may also assist you in establishing the space efficiency obtained from new ways of working, or through improved workstation designs. An example of this would be the large areas (of desktops and circulation space) opened up through moving from old visual display screens to flat panel displays.

The workplace audit, considered in conjunction with your company projections, will help you, advised by your fit-out specialist, to decide whether your existing premises could be re-planned and refurbished to meet the future needs of the organisation or whether you need to appoint a commercial premises agent to seek out a choice of possible buildings as a new base for the organisation.

Your fit-out specialist will be able to provide invaluable guidance and informed advice based on a wealth of experience.

Jargon Buster

Space standards	The area of floorspace needed for various kinds of work
Space audit	Similar to a workplace audit – a thorough survey of the needs of an organisation
Space plan	A plan that sets out where individuals should be located according to work type
Hoteling	Provision of bookable desks, making reservations in the same way as booking rooms in a hotel for staff or outsourced consultants who spend limited time in the office, see *Chapter 38*

3

PLAN FOR THE FUTURE – MAKING THE DECISION TO REFURBISH OR RELOCATE

First Principles

- Always think beyond the move or refurbishment
- Consider the long-term implications for your business
- Make sure that all departments are involved in the process
- Ensure you allow for expansion space if your business is growing
- Select the location of your premises with your staff in mind
- Select a fit-out specialist who can help you professionally

Companies who adopt a high-level view of their markets will know that the real reason for their success rests in consideration for the long-term strategy for the business. It is widely accepted that short-term business strategies rarely work.

The same principles apply when considering the brief for your new office design. Do you refurbish your existing premises or do you relocate?

Your business plan should drive the process, identifying potential issues such as expansion and operational efficiencies. Your department heads will have useful insights and should be consulted about the operations for which they are responsible. All the information gathered should be incorporated into the brief.

Some companies decide to go into serviced offices, which may prove to be an expensive route in the long term. However, such a move does offer certain flexibility.

A fit-out specialist will need to be selected. They will need to be knowledgeable about your business needs and aspirations. It is therefore vital to allocate time to briefing meetings where ideas and suggestions can be discussed. *Chapter 9* highlights some of the qualities you should seek for in your fit-out specialist.

Jargon Buster

Blue sky thinking	Keeping an open mind on a variety of issues
D&B	Design and Build
Common parts	Parts that are shared with other tenant companies, e.g. stairs, lifts, ducts, toilets, etc
Net internal area, NIA	Total useable floor area excluding common parts
Gross internal area, GIA	Total area of a floor, or of a building including common parts

4 PREPARE YOUR BRIEF

First Principles

Your brief must cover the following areas:

- Current workplace issues
- Office layout preferences
- IT infrastructure
- Specialist requirements
- Corporate image and branding
- New or existing furniture

Your brief should provide a strategy that will allow your chosen fit-out specialist to consider all the design and practical considerations. When preparing your brief you should consider the relevance of the following factors:

Workplace considerations
- Numbers of staff
- Department locations
- Adjacencies
- Expansion or contraction

Office layout preferences
- Cellular or open plan
- Privacy
- Flexibility

IT strategy
- Future capacity
- Cabling versus wireless
- Communications/IT room

Corporate image
- Use of colour and materials
- Branding requirements
- Contemporary or classic

Specialist areas
- Studios
- Kitchens and break-out areas
- Meeting and board rooms
- Laboratory or workshops

Landlord requirements
- Hours of working
- Shared facilities
- Existing mechanical & electrical systems

This is not an exhaustive checklist. Your brief should give consideration to all aspects that are important to your business and the achievement of your objectives.

Jargon Buster

Adjacency	Who needs to be physically near whom?
Sound attenuation	Reduction in, or deadening of, noise
Blocking and stacking	A guide to where departments will be located, vertically and horizontally

5

SELECT YOUR IN-HOUSE PROJECT COORDINATOR

First Principles

- Analyse your own workload and contribution to the business
- Consider whether you have the time to devote to the move or refurbishment
- Carefully consider appointing an in-house project coordinator
- Clearly identify the role of the project coordinator
- Ensure the project coordinator has the authority to make decisions
- Set up the reporting procedures

Be under no false illusions, if you try managing the project yourself, it will mean that you will take your eye off the day-to-day running of the business. It will add another responsibility to your already hectic workload. As well as this stress, you have a private life to lead and need to sleep at night, knowing that your responsibilities are under control and going to plan.

You need to appoint an in-house project coordinator. Ideally your candidate should have some experience in managing projects. He/she needs a clear brief from you as to your expectations, and needs to be enthusiastic: he/she will be an ambassador for the process.

Once you have appointed your in-house coordinator, you should empower that person with the appropriate authority to make decisions on your behalf. There has to be a clear understanding of the budgets and timescales you are expecting.

5

You need to instigate regular reporting to assist you in keeping abreast of progress, without you having to get personally involved. You will need to recognise the pressure that the project coordinator is under and convey these facts to your staff. Communication with all the staff is vital – they will feel involved and even more a part of your company.

Jargon Buster

Project Champion	The project coordinator
MAN	The person with the Money, Authority and Need
Churn	The number of people who relocate within a workspace within a year divided by the total number of occupants, times 100
CAPEX	Capital Expenditure

6

SELECT YOUR IN-HOUSE TEAM

First Principles

Your in-house team must have expertise on these subjects:

- Operations
- Human Resources
- Finance
- IT and Communications
- Health & Safety
- Legal issues

The relocation or reorganisation of your business calls for input from every employee, manager and director. While you must listen to personal whims and concerns, your key and primary focus must be on the operation of your business, including HR, Finance, IT and communications, Health & Safety, and legal issues.

Consequently you need to select a team of people who have relevant experience for each of these disciplines. In some cases one person may be able to cover more than one subject, but often an individual from each discipline will join the team.

The project team will provide a key contribution in formulating the brief and providing vision and strategy for the future needs of the business.

Clearly, personal accountability, integrity and an ability to communicate are pre-requisites. Errors and misunderstandings need to be eliminated quickly through regular detailed meetings which should be minuted with agenda and action points for clarification.

In sum, detailed planning will ensure the success of your project.

Jargon Buster

Downsizing   Reducing headcount or overheads

Value engineering   Stripping out unnecessary costs from a project

Cascade effect   Sending messages throughout an organisation from the top down

7 SELECT A COMMERCIAL AGENT

First Principles

The responsibilities of a commercial agent are to:

- Assess your current building and the implications of your organisation vacating the property
- Draw up a shortlist of suitable premises
- Analyse the financial implications of each property
- Assist in the selection process
- Negotiate on your behalf
- Draw up heads of terms and finalise the lease

Your property consultant will have a considerable impact on the project and your potential exposure to liability. The brief you provide to your agent will be key to ensuring you obtain appropriate and relevant advice at an early stage.

Your agent should have relevant expertise and knowledge of the local and area property market. Some agents offer national coverage with a range of local offices, while others are local players. Select the agent that fulfils your criteria and one with whom you feel comfortable working.

You will need to have open and frank discussions about your business and its financial performance. There are often issues connected with a building that will produce negotiation points at the stage when terms are being agreed. For example, if the space being offered has an inefficient floor plate, you may need to take a greater area to compensate. In this instance, your agent may be able to negotiate a reduction in rent – or (more likely) a rent-free period or fit-out contribution – to reflect this scenario.

A good commercial agent should more than justify their fee as a result of their knowledge of the market and their negotiating skills. Many landlords are offering significant contributions to fit-out costs to attract tenants in a difficult marketplace and your agent should be able to advise you.

Lease negotiations on a particular property can occasionally fail. Consequently, you will need to arrange a "plan B" to guard against such an event.

Jargon Buster

Term	The length of a lease
Terms	Conditions of a lease
Break clause	Provision in a lease that may allow you to terminate it part way through the term
Rent-free period	An agreed period at the beginning of a lease when no rent is payable

8 CONSIDER WHO ELSE NEEDS TO BE INVOLVED

First Principles

- Check whether your lease obliges you to utilise certain suppliers or contractors to carry out all or part of the works
- Contact adjoining occupiers and inform them of your move
- Tell your adjacent occupiers if there are likely to be disturbances, for example, construction noise or large vehicle movements

Do note that landlords sometimes require you to employ specific contractors or suppliers. Be careful to understand the implications and financial effects of any preferred suppliers or maintenance contracts that the landlord has already set in place. These parties may need to be approached at an early stage with a view to incorporating their works into the design scheme. Failure to observe your obligations could result in costly reinstatement works or legal issues.

If your office space is adjacent to or within a multi-tenanted building, you may need to involve the building managers or facilities managers within these organisations. This process will effectively become a Public Relations exercise to eliminate concern, frustration and getting off to a wrong start with your near neighbours. This will apply particularly if the work is likely to be noisy, during working hours, or involve potential obstructions from large delivery vehicles.

8

The details of your lease will need to be closely scrutinised by your legal representatives. You will need to become conversant and comfortable with such terms as party structure, party wall agreement and restrictive covenants. Again, both your legal team and fit-out specialist will be able to offer assistance and guidance so that you can achieve satisfactory results.

Experienced legal practitioners and proven fit-out specialists will have a wealth of experience in all these matters that can be called on to produce practical and actionable advice. If ever there is uncertainty over a point, no matter how trivial it may seem, do not be afraid to ask questions. Your fit-out specialist will have the necessary experience to be able to provide the answers.

Jargon Buster

Party structure	A wall or floor that divides two properties or demises, as defined by the Party Wall Act, 1966
Party wall agreement	A legal agreement relating to party structures
Restrictive covenant	A legal agreement that enforces or prevents certain actions

9 SELECT YOUR DESIGN AND BUILD FIT-OUT SPECIALIST

First Principles

- Design and Build delivers everything you need from a single source
- As with every other business, there are good, bad and unscrupulous organisations
- The fit-out specialist is the most important member of the team
- Choose carefully, after extensive and detailed research
- Avoid engaging a large company for whom your project may well be relatively insignificant

Broadly there are two routes to achieving an office fit-out for most organisations:

- The traditional route requires you to coordinate the input of architects, designers, engineers, quantity surveyors, consultants and contractors individually, which can be very time-consuming. Other disadvantages of the traditional route can include a larger initial outlay, an inability to finalise the budget until much later in the project and a longer overall timescale.

- Design and Build (D&B) is the more effective way of achieving an office fit-out for most organisations. The D&B specialist provides you with a single point of contact for the design and construction process. This enables you, the client, to concentrate more on your business without distraction. D&B is usually faster and allows the people who will actually fit-out your offices the chance to be involved from the outset.

9

Because the D&B route involves delegating responsibility to a specialist outside organisation, we have identified some key areas to look for in assessing their competence and checking that they have a clear understanding of your requirements.

From day one, what your specialist should provide is a "can do, will do" attitude which demonstrates that the challenges are being thought through and dealt with logically. A genuine interest in the needs and aspirations of your business, and the opportunity to present solutions, is a good indication of a responsive attitude and a can-do approach.

Do not assume that your project is right for every organisation that knocks at your door. It would be disastrous if your project was found to be beyond the capability of the contractor. The project could go badly wrong, including delayed completion, poor quality design or workmanship, and budget over-runs.

Similarly, avoid appointing a large company for whom your project is relatively insignificant. It may lead to you being considered too small and receiving service and attention that is second rate.

At this stage, it is advisable to take time to carefully analyse previous projects and case studies that have been undertaken by your potential contractor. Any genuine fit-out specialist will have many case studies to present to you and will openly discuss these with you, including project size, value, scope of works undertaken and project timeframe. You should take the time to arrange visits to completed projects and to discuss the project in detail with previous clients. **[Continued on next page]**

9 SELECT YOUR DESIGN AND BUILD FIT-OUT SPECIALIST

Any initial presentation from a fit-out contractor will no doubt sound convincing, but be sure you know exactly what their credentials are. Choose a specialist that has all the key disciplines in-house to fulfill your project, including project management and space planning. Sometimes these important roles get outsourced to freelance individuals; such moves can lead to unsatisfactory performance and service levels.

Check out the financial stability of your D&B contractor which should provide a relatively accurate appraisal of their long-term viability.

To give you confidence in how your project will be managed, visit the offices of the company that may manage the project and meet their staff. Insist on meeting the project team, the designer, the planners, the project managers and the CDM coordinator. See *Chapters 68 and 69* for more details.

Ask to speak with the Health & Safety manager who will fulfil a key role under the CDM Regulations – for which you are ultimately responsible. Carefully assess the competence of this person and those managing your site because the penalties for getting this wrong are severe. Consider also speaking with other clients to assess how their Health & Safety issues were managed. The track record of your fit-out specialist should also be exemplary and nothing less should be acceptable to you.

If you are not already fully knowledgeable, it is recommended that you make yourself aware of the following words and phrases, which you will undoubtedly encounter in the many discussions surrounding the selection of your fit-out specialist: warranty, collateral warranty, retention and defects liability period.

Be sure to check out the management structure of the business you intend to engage; it is important that you possess a clear understanding of who the management team are and their responsibilities. These people need to be accessible to you throughout the project from briefing to completion.

Communication routes should be established early and your project manager should be visible regularly throughout the project. Further, as your main point of contact, they should be readily available day-to-day and hour-by-hour. Remember, in this business, there can never be too much communication.

Jargon Buster

Warranty	A term in a contract, breach of which could result in a damages claim, but not termination of the contract
Collateral warranty	A warranty that runs in parallel with the main contract involving a third party
Retention	An agreed sum of money retained by the client until defects have been put right at the end of the defects liability period
Defects liability period	A period after completion where the contractor is liable for correcting any defects that arise in the construction

10 TERMINATING YOUR LEASE

First Principles

- Business leases are governed by a statutory code in the Landlord and Tenant Act 1954
- A lease can only be terminated by one of the methods detailed in the Act
- The Act applies to most business leases, unless the parties opt out before the lease starts

The 1954 Landlord and Tenant Act broadly gives business tenants security of tenure – a statutory right when their lease ends to remain in their business premises under a new tenancy. If the landlord and tenant cannot agree on a new lease, the tenant can apply to the court, which will fix the terms of a new tenancy, reflecting the terms of the existing tenancy, except that the new rent will reflect the current open market rent.

There are certain grounds under which the landlord may oppose renewal. For instance if the tenant has failed to pay the rent or meet other lease obligations, but also certain grounds where the tenant is not "at fault" – such as the landlord providing the tenant with alternative accommodation, or wishing to redevelop or re-organize the premises. A landlord successfully opposing the grant of a new tenancy under the "no fault" provisions may be obliged to pay compensation to the tenant.

The Act, however, permits parties to agree to a lease excluding security of tenure or "outside the Landlord and Tenant Act". For such an agreement to be valid, the parties must follow specified procedures; and where this is done, the tenant has no statutory right to renew the tenancy, and no entitlement to compensation at the end of the tenancy.

The renewal or termination process begins with either the landlord serving a notice of termination on the tenant (sometimes called a section 25 notice) or the tenant submitting a request for a new tenancy (sometimes called a section 26 request).

A landlord wishing to oppose renewal must serve a counter notice to the tenant's request. The parties can then agree terms for a new tenancy without going to court. If there is no agreement, the tenant must apply to the court within certain time limits or he or she loses the right to renew. There are also special provisions enabling a landlord to apply to the court for the renewal or termination of the tenancy.

Jargon Buster

Term	The length of the lease, once a long-term commitment of 25 years, now more commonly, three, five or seven years
Security of tenure	The right to have a new lease granted when the current lease expires, subject to the following of a detailed notice and court procedure
Use	The lease will specify how and for what purposes the premises can be used (for example, office, shop) and these restrictions can be enforced by an injunction
Break clause	A term in a tenancy agreement that allows a tenant to leave on a set date or dates within the tenancy period, without incurring any financial penalty

11 NEGOTIATING WITH THE LANDLORD, INCLUDING HEADS OF TERMS

First Principles

- It is unlikely you will find the perfect building
- Look at how your needs are met by each building
- Use any problems to negotiate with your landlord
- Negotiate for rent reductions, rent-free periods and contributions towards fit-out
- Heads of Terms set out the agreement between you and your prospective landlord

Your office will typically involve a compromise unless you are building a purpose-designed facility. Your commercial agent should show you a range of premises available that may meet your needs. However, there may be deficiencies – like odd-shaped floors – which could present an opportunity to negotiate. Odd-shaped floors make it difficult to space plan efficiently. A circulation factor of 15% of gross area is usual but if this increases due to poor building design, there may be scope for negotiation.

Heads of Terms set out the agreement in principle between you and your prospective landlord. They typically are issued after a prospective tenant has viewed a property and made an offer. After the landlord has decided the proposed rent, the successful bidder is advised in writing of the main Heads of Terms.

The Heads of Terms are usually issued by the landlord's agent and have to be copied to your commercial agent and lawyer for comment. The status of the property has to change to "under offer" once the Heads of Terms have been agreed, until the lease is completed. You should aim to include an exclusivity agreement to ensure the landlord negotiates solely with you for a given period.

The landlord may prefer to negotiate a rent-free period or a contribution towards fit-out costs in lieu of a reduced overall rental/lease, which can adversely affect the building's market value. Contributions towards fit-out costs are common, but may be affected by the prevailing market conditions and the desirability of the property.

Please allow plenty of time for legal negotiations especially if you are dealing with an underlease or sub-tenancy.

Jargon Buster

Floor plate	Single floor in a multi-story building
Circulation space	The area within your demise that is given over to corridors, whether closed or open-plan
Demise	The area that you are leasing

12 DILAPIDATIONS – DON'T IGNORE THIS IF YOU ARE RELOCATING

First Principles

- Dilapidations concern any disrepair or damage to a rented property
- One basic common problem is not understanding the terms of the lease – if in doubt, ask your lawyer to interpret it for you
- It is vital you work closely with your design and build fit-out specialist and commercial agent
- Using their advice, negotiate hard to get the most out of your lease

You need to be aware that full repairing leases give rise to dilapidations clauses. "Dilapidations" specifically concern any disrepair or damage to a rented property. Under this term, the intention is to identify and compensate landlords for the cost of reinstating the property to the original condition at the start of the lease.

As a dilapidations clause may demand you leave the property in the same condition at the end of your lease as it was on the day you first took over the lease, you are advised to consider a schedule of condition photographic survey before actually taking up occupation. One basic common problem affecting a lot of tenants concerns them not fully understanding the terms of the lease. Take professional advice if there is anything you do not understand. It is vital you work closely with your design and build fit-out specialist and commercial agent as dilapidations are a highly complex area and beset with financial traps that can easily affect the unwary. It is important that you take all the advice you need.

Be aware that even if you have made significant improvements to the building, you may still have to remove them to comply with the terms of your lease when you vacate the premises, unless you have specifically agreed otherwise with the landlord.

You should factor dilapidations into your budget for the total cost of occupation of your leased premises.

Your fit-out specialist should be able to assist you in compiling a list of repairs and items which may need to be removed from your premises prior to your lease expiry and provide an estimate of the costs involved. You are wise to take advice from your property lawyer to ensure that you are correctly advised and allow adequate time to carry out the dilapidations works to your Landlord's satisfaction.

Jargon Buster

Dilapidations Forum	Influencing change in dilapidations practice proactively, check RICS website for information
Vacant possession	All chattels should be gone; the landlord has the keys and can access the building at will
FRI lease	Full repairing and insuring lease

13 RENT REVIEWS

First Principles

- The tenant usually pays the rates and taxes imposed on premises
- There are no statutory limitations on the rent payable
- Leases specify the rent payable and when (usually quarterly or monthly)
- Many leases contain rent review provisions

Rent reviews are a mechanism for adjusting a tenant's rent to the current market level. Similarly, the revaluation of rating assessments adjusts the rates an occupier pays, bringing it into line with rental values. There are no statutory limitations on the rent payable. If the landlord has opted to tax the building, you will have to pay VAT on the rent.

You negotiate rent reviews (if your lease provides for them) with your landlord. The key questions are whether an increase in rent is reasonable and if you should challenge it. Many leases contain rent review provisions that protect the long-term investment of property from the landlord's side by enforcing upward only rent reviews. This means that the rent cannot fall.

These provisions can be complex. Dates for the reviews and the basis of the review will be set out in your lease. You should enter dates into a diary and engage a solicitor and surveyor to advise you on the review's conduct. Typically, the lease will allow you and the landlord to agree the new rent between yourselves for a period before the review date. If you cannot agree, the review may be referred to an independent surveyor to decide.

Look to get the most out of your lease arrangements by pursuing tough but fair negotiations with landlords, having well briefed yourself beforehand with actionable advice from your design and build fit-out specialist and commercial agent. This cannot be stressed enough. A lease will contain restrictions on a tenant disposing of its lease outright (known as assignment), subletting and sharing or disposing of occupation.

Jargon Buster

Service charges	Payments made by a tenant, in addition to rent, to cover the cost of such items as, building security, cleaning and lifts
Assignment	Where a tenant disposes of the whole lease to another tenant or tenants. Landlords may require you to get approval for any such assignment
Subletting	Where a tenant disposes of part of the lease to another tenant or tenants. Landlords will require to approve any sub-letting
Late payment interest	Monies paid at a high rate, e.g. on any late payments of rent and other sums due to landlords under the lease
Headline rent	The rent paid disregarding any incentive given, e.g. on rates or a rent-free period
Net effective rent	The rent paid adjusted to reflect any incentives. Where incentives are given to a tenant, the headline rent will be higher than the net effective rent

14 COMMISSION A BUILDING SURVEY

First Principles

A building survey should cover:

- Dimensions of the space to be taken
- Locations of services risers and incoming mains
- Schedule of condition
- Mechanical and electrical services

It is not considered wise to rely on the landlord's opinion or his maintenance contractor to provide a schedule of condition for the existing building infrastructure or heating and ventilation systems.

Experience has shown that a detailed survey at an early stage will highlight any defects or remedial work that is required before the lease is signed. This could have far-reaching implications, for example, the lease may require you to reinstate the air conditioning system at the end of your tenancy to a specification that is of higher quality than when you took on the lease.

Another important reason for commissioning a detailed survey of the condition of the premises prior to your signing the lease and taking up occupation is that the terms of the lease may well obligate you to pay for reinstatement to condition at the termination of the lease period.

Without documented and perhaps even photographic evidence of preexisting damage or wear and tear, the landlord could seek to get you to pay or reimburse him to reinstate the building to its as-built condition. See *Chapter 12*.

Your fit-out specialist should be able to recommend a suitable expert to commission this survey for you, providing a detailed report with attached notes and photographic evidence of its condition.

Your fit-out specialist may consult with the Building Control Officer to ensure that the building complies with the building regulations and discuss the implications of any changes you might make. Building regulations are covered in *Chapter 17*.

Jargon Buster

Mechanical services	Heating, ventilation, air conditioning and water
Electrical services	Power and lighting
M&E	Both of the above
Riser	A vertical shaft within a building allowing cables and pipes to pass between floors

15 SELECTING YOUR NEW OFFICE – CAT A OR CAT B?

First Principles

- Two common types of office fit-out are known as Cat A and Cat B
- Shell & Core developments include finishes to the landlord's area only
- Cat B fit-outs take the work to a stage further toward from Cat A

When selecting a new office, you will notice that there are various levels of fit-out, which will no doubt be reflected in the rent payable, but which will also impact upon the initial cost of setting up your office on the premises.

The most basic condition in which potential office space is usually offered to the market is often termed "Shell & Core". A Shell & Core development may include finishes to the landlord's spaces only, with services distribution for the building's tenants capped off at the risers to each office floor. Rent for such accommodation may seem cheap but fit-out costs will be high.

At the other end of the spectrum, fully-fitted serviced offices are widely available, where all facilities are provided, often including a manned reception and additional bookable conference facilities.

Between these extremes, there are many variations in how much the landlord provides. Two levels of fit-out often offered are widely known as Cat A and Cat B.

15

A Cat A fit-out, which is sometimes known as "developers finish", includes the provision of suspended ceilings, raised floors, carpets and basic M&E services into the office space. According to Building Magazine, compared with Shell & Core, a Cat A fit-out adds up to £425 per square metre (sq mtr) of net internal floor area for offices in the City of London or West End, and up to £325 per sq mtr for outer London locations.

A Cat B fit-out takes the work a stage further forward. The fit-out is completed by the landlord or developer to the future occupier's specific requirements, and can include the partitioning of cellular office space, all furniture and fittings, and IT and communications deployment. Such a fit-out can also include the modification to Shell & Core; Cat A finishes and services provisions to accommodate a client's space planning and operational needs.

If all this leaves you confused, you are not alone. It pays to retain a commercial agent and work with a fit-out specialist in order to advise you on the best balance between the cost of fitting-out your offices initially and the ongoing rental charge. Exit costs and dilapidations at the end of the lease also need to be factored into the equation. See *Chapter 12*.

Jargon Buster

M&E	Mechanical and Electrical services
Shell & Core	A building that provides only a structure and common parts such as toilets; all fit-out elements are usually provided by the tenant
Risers	Vertical ducts carrying services such as electrical wiring and communications between floors

16 LICENCE OF ALTERATION

First Principles

- The licence of alteration is needed when a tenant wishes to make additions or alterations to a building, usually structural or affecting the M&E elements
- The works may improve the property in the long term
- If the lease is registered at the Land Registry, the licence of alteration will need to be registered too

The licence of alteration is usually a requirement of the lease and requires the tenant to get a formal approval from the landlord before making some changes or alterations to the building. The lease may provide that you need the landlord's consent for the intended works or it may impose an absolute prohibition on any works being carried out. The licence deals with each situation. This often includes items like the external positioning of ductwork or air conditioning units.

Obviously the landlord or his agents will consider whether or not to give you permission for the works to be carried out. They may consider aspects such as whether the works will improve the property in the long term.

Your landlord may be the owner of the freehold. Or the landlord may hold a lease of the property, in which case the consent of the freehold owner may be needed. If the property is mortgaged by the landlord or if the lease is mortgaged by you, the consent of the lender may also be needed to carry out the works.

16

If the lease is registered at the Land Registry, the licence of alteration will have to be registered too. If the lease is not registered at the Land Registry, it is best to endorse a note on the cover/title page that the licence has been granted. It is assumed that the landlord and you are the original parties to the lease (if not, the licence will need modification).

It is assumed that you will not need any special rights of access to carry out the works. If extra rights are needed, you will have to obtain these too.

If you are carrying out works which improve the building rather than just suiting your organisation's needs (for example, installation of air conditioning) you may be able to negotiate a landlord contribution to the cost and agreement that the works may without penalty be left in situ at the end of your lease period.

Jargon Buster

Land Registry	Registers title to land in England and Wales, and records dealings (e.g. sales and mortgages) with registered land
Lease	Contract granting use or occupation of property during a specified period in exchange for a specified rent

17 BUILDING REGULATIONS

First Principles

- Most alteration works will require approval under the Building Regulations and some will also require Planning Permission
- The Building Inspector will visit the site as work progresses
- Building Regulations Part L deals with energy conservation

Obtaining relevant consents from a local authority is a key milestone to be achieved in any office fit-out or alteration works. The consents that may be needed include Building Regulations and Planning permission. See *Chapter 18*.

As well as existing to ensure the health and safety of people in and around all types of buildings, the Building Regulations also cover energy conservation and access and facilities for people with disabilities. In fact, the regulations deal with 13 parts, each dealing with individual aspects of building design and construction: structural matters, fire safety, energy conservation, hygiene, sound insulation, access and facilities for disabled people, ventilation, drainage, resistance to moisture, combustion appliances, glazing, protection from falling, and use of toxic substances.

Each part of the regulations sets out the objectives that the individual aspects of building design must achieve. The parts are accompanied by "approved documents" which contain practical ways in which to comply with the requirements.

The responsibility for complying with Building Regulations rests with the person or organisation carrying out building works. It is vital to ensure that your fit-out specialist makes the application as it's the building owner who is served with the enforcement notice if the building works fail to comply with the requirements.

As soon as your plans are finalised, your fit-out specialist will submit them to the Building Control department for their comment and to ensure compliance at pre-construction stage. To proceed without making a Building Control application is illegal and thus means potential litigation procedures being brought if the works undertaken do not comply. This can be costly and we strongly recommend that this important milestone is accorded due consideration at an early stage in the project.

Each local authority has its own Building Control department or alternatively licensed inspectors are authorised to carry out this function.

Jargon Buster

Building Regulations — The rules applied to buildings enforced by the Building Control department

Enforcement notice — A notice requiring a certain state or action to be taken or to cease. In the context of Building Regulations, a notice requires a building owner to alter, remove or amend works which contravene the Building Regulations within 28 days

EPBD — Energy Performance in Buildings Directive

18 PLANNING APPLICATIONS

First Principles

- Some alteration works will require Planning Permission
- Listed buildings will require Listed Building consent
- Planning applications can take up to 13 weeks for determination

Planning Permission may be required from the local authority for any major alteration works you may be undertaking at your offices. Planning consent is not normally required for a re-fit, but will apply to any external alterations, change of use, or if your building is in a conservation area or listed by English Heritage. See *Chapter 20*.

Planning applications need to be considered in your critical time path as they can take up to 13 weeks for determination, following which, if amendments are required, additional time may be needed.

While grants for works on listed buildings are available, you are most unlikely to get any sort of grant for a Grade ll or C-listed building. See *Chapter 21* for further details.

Whether the works you propose need Planning Consent or not, you need to consider whether, under the terms of your lease, you need written approval from your landlord before work starts. See *Chapter 16.*

With external signage, note that planning approval is generally required for large, high or illuminated signage.

Jargon Buster

Reserved matters   Items that are still to be agreed although planning permission has been granted

Determination   Making a decision

19 THE INFLUENCE OF THE GLOBAL WORKPLACE

First Principles

- There are currently profound changes in workplace design, influenced by globalisation
- Furniture ranges are available globally
- Check local regulations and cultures before making changes

All types of businesses are experiencing the trend towards globalisation including banking, carriers, vehicles and design. Even healthcare is going global, with patients shopping for the best value surgery in emerging countries such as India and Singapore.

The global explosion is driven by costs and enabled by technology. Transactions around the world that once took months to effect are now conducted instantly and seamlessly.

Little wonder that globalisation has affected office design within almost every international company looking to reduce costs through standardisation of design, finishes and furniture.

Furniture manufactures in particular have responded to the demand for ranges which are available globally and some manufacturers have showrooms in most major cities worldwide and have developed a range of products which can be specified globally.

However, the cultural differences between nations remain, and different languages and behaviours all have an implication on work. The biggest mistake companies make is to assume that what works well at home will also work abroad. In Japan age and experience are revered and young people however talented may not be given top management positions. This is the opposite of the USA where young entrepreneurs are given executive powers to drive international companies forward.

Many organisations are developing "Agile" working strategies (see *Chapter 43*) to respond to the challenges of a highly mobile and global workforce. This new way of working empowers staff to select an appropriate work zone that is suitable for the task rather than allocate everyone a fixed desk position. It allows for superior space utilization and more flexibility, potentially reducing costs and saving space.

Regulations also differ from country to country even within Europe and whilst Health and Safety legislation may appear to be similar, the way it is interpreted and managed can be very different.

Finally, globalisation is here to stay and will continue to shape the places we work in. To adapt can mean significant cost savings and benefits, but it does need to be handled sensitively at a local level to ensure staff are properly trained and educated.

Jargon Buster

The MacDonalds effect   Consistent standards throughout all areas of the business to give global consistency

ABW   Activity Based Working – another term for the "Agile Office", see *Chapter 43*

20 LISTED BUILDING AND CONSERVATION ISSUES

First Principles

- "Listing" is not intended to fossilise a building
- Some 500,000 buildings are listed, most being Grade II (or C)
- Listing does not prevent change

Listing is not intended to fossilise a building. Indeed, such buildings' long-term interests and conservation are often best served by putting them to good use. If this cannot be the one it was originally designed for, a new use may have to be found. Listing ensures that the architectural and historic interest of a building is carefully considered before any external or internal alterations are agreed.

Buildings are graded to show their relative architectural or historic interest, using the following classifications:

- Grade I buildings are of exceptional interest

- Grade II* are particularly important buildings of more than special interest

- Grade II are of special interest, warranting every effort to preserve them

Listing currently protects some 500,000 UK buildings, of which most (over 90%) are Grade II. Grade I and II* buildings may be eligible for English Heritage or Cadw (Wales) grants for urgent major repairs (Grades A, B and C for Historic Scotland and

Ulster Architectural Society, N. Ireland). You are extremely unlikely to get any sort of grant for a Grade II or C-listed building.

The demands of workplace technology and other external forces such as the Health and Safety Executive often call for radical alterations to a building's make-up to allow the tenant organisation to remain competitive in their marketplace and compliant with workplace law. The demands often mean the building is unsuitable and needs extra alterations to make it competitive and compliant.

Listing does not prevent change, but it does mean owners and occupiers of listed buildings may need listed building consent (LBC) if they wish to undertake work to their buildings. It is possible to adapt to modern technology and ensure DDA compliance if done sympathetically and approved by the Local Authority.

CAFM software (see *Chapter 22*) can provide an early warning of listed status, and also offer easy access to associated information, such as data and contacts relating to covenants and restrictions. Building plans and photos can also be linked into the software, with photos providing evidence of the original condition or required condition of a building, which is pertinent where certain standards need to be met.

Jargon Buster

Disability Discrimination Act	See *Chapter 24*
Listed Building Consent	Following strict guidelines will avoid heavy fines and potentially six months imprisonment – beware

21

WHY SELECT AN INTELLIGENT BUILDING?

First Principles

- Intelligent buildings promise terrific innovation
- Internet Protocol (IP) backbones are expected to play a key role
- Building operations will be high performance and cost-effective

An intelligent building is difficult to define – one attempt is "the use of technology and process to create a building that is safer and more productive for its occupants and operationally more efficient for its owners."

There are many buildings offering excellent intelligent features around the UK today, with attributes including computerised lighting controls, innovative heating and cooling solutions, leading edge architectural design, spectacular façade engineering, ergonomically-designed furniture and fittings and the latest IT and communications technologies and systems.

Future drivers for intelligent buildings are expected to be IT and communications, robotics, smart materials, sustainable factors and the impacts of social change. Aside from technological developments, other factors are expected to include climate change, regulatory change and how people work and live within these buildings.

Any innovation that simultaneously reduces cost over time while enhancing building performance must be appealing – and indeed intelligent buildings are designed to promise such innovation. For example, most buildings today feature many low-voltage systems, each calling for its own control, management and monitoring over the building's lifetime. Without a common infrastructure that can link them together, these systems can create a lifetime accumulation of unnecessary cost. This is something an intelligent building is designed to rectify.

With a single backbone – expected to be Internet Protocol (IP) based – supporting all systems from fire and security to lighting, HVAC, IT to communications, building operations can become high performance and cost-effective. The UK's BRE started the ball rolling with its BREEAM rating system, while the US Green Building Council has released the LEED system. Both are designed to improve the environmental performance of buildings.

Jargon Buster

IP	Internet Protocol
BRE	Building Research Establishment
BREEAM	BRE Environmental Assessment Method, a voluntary measurement rating for green buildings
LEED	Leadership in Energy and Environmental Design

22 BUILDING MANAGEMENT SYSTEMS

First Principles

- Running on computers, BMS utilise many technologies to effect energy management and building control tasks
- BMS can diagnose maintenance and service needs
- Other diagnostic functions can be created, such as predictive maintenance

Building management systems (BMS) utilise many technologies to effect energy management and building control tasks. BMS control, monitor and optimise such building services as heating, ventilation, air conditioning, lighting and alarm systems. They can form part of an intelligent building when integrated with other systems.

Typically, a central control unit runs the system, based on information supplied by some of the peripherals and on pre-set instructions for some of the devices. Commands are transmitted through two-wire fieldbus systems, power lines, phone lines, fibre-optic cables or in the future in wireless set-ups. Systems are based on distributed-intelligence microprocessors, where intelligent peripheral units manage local tasks and functions, while the central unit acts as a supervisor.

The benefits of technologically sophisticated BMS', are already being realised by savvy Facilities Managers. For example, the provision of temperature sensors allow meeting rooms to switch off the heating by synchronising with the lighting to turn off when people leave the room.

Systems exist to allow the various elements of the building's information systems to integrate seamlessly. The key concerns now are far more than generating data and more about using that information to create a response. The integration of BMS-controlled assets with a CAFM system allows alarms raised in the BMS to automatically trigger a maintenance request. This ensures a rapid response and ultimate business continuity. Similarly, bi-directional links between BMS and CAFM should ensure lighting and HVAC systems are provided only when they are needed to minimise energy use.

Going beyond preventative maintenance, predictive maintenance is a method of monitoring and collecting asset data in order to predict impending equipment failure. This method maximises equipment uptime and provides a proactive tool to complement planned maintenance scheduling.

Acceptable energy efficiency thresholds will tighten again in 2014. So it is clear that forward thinking Facilities Managers should stay ahead of the trend and select seasonably efficient air conditioning systems that comply with new SEER energy consumption recommendations and reduce energy through innovative control systems.

Jargon Buster

Fieldbus	A standard means of communication between devices in a building
HVAC	Heating, ventilation and air conditioning
CAFM	Computer-aided facilities management
CPU	Central processing unit, as found in computers, microprocessors

23 THE ASBESTOS SURVEY

First Principles

- Asbestos in a building is only generally harmful if disturbed
- Many buildings constructed in the 20th Century may contain asbestos
- Special precautions must be taken if asbestos is going to be removed or disturbed
- Asbestos kills over 3,000 people in the UK every year, while by 2020, 10,000 people a year are predicted to die

It is a legal requirement that all buildings are surveyed for the presence of harmful materials and asbestos – and if you are purchasing or leasing a building this specialist report should be made available to you. There is no safe level of exposure and repeated low-level exposure can also cause asbestos-related diseases. It takes 15-60 years for the symptoms of mesothelioma, asbestosis of the lungs or asbestos-related lung cancer to appear.

If asbestos is contained within the building fabric, your fit-out specialist should be made aware of this immediately so as to avoid any disturbance of this material. This does not necessarily mean you should avoid the building as it depends on the type of asbestos, its location, and whether the proposed alterations will impact on the areas of asbestos.

You may need to provide disposal of asbestos in the event of major refurbishment or alteration works which must be carefully surveyed by a specialist and removed by approved and competent contractors. HSE-licensed contractors must carry out the work. They must double-bag the waste, clearly label it and dispose of it at a licensed site.

23

You should always check the level of asbestos awareness training that operatives from all contractors have unless they know that the buildings in which they operate are totally asbestos free. Blue asbestos is lethal and most likely to be found in any buildings built between 1950 and 1980. While 3,000 die from asbestos exposure every year now, by 2020 the numbers are expected to be 10,000 a year and could escalate unless we all follow the advice given here.

The HSE issue a good guide called "Asbestos - the survey guide" which may enlighten you as to the dangers and requirements of the law.

If you fail to manage the asbestos on your premises or manage it poorly the implications are significant – civil actions, legal actions, clean-up costs or even closure of the building. It all equates to serious financial and possibly reputational costs.

Jargon Buster

Deleterious	Harmful
Blue asbestos	Most dangerous type of asbestos
Asbestosis	The common or medical name for the respiratory condition caused by asbestos; fatal
Mesothelioma	A form of carcinoma of the mesothelium lining lungs, or abdomen, or heart, usually associated with exposure to asbestos dust; fatal
HSE	Health & Safety Executive

24 CHECK YOUR DDA COMPLIANCE

First Principles

- DDA applies to all commercial and public buildings
- The regulations go beyond the needs of wheelchair users
- Disabilities such as impaired sight and hearing are also covered
- DDA 2005 requires people with a disability to have the same opportunities as able-bodied people

The Disability Discrimination Act (DDA) 1995 was amended by the DDA 2005 which introduced new requirements for transport, public authorities and private members' clubs. The DDA also applies to all commercial and public buildings. While it may not prove necessary to implement all of the DDA's requirements immediately, during any refurbishment within your building, consideration should be given to the requirements to avoid costly remedial works at a later stage.

The DDA defines "disability" as "a physical or mental impairment which has a substantial and long-term adverse effect on a person's ability to carry out normal day-to-day activities." And "long-term" means the disability must last or be expected to last for at least 12 months.

The DDA 2005 has also seen the definition of disability extended to include individuals with mental illnesses that are not clinically recognised to be mental impairments (e.g. dyslexia, obsessive compulsive disorder, ADHD, attention deficit disorder), and people with cancer, HIV infection or multiple sclerosis, whether or not the conditions have an effect on their ability to carry out normal day-to-day activities.

24

The DDA outlaws discrimination by those who hire contract workers. If you contract work out to a disabled person or someone who becomes disabled, you must not discriminate against them for any reason.

Your fit-out specialist will be able to arrange for a DDA consultant to assess how the requirements of the law apply to your business. There are special responsibilities for occupiers of buildings where the public have access and for developers/designers of new buildings.

The use of contrast colours is crucial for design compliance with the DDA regulations. Partially-sighted users need colour contrast to identify an item or object, i.e. light switch, handrail, leading door edge or door handle.

Jargon Buster

Part M	The section of the Building Regulations that deals with disabled access
Access statement	The document outlining the issues related to a building and its accessibility for disabled users

25 ENVIRONMENTAL CONSIDERATIONS/SUSTAINABILITY

First Principles

- The sustainability, carbon footprint and energy efficiency of buildings are strategically important
- Europe's total building stock consumes over 40% of its energy consumption and creates over 40% of its carbon dioxide emissions
- Deploy energy efficient solutions wherever possible
- Get buy-in to your energy efficiency measures from your staff and suppliers

Sustainability issues have impacted business dealings across the world in the past few years. The sustainability of buildings has assumed a strategic importance and become much more significant in day-to-day business. Business premises are responsible for a high and rising percentage of carbon dioxide emissions and energy consumption.

To increase awareness of energy performance in UK buildings, Energy Performance Certificates are required. April 2010 saw the introduction of the Carbon Reduction Commitment (CRC), one of a raft of measures introduced by the UK government to curb energy consumption. The CRC is aimed at reducing carbon emissions from large commercial and public sector organisations by 1.2 million tonnes of carbon per year by 2020.

Whilst many organisations will not need to participate in the CRC, the focus on measuring carbon footprints and deploying energy efficient solutions is highly strategic and relevant to everyone, both organisations and individuals alike.

Buildings are now having to meet legislative targets in terms of energy saving. DEC certifications have for some time been a mandatory requirement for all public and private buildings when they are sold or leased and this is encouraging facilities managers to drive through energy efficiency measures.

25

The UK has committed to reduce greenhouse gases by at least 80% by 2050. This is a tough target – which will require every part of our economy and society to do their bit.

Simple basic solutions can be applied by your staff to include turning off lights wherever possible, fixing thermostats and closing doors. Where reasonably practical ensure that energy efficiency is included in the buying specifications for all your equipment, and consider specifying recyclable products, including long-life low energy bulbs, and blinds that reflect solar heat gain.

RICS has led the development of the Ska Rating tool, assessment methodology, and scheme that focuses 100% on fit-out and allows for the measurement, labelling, quality-assured certification and benchmarking of workplace projects. Ska Rating helps organisations achieve more sustainable fit-outs – it covers a holistic range of sustainability considerations including waste, water, pollution, transport, materials and wellbeing, plus energy and carbon dioxide. See *Chapter 28*.

It informs you about the impact your fit-out will have on energy efficiency. If you are ISO 14001 accredited, a Ska certificate helps ensure a fit-out project is rated accurately and can be used to support an environmental management system.

You may wish to work with your fit-out specialist to specify elements and materials which satisfy environmental guidelines. Your fit-out specialist should have ISO 14001 and will be able to guide you through this process.

Jargon Buster

EPBD	The EU's Energy Performance in Buildings Directive
EPC	Energy Performance Certificate
CRC	Carbon Reduction Commitment
ISO 14001	International standard on environmental management

26 MEASURING YOUR CARBON FOOTPRINT

First Principles

- Everything has a carbon footprint.
- Carbon emissions need to be measured on a life cycle approach.
- Carbon footprinting is now regarded as a very key part of good corporate governance.

Firstly, let us define; what is a carbon footprint?

A carbon footprint is the total emission of Carbon Dioxide and any other greenhouse gases (GHG3) in terms of carbon equivalents (CO2e) for a defined system or activity. It measures the total contribution to climate change and can help to identify where the biggest carbon impacts and potential costs and savings occur. Everything has a carbon footprint.

Many people question the benefit of carbon footprinting but it is increasingly becoming a key criterion by which successful organisations are judged. It can help to:

- Reduce emissions of carbon
- Identify cost savings or new, more efficient ways of working
- Comply with tightening regulations
- Enhance your company's reputation

Many companies focus on business travel as a major impact but ignore other high energy usage activities in buildings such as heating and refrigeration. Focussing on the big issues in your business pays dividends. See *Chapter 27.*

Engage with your office fit-out specialist and explain your company's policies and targets regarding carbon footprinting and decide how you want it to impact on the way your office works and the materials that are specified.

Jargon Buster

FISP	Furniture Industry Sustainability Programme
DECC	Department of Energy and Climate Control
WBCSD	World Business Council for Sustainable Development
Footprint Expert	Software produced by the Carbon Trust to measure carbon footprinting on a fast and consistent basis

27 CARBON EMISSIONS CONTROL; CARBON REDUCTION

First Principles

- In the UK two-thirds of energy delivered to buildings is used for space heating
- All new commercial buildings must meet zero carbon targets by 2018/19
- Energy Performance Certificates have been required since October 2008
- Lighting energy consumption can be reduced by 50% through deploying energy-efficient lighting technology

Over 40% of the delivered energy in Europe is used in buildings, while in the UK two-thirds of that energy is used for space heating, while in commercial buildings 20% of the energy is used for lighting. The Carbon Reduction Commitment (CRC, see *Chapter 26*) is one government tool designed to reduce carbon emissions from large commercial and public sector organisations by 1.2 million tonnes of carbon per year by 2020. With stipulations that all new commercial buildings must meet zero carbon targets by 2019, and the public sector by 2018, there are an emerging number of other ways to assist in the delivery of these tough targets.

Energy performance certificates (EPCs) have been required for all commercial buildings since October 2008. The core aim of the EPC scheme is to increase awareness of the energy used in buildings, and to promote increased investment in energy efficiency by setting up measurements of relative energy performance and introducing regular inspections and re-evaluations. There are some exemptions, detailed in information that can be obtained free from the government website **www.communities.gov.uk/publications**

Energy efficiency equally applies to walls, roofs, and windows, including glazing, shading, complex glass and frames. The Carbon Trust estimates that some 25% of a building's heat can escape through an un-insulated roof. There are many green ways to rectify this by utilising sheep's wool or rock mineral wool. A raft of new legislation is set to be introduced across Europe relating to window and glazing, blinds and shading, linked in part to use of air conditioning systems. One example is the use of integrated blinds to cut air conditioning energy use through the ventilation and cooling benefits they provide.

Looking at lighting, low carbon refurbishment can deliver increased sustainability without excessive capital expenditure and disruption. Indeed significant savings can be made by installing relatively simple solutions. Switching to energy-efficient lighting technology can decrease lighting energy consumption by over 50%, and retrofitting can be less costly and less disruptive than system replacement.

There are government-funded loans available to assist in the installation of energy-efficient lighting and for other green refurbishment works, for example the Carbon Trust interest-free loans scheme and Energy Saving Scotland loans for SMEs.

Jargon Buster

T5 lamps	Triphosphor high frequency lights
Salix	Energy efficiency loan scheme (funding for public sector), see **www.salixfinance.co.uk/loans.html**

28 WHY SKA?

First Principles

- Ska measures the sustainability impact of an office interior fit-out
- It is administered by the Royal Institute of Chartered Surveyors
- Many organisations favour it because it is cost effective

Against a background of growing pressure for property occupiers and owners to improve the sustainability of existing as well as new buildings, RICS has led the development of an assessment methodology, rating tool and scheme that focuses on fit-out and allows for the measurement, labeling, quality-assured certification and benchmarking of workplace projects.

Simply, Ska Rating helps organisations to achieve more sustainable fit-outs, obtain clear guidance on good practice in fit-out and how to implement it and benchmark the performance of fit-outs.

Ska Rating is designed to encourage good practice in fit-out work and has been developed collaboratively by consultants, contractors and occupiers. The fit-out sector until recently was underserved with specific benchmarks and labeling and the new Ska Rating was intended to fill this gap.

28

The current economic climate is extending real-estate life-expectancy. Occupiers are now more likely to refurbish their existing offices than seek new ones, but while there are proved methods for labeling the environmental performance of whole building, fit-out has been a sustainability blind spot.

With its in-depth focus on fit-out, Ska complements other labeling methods, such as BREEAM and LEED. Ska rating focuses 100% on fit-out and considers energy, waste, water, pollution, transport, materials and wellbeing as well as carbon dioxide emissions.

It has been a principle from the outset that Ska Rating should be accessible even for the smallest organisations. For businesses seeking the credibility of a professional certificate an assessor can be engaged to rate and certify the project. Costs are relatively low.

No matter what your starting point, a Ska Rating will enable you to measure 100% of the environmental performance of an office fit-out since it does not consider the base build, it measures only what you do to add value to your property.

The Ska assessment process is broken into three stages: design/planning, delivery/construction and post-occupancy assessment.

Your fit-out specialist will usually have trained Ska Assessors to help you engage in this valuable process.

Jargon Buster

RICS	Royal Institute of Chartered Surveyors
Ska	A tool originally developed by a company called SKANSKA to measure sustainability in the workplace

29 CHECK YOUR RATES

First Principles

- UBR (uniform business rate) is a means of taxation of business premises based on the notional rental value of the property
- HM R&C assesses all commercial properties at prevailing market rent levels and a rateable value is calculated on which the UBR is based
- Property expenditure includes payments for rent, rates, insurance and service charges – a significant cost

As the tenant, you will usually pay the rates and taxes imposed on your premises.

Within the UK, a uniform business rate or UBR exists as a means of taxation based on the value of your property. All commercial properties are assessed at prevailing market rent levels by HM Revenue and Customs Valuation Office, and a rateable value is calculated and fixed for a certain period. This will be reviewed every five years, and values become fully effective after a further two years.

For occupied property, the UBR is added to this value to calculate the total sum payable for rates. You need to be apprised of these rules, together with the information following to enable you to ensure effective financial management (correct at the time of going to press).

Since April 2008, unoccupied commercial property has been relieved of business rates for three months, after which period the full sum becomes payable. Appeals may be made against rating assessments for which you should seek an expert surveyor's services.

You may want to check whether rating liability may be reduced where the property has suffered materially, for example, through part demolition. External factors, such as nearby road works or building works, can reduce the rateable value.

Property expenditure is typically associated with payments for rent, rates, insurance and service charges. You will appreciate that these costs together can constitute around a third of the business overheads, which is a significant amount, exceeded only by payroll costs.

Jargon Buster

Rateable value	The notional rental amount for which a property (or part thereof) could be leased at the base date for valuation purposes
Transitional relief	Where rateable values have risen considerably, to cushion the rise, the government introduced arrangements so the ratepayers would not have to pay the whole increase at once
Transitional surcharge	Where rateable values have decreased, ratepayers receive a percentage of the reduction over a period of up to four years

30 TRAVEL PLANS, CAR PARKING AND ACCESSIBILITY

First Principles

- Transport is one of the highest costs after personnel
- Travel plans aim to combat overdependence on cars
- Car parks are often the first thing visitors will see of your organisation

For many organisations, transport is one of the highest costs after personnel. Travel plans are aimed at reducing adverse environmental impacts of transport to and from specific sites and buildings. But many energy-unfriendly operations need to be reduced, such as transport-derived air pollution, carbon dioxide emissions and traffic congestion. Travel plans also produce time and cost savings, greater flexibility and accessibility for staff.

Travel plans aim to combat overdependence on cars, in favour of more environmentally-friendly modes of transport, such as public transport, walking and cycling. These plans also seek to reduce the need to travel – for example, you could suggest videoconferencing and/or conference calls in certain cases.

Car parks are often the first thing visitors will see of your organisation. You should ensure your organisation's car park is clean, well signed and lit, with well-manicured grassy areas where appropriate – this is the image your visitors will take away with them.

Current guidelines allow you to have one car parking space per 30 sq mtr for all office developments above 2,500 sq mtr. If this is insufficient to accommodate your staff, you will have to consider car sharing schemes, public transport options, cycling and walking, within your travel plan.

You need to be aware that under the workplace parking levy order, companies with more than 11 parking spaces could be liable for annual charges of up to £380 per space. This charge was implemented in 2012 by Nottingham City Council, and other Local Authorities are following. Businesses which allow employees and visitors to park on company premises and exceed a given number of car parking spaces will be taxed. Unsurprisingly, it is not very popular.

The Government has introduced a tax exempt cycle to work loan scheme for all employees which covers bicycles and safety equipment. Employers may consider offering shower facilities and cycle storage racks.

Jargon Buster

(Green) travel plan An effective site management tool that also meets the need for continuous improvement in environmental management

Fleet management Running a number of vehicles (cars, vans) owned or leased by an organisation for use by its staff

Vehicle Excise Duty Tax applied to a vehicle depending on the gram per kilometre of carbon dioxide emitted – those with 130 grams per kilometre or less pay nothing

31 FORMULATE YOUR FIT-OUT BUDGET

First Principles

- The fit-out budget is one of the biggest items of business expenditure with which you are likely to be involved during the relocation process
- Partner with an experienced design and build fit-out specialist
- It is vital to ensure everything is factored into your budget – it is always the unexpected elements that are going to pose the greatest challenges

Budgeting for an office fit-out, relocation and refurbishment ranks amongst the largest chunks of business expenditure with which you are likely to be involved. Setting your budget demands a rigorous and exacting approach, stretching across your entire corporate structure.

There are mistakes galore peppering the formulation of budgets. To ensure you will make the best plans for your organisation, partner with an experienced design and build fit-out specialist who can provide input from a project consultant with demonstrable and proven experience. If nothing else, this move will drastically reduce the chance of any budget surprises keeping you awake at night.

It is always the unexpected elements that are going to throw up severe challenges to your carefully prepared plans. For example, do not forget to factor dilapidations into your budget. If you are refurbishing a listed property, check to see whether your network and IT systems can be accommodated.

Check also whether any alterations proposed under the Disability Discrimination Act are mandatory, and factor in all costs. Maybe this is a time to consider leasing your fit-out. See *Chapter 32*.

It is key to ensure everything is factored into your budget – floor coverings, partitions, furniture, lighting, ceilings, reception, restaurant facilities, even car parking and travel plans. Check, check and check again with your fit-out specialist – you can never do enough checking. For instance, there may be elements to do with a building control application that you have not considered. Include a budget element to cover communication with your organisation's staff about the fresh, new appearance of their working environment. It is wise to build a contingency allowance into your budget to allow for the unforeseen.

Jargon Buster

Budgetary control	Ensuring the financial management plan that has been agreed with the board is achieved
Zero-based budgeting	Construction of a new budget for each service/element from basic principles
Cost centres	Units for forecasting expenditure and quality
BCP	Budget Cost Plan

32 LOOK AT PROJECT FINANCE OPTIONS

First Principles

- Funding may be derived from many sources
- Ensure budgeted maintenance and IT finances are factored into the project
- All items of expenditure should be considered for tax efficiency purposes
- Leasing may prove to be a better option than outright purchase

Not everything involved in an office fit-out needs to be treated as capital expenditure. You should, for example, carefully consider the tax efficiencies of leasing your office fit-out and furniture package. Such an exercise will release capital for injection into the business.

Your fit-out specialist should be able to recommend or provide costing options for you to evaluate along with your existing finance option.

If you own your premises there are other options open to you, including sale and leaseback. This exercise releases capital which can be applied directly to your business, and/or for any expansion plans.

It can prove to be advantageous to own your own property as the capital growth in property can be significant. Many companies elect to set up a pension fund that owns the property and leases it back to the organisation.

Finding freehold office property is difficult, and in seeking it out, you may find yourself in stiff competition with developers and investors.

Most organisations find that leasing property is the preferred option as there are tax advantages in doing this, while capital expenditure and risk are minimised.

Jargon Buster

Sale and leaseback	Selling your property to a third party and renting it back from them
Dilapidations	Deterioration of a property compared with its condition prior to occupation, see *Chapter 12*
Feuhold	Scottish for freehold
Revenue expenditure	Purchasing goods and services in the short term, including any associated business input costs
Capital expenditure	Cost associated with acquiring fixed assets

33 COMMUNICATE WITH STAFF

First Principles

- PR works
- Unanswered questions affect morale
- Commence staff consultation sooner rather than later

Your organisation's staff are one of its most valuable assets. Communication with them about the project should start early and be maintained throughout the life of the project, to influence their buy-in and approval. Unchecked rumours can be highly damaging to a business and staff will quickly become disillusioned.

Communication and consultation with staff is a pre-requisite to ensure an effective office relocation. It has been proven many times over that if this process is handled correctly and with due consideration for staff needs, the results can be extremely productive and work for the good of the organisation.

Your fit-out specialist may be able to assist you if you find you do not have sufficient time to devote to the task. Some organisations prefer an outside specialist to coordinate the approach to the staff, since it gives a more proactive and consultative appearance to their suggestions and input.

33

Indeed, a relocation is a good time to re-evaluate your working practices. An example of this is to introduce more open-plan working environments. If you involve your staff and your design and build specialist in this process at an early stage, you will maximise your chances of success. No question.

There are naturally some decisions that are best made at senior level. You need to make it clear from the outset what the areas are that can be influenced by the staff and those that are not negotiable. Staff will respect the management for a firm approach, rather than for one that appears receptive to ideas but which is in fact already closed and decided.

Jargon Buster

PR	Public Relations – a consultative process of communication
Buy-in	Influencing people to accept your ideas
Rumour mill	The often damaging tendency for an incorrect report to spread through an organisation

34 WORKING WITH YOUR DESIGNER

First Principles

- Let the designer design – but you can also have an opinion
- Use pictures to show your designer what you like and dislike
- If the result is not better than you could have imagined, do not accept it

To direct a designer too closely is rather like telling a master chef how to prepare his or her signature dish, or a taxi driver exactly which route to follow to your destination. Giving your designer a free hand often results in a better outcome than you could possibly have imagined.

It is a good idea to let your designer know the kind of design you like and the one that will reflect your organisation's image. There will sometimes be images from magazines or photos that will convey not only the styles or features that you appreciate but also those that you could not accept.

All good design and build contractors should possess the ability to interpret your brief and turn it into an exciting concept. They will be able to provide you with CGIs of their design proposals. These should be of high quality, with the appearance of panoramic photographs of your space. They are an excellent way of communicating the design to staff and senior management. Do note, however, that the fit-out specialist may charge extra for this service.

If you wish to reflect your organisation's brand in the design, make the designer aware of functions, styles and anything that may affect the design process, to enable him/her to get a feel of the organisation's ethos, so that this may be embodied in the finished results.

The final outcome of the design process should be better than you could have imagined, nothing less. If this is not the case, why employ a designer in the first place?

Jargon Buster

CAD	Computer-aided design
CGI	Computer generated image
GAs	General Arrangement drawings (plans)

35 CHECK YOUR INSURANCE COVER

First Principles

The minimum insurance cover that should be provided by your design and build specialist is:

- Employers liability
- Public liability
- Professional Indemnity

You are strongly advised to obtain copies of and scrutinise your fit-out specialist's insurance policies carefully. You should also check with the insurers that the policy is still current. The claims history will identify any previous occurrences that may indicate negligence. Check carefully.

As well as the contractor's insurance, you need to be aware of your own situation – you should investigate your own buildings and contents insurance to ensure that you have sufficient cover. You must make sure that you have the appropriate buildings insurance from the day of commencement of any new lease. If you are in any doubt, your legal advisor or insurance broker will be able to advise you of the best course of action.

Also, if you are undertaking a business-critical relocation activity, you may need to consider business interruption insurance. You are advised to discuss your requirements with your insurance broker or a specialist with relevant experience.

Also you might like to consider the captives market. Captive insurance companies are insurance companies established with the specific objective of financing risks emanating from their parent group or groups, but they sometimes also insure risks of the group's customers as well.

Using a captive insurer is a risk management technique by which a business forms its own insurance company subsidiary to finance its retained losses in a formal structure. It might be worth a discussion.

Jargon Buster

FRI lease	Full repairing and insuring lease, where the costs of all repairs and insurance are borne by the tenant
PI	Professional Indemnity insurance carried by an architect or designer

36 HEALTH AND SAFETY IN THE OFFICE

First Principles

- A safe and healthy environment is key to producing happy and healthy workers, which in turn can lead to a successful organisation
- HSE regulations to improve the health, safety and comfort of office staff are now mandatory
- Having happy and healthy workers means increased productivity and reduced rates of sickness absence
- Modern health and safety law in the UK is goal-setting rather than prescriptive

The health and wellbeing of employees is a key factor in the success of any organisation. HSE regulations to improve the health, safety and comfort of office workers are now mandatory. The directives have far-reaching implications for the design and provision of office furniture, the use of display screen equipment, space allocation, environmental control and office design, for example.

It is the duty of the employer to ensure every workstation – including those used by staff at home – is assessed and a record kept of the details. There are minimum standards relating to the operations of the workplace that must be adhered to: noise levels should not distract attention or disturb speech; satisfactory lighting conditions must be provided; chairs must be comfortable for the individual and height adjustable; and the space in front of keyboards has to be sufficient to provide support for the hands and arms. And that's just for starters.

Building Regulations Part F requires the minimum provision of 10 litres of fresh air per person per second. This needs to be given careful consideration. Mechanical ventilation has to be designed to provide a supply of fresh air in litres per second per sq mtr of floor area. Ask your fit-out specialist for guidance.

Being successful in creating a safe and healthy environment in the office comes down to a mix of following the right directives and regulations, asking staff what they need and want, getting the right design, temperature and air quality, and having programmes in place to deal with stress. The benefits of having happy and healthy workers are increased productivity and reduced rates of sickness absence.

Modern health and safety law in the UK is goal setting rather than prescriptive. The responsibility is on you the employer to apply broad legal principles to suit your particular organisation, rather than following fixed rules which may not be appropriate to your circumstances. Just answer the question: "how do I know I've done enough to comply with the law?" Answers will probably involve the use of the word "reasonable".

Jargon Buster

DSE	Display Screen Equipment
HSW Act 1974	Cornerstone of health and safety legislation – it's an "enabling" Act under which detailed regulations on particular work-related risks are made

37 HOW TO REDUCE STRESS AT WORK

First Principles

- Stress is the second-biggest cause of work-related illness after back-related issues
- Key strategies must be implemented by senior management
- Communicate that stress-related problems are not a sign of weakness

According to the HSE, stress at work may lead to high staff turnover, an increase in sickness absence, reduced work performance, poor time keeping and more customer complaints. Stress is the second-biggest cause of work-related illness in the UK after back-related issues, and costs employers some £400 million per year, while the wider cost to society is reckoned to be £4 billion a year.

You can make jobs more interesting, and ensure they do not make unreasonable demands – are long hours and taking work home considered normal? You could provide an awareness programme with information on the existence, manifestation and management of stress. You could boost individuals' feelings of competence through personal development planning, by improving the physical environment and by ensuring heat, light, ventilation, water, etc are available. Your fit-out specialist should be able to help here, and can for example advise you on the best form of seating to deploy to avoid stress and tension. Provision of a "break-out" zone where staff can relax is often recommended.

Develop a supporting culture and improve your organisation's coping techniques. Ensure you are accessible to all staff to discuss problems/anxieties. Devise effective induction and introduction programmes for new staff. Encourage staff to talk about their feelings and effects of stress. Encourage and recognise supportive behaviour of others. Develop cooperative as opposed to adversarial management styles. Engender team spirit. Encourage group problem solving to discuss perceived causes of stress.

Do communicate to your staff that stress-related problems are not a sign of weakness. While maintaining this culture you should not lose sight of the fact that stress can affect management too. It is recommended that private and regular assessment is available.

Dealing with and preventing exposure to stress in the workplace before it affects your employee will cost you far less than having to manage their rehabilitation and return to work. In addition if it can be proved that you as an organisation have failed your duty to take reasonable care of your employee you could end up on the "wrong side of the law".

Jargon Buster

HSE	Health and Safety Executive
Stress	"The adverse reaction people have to excessive pressure or other types of demand placed on them" (HSE definition)

38 OPEN PLAN OR CELLULAR OFFICES?

First Principles

- One person's communication may be another's disturbance
- Open-plan offices are more space efficient than cellular alternatives
- Glass partitions need not be see-through
- Mass is the only acoustic insulator

Consideration of your operational business needs will determine the balance between open-plan and cellular environments, as the situation of choosing one environment over another is not straightforward.

First, you should carefully consider the job roles within your organisation and decide whether they are best carried out in an open-plan or cellular environment. Cellular offices are often associated with status, so getting the correct balance is vital.

Open-plan environments tend to promote team working and communications, and are often space and cost efficient. However, open-plan environments can be distractive and this can be counterproductive if not properly planned as can be seen in *Chapter 39*.

Sound deadening products such as partitions, glazing, suspended ceilings and flooring can help in reducing noise and provide an optimum environment in which you and your staff can operate. Putting up glass partitions does not mean staff have to see each other through them – there are various translucent and shaded film work options.

It is worth paying particular attention to ceiling finishes, which can significantly affect the acoustics in a busy office or call centre. Equally, it should be noted that mass is the only true acoustic insulator. See *Chapter 39*.

Jargon Buster

Manifestation	The treatment of glass to make it visible
Burolandschaft	The original name for open-plan (German origin)
White noise	A sound that contains every frequency within the range of human hearing (generally from 20 hertz to 20 kilohertz) in equal amounts

39 ACOUSTICS IN THE OFFICE

First Principles

- Most open-plan offices suffer from the distraction of noise
- Five office elements as below need to be addressed to control noise
- There is potential to regain productivity and privacy

For all their advantages, most open-plan offices still suffer from the distraction of noise. Ambient noise levels have been rising along with the population densities of open-plan spaces to the extent that noise intrusion has begun to impact on privacy and productivity. Informed advice from noise experts is that to solve the problems, there are five systems which need to be addressed: furniture; ceilings; walls and windows; floors; and noise-masking systems. We address these points briefly:

Furniture – modular screens create workplaces where acoustic privacy is achieved (in certain cases there will be advantages over partitions); moveable screens offer immediate sound screening properties; acoustic foam linings can be fitted to seating; and sound absorption materials can be applied to storage systems.

Ceilings – sound that travels over screened areas in your open-plan environment is most commonly reflected off ceilings, so there are suspended ceilings with special sound absorption qualities engineered in; another method involves the use of overhead baffles, while another utilises suspended panels.

Walls and windows – sound-absorbing wall panels work well with absorptive ceiling systems; wall-mounted acoustic foam-lined panels can feature as wall art; blinds can be made from low-emission fabrics (windows will be double or triple glazed) which absorb reflected sound off window surfaces; and room dividers can have sound-absorption properties while having artistic appearances.

Floors – represent the largest continuous surface in any office, making significant

contributions to unwanted noise. Acoustic absorption is typically provided through state-of-the-art carpet with a special backing (that is superior to any alternatives).

Noise masking systems – applicable to certain environments, this system artificially introduces a low level of noise across a broad band of frequencies which is played by speakers in the ceiling void; ambient noise levels are increased (unobtrusively) in a noise-sensitive room, acting to mask noise from other sources. Noise is a distraction only if specific sounds (speech) are distinguishable against the background level of sound.

Your open-plan environment will require a balance of productivity and privacy, and your design and fit-out specialist should be able to help with practical advice and solutions.

Sound is measured in terms of the frequency of the wave expressed in hertz (Hz) and the wavelength and pressure level expressed in decibels (dB). A whisper would normally register about 20 dB, a normal conversation would be 40-50 dB and a night club about 100 dB. The threshold for pain is 120 dB.

Acoustics are not governed by Part E of the Building Control regulation (resistancy to the passage of sound) which means any available guides are not mandatory. It pays to take good advice if privacy and good working conditions are a prerequisite.

Jargon Buster

dB	Decibel – the measure of sound; a 4 dB increase to sound insulation properties will double its performance; an increase of 10 dB is often considered to be a doubling of loudness
Acoustics	The interdisciplinary science dealing with the study of sound
SNR	Signal-to-noise ratio
STI	Speech Transmission Index

40 PARTITIONING SYSTEMS AND MOVEABLE WALLS

First Principles

- Workplaces today are generally open-plan arenas
- Using partitions and moveable walls means the workspace can be reconfigured at short notice
- Team spaces can be quickly set up, and equally fast taken down

Modern workplaces are typically open-plan areas. Corridors of private offices have mainly been swept away, apart from some senior executives offices. What are available for open-plan spaces today are screens, partitions, suspended and wall-mounted panels, and moveable walls. Such systems can be used to tackle acoustics issues in the office, see *Chapter 39*.

Screens and non-fixed partitions are typically capable of being moved by hand into required spaces to create work areas. De-mountable partitions and wall-mounted panels are more difficult to move but can be moved relatively easily by your fit-out specialist. Moveable walls are so constructed to allow you to subdivide a larger room quickly at short notice, while retaining good acoustic values. For example, a large board room or training room could be subdivided into two small meeting rooms. The ability to reconfigure the workplace at short notice, without small-scale demolition involved, is highly desirable and most useful.

40

When looking for a partitioning system, your fit-out specialist will help you to consider the following key factors: fire resistance; compatibility with other structural elements, such as raised floors and suspended ceilings; load-bearing capacity – you might want to put up shelves on some partitions, for example; ease of relocation; and acoustic properties.

Different colours and finishes can also be used on partitions and screens to mark out teams and denote departments. In sum, team spaces can be quickly created, and equally quickly taken down.

One of the most commonly overlooked aspects is how the partitioning integrates with its surrounding materials. Many demountable partitioning systems only extend to the underside of a suspended ceiling and careful consideration needs to be given to the acoustic value of the ceilings, floors, air conditioning ductwork and lighting system. It is useless to specify a partitioning system with excellent acoustic properties if the noise or conversations are heard in adjacent rooms or areas via the poorly fitted or designed ceiling!

Glass partitions are very popular since they allow light to be transferred but careful consideration needs to be given to ensure that visual privacy is maintained. The use of filmwork manifestation can be used to provide obscuration to varying degrees to overcome this problem.

Jargon Buster

Planning grid	A means of imposing a notional structure to help plan the occupants into the floor space
Carrels	Or study booths – these are hot desks with some form of screening to provide enclosure for concentrated work in open space; flexible alternative to permanent enclosures

41 ALTERNATIVE WORKING ENVIRONMENTS - HOT DESKING AND HOME WORKING

First Principles

- Not all work needs to be done at a desk
- IT tends to have taken over administrative roles
- Hot desks, break-out areas and chill zones are space efficient
- Open-plan workers often need to break out into quieter areas
- A variety of working environments can act as meeting rooms
- Some people will always need a desk every day, while many will not

Offices today typically offer a range of environments including traditional workstations, hot desks, meeting rooms, break-out areas and chillout zones.

In current competitive markets, space is at a premium. Consequently, over recent years, many organisations have implemented alternative desking solutions and space-efficient ways of working, driving down office accommodation costs and increasing productivity. Indeed where a range of working environments has replaced a desk-only solution, research has reported improved use of space of between 10% and 35%. See *Chapter 43*.

In some offices you will find that desks are only occupied for 15% of the working day, so it is no surprise that organisations will look to home working to improve efficiency. That said, however, you will need to ensure the same attention is paid to home workers' Health & Safety issues as those in the office. But you will also need to recognise that home working does not suit everyone.

41

Also, many workers now have the right to flexible working. You should also be aware that flexible working practices are different from flexitime. There may be part-time workers and job sharers in the employee mix. All will need workspace at some time.

Face-to-face communication remains the best method of communication and informal areas in an office can often provide the perfect environment for impromptu meetings or for meeting customers over a cup of coffee. Hence break-out areas and chillout zones have become increasingly popular with the advent of space-efficient open-plan office areas. This all makes for interesting challenges for you and your fit-out specialist.

Jargon Buster

Hot desk	A workstation not assigned to an individual worker
Break-out area	An environment providing an informal meeting or rest area within the office
Chillout zone	A quiet lounge area where staff can relax, drink and socialise

42 THE PSYCHOLOGY OF COLOUR

First Principles

- Colour tends to have an effect on the behaviour of people
- Certain colours can be stimulating
- Other colours are more restful
- Colour-blind people are also affected in the same way

Colour is known to have an effect on morale and influence the level of activity of people. The selection of colours is therefore a key decision.

Busy meeting rooms used for brainstorming sessions might be painted red, yellow or orange, which are all very energising colours. However, you should be aware that their over-use can lead to irrational and unpredictable behavior!

Quiet rooms for contemplation and problem solving can be finished in blue or purple, which are both colours associated with serenity and truth – but too much of these colours can have a very cold effect.

White and grey are often used in office environments as they are neutral, but the effect can be bland if they are over-used.

Green is a popular colour reflecting the physical creation and is often used to promote an image of the value of the environment.

Are black and white colours? This is a question which has long been disputed. Technically white is the absence of colour and black is achieved by the mixing of primary colours together. White is often used to reflect purity and a minimalist culture whilst black can be used to create a mood of solidity.

Blue is often used by banks and financial institutions and is often said to reflect security, trust and reliability.

Your design team should provide you with mood boards and samples of all the finishes that are proposed for your new interior. You should make sure that these are presented to you in the proportions that they will be seen in your new offices, otherwise a completely false impression might be given.

Do not forget that colour is a very emotive and subjective subject. Not everyone will agree with your colour choices.

Jargon Buster

Mood board	A collection of images that reflect the mood of the interior design
Sample board	A display of the fabrics and finishes that will be used in the interior
Colour swatch	A demonstration of the colours available in a particular finish. Note that printed colours may not be exactly the same as the finished article

43 THE AGILE OFFICE

First Principles

- Agile Workplaces provide flexible solutions for today's highly mobile workforce
- Agile Workplaces tend to reduce dilapidations liability due to a reduced "built" environment
- 90% of staff who work in Agile Workplaces prefer it to the traditional office
- Statistics tell us that 45% of workplaces are underutilised

In recent years the advent of mobile technology has changed the way we worked for ever. Instead of being fixed to a PC on a desk, staff could now roam, and hence the word the "virtual office" was coined.

In the increasingly mobile and globally distributed workforce with pressures being placed on FM's to reduce costs, improve mobility and reduce carbon footprints many organisations are reviewing their property strategy. They no longer want to pay for vast swathes of floor space which support unused desks or large meeting rooms designed for 12 persons that on average are used by 2 or 3.

The "one size fits all" standardisation is history. Today's organisations need to scrutinise their work habits and provide efficient solutions for their user groups.

Most surveys reveal startling statistics; many companies find that their real estate is only occupied effectively for 20-30% of the time. Until they see the data they hardly realise how much their employees' work habits have changed.

43

Agile Working recognises that different activities require different environments and that throughout a working day employees undertake tasks that require different levels of collaboration and concentration. Rather than achieve everything from their own individual workstation or desk, the agile workplace empowers individuals to choose their setting to suit their activity. Agile working empowers staff and saves space, ensuring that everyone in the office space works hard! Welcome to the Agile Office.

Your fit-out specialist will be able to provide specialist advice on this important workplace revolution and will probably begin a workplace assessment to evaluate how efficiently you are using your office space. Research from the assessment will allow experienced designers to use the results to design a workspace which is flexible, cost effective and which allows the staff to achieve the best results for your

Jargon Buster

Discovery Workshops	A group discussion of selected employees to discuss issues in the workplace
Follow-me Printing	Solves the problem of finding the closest printer and finds or prioritises the printer based on location
TOIL	Time Off In Lieu; allows flexible working hours that can be varied across days by paying back extra hours worked on one day with time off on other days

44 FENG SHUI

First Principles

- Feng Shui is used by some people as a guiding principle in interior design
- Its roots are in ancient China (stretching back 3,500+ years)
- While there are millions of Chinese, and many others globally, who believe in Feng Shui, there are those who believe it is preposterous

Feng Shui (pronounced "fung shway" in English) is a set of (Chinese) principles that some practitioners believe greatly influence the wellbeing of the occupants of a room or building. It is fundamentally about the alignment of a building or elements of a building to coincide with natural forces such as space, the weather, the stars and geo-magnetism.

It is said that the correct placement and arrangement of spaces and components within a building can achieve harmony with the environment.

A building that is designed and planned in accordance with Feng Shui is believed to enhance the health, wealth and personal relationships of the occupants.

You may wish to discuss Feng Shui with your fit-out partner as some interior designers work within its compass to create buildings with good "Qi" or flow of energy. The goal of Feng Shui as practiced today is to locate the human built environment on spots with good "Qi".

44

One tip is: "The arrangement of tables and chairs should be in a harmonious position so that Qi is able to flow smoothly" while another is "to always sit with a solid wall behind your back to ensure that you have support in your life, never sit with a window behind you."

Some believe that Feng Shui can positively influence the morale of employees in the workspace, especially if they have been introduced to its principles during the design and fit-out process.

There are of course those who choose not to believe in the principles, but believe it is preposterous.

Jargon Buster

Qi	Flow of energy (pronounced "chee")
School	A technique of Feng Shui

45 ERGONOMICS

First Principles

- Ergonomics deals with the "fit" between people and their work
- Ergonomics draws on many disciplines in its study of humans and their environments
- The field of ergonomics has been called one of the top 10 emerging practice areas
- Workplaces take either the reactive or proactive approach when applying ergonomics practices

Ergonomics deals with the "fit" between people and their work. It takes account of the workers' capabilities and limitations in seeking to ensure that tasks, equipment, information and the environment suit each worker.

To assess the fit between a person and their work, ergonomists consider the job being done and the demands on the worker, the equipment used (its shape, size and how appropriate it is for the task), and the information used (how it is presented, accessed, and changed). Ergonomics draws on many disciplines in its study of humans and their environments, including biomechanics, anthropometry, mechanical engineering, industrial engineering, industrial design, kinesiology, physiology and psychology. Indeed, the field of ergonomics has been given the accolade of one of the top 10 emerging practice areas.

Workplaces may adopt the reactive or proactive approach when applying ergonomics practices. Reactive ergonomics is when something needs to be fixed, and corrective action is taken. Proactive ergonomics is the process of seeking areas that could be improved and fixing the issues before they become a problem. Such problems may be fixed through equipment, task or environmental design – the first changes the physical devices people use; the second changes what people do with the equipment; and the third changes the environment in which people work, but not the physical equipment they use.

Your design and fit-out specialist will be able to discuss any questions you may have on ergonomics and its application to your workplace.

Employers should make greater use of ergonomic guidelines when specifying furniture to avoid purchasing unsuitable furniture. An international standard that can help is ISO9241-5 "workstation and postural requirements".

There is a strong argument that correct or best practice ergonomics make people more productive and certainly help to reduce absenteeism and ill-health. Not only will people be more productive but also happier and that has to be good for your business! See also *Chapters 51 and 52*.

Jargon Buster

Anthropometry	Measurement of the individual for the purposes of understanding human physical variation
Kinesiology	The science of human movement; derived from the Greek words kinesis (movement) and kinein (to move), also known as human kinetics

46 RECEPTION AREAS – FIRST IMPRESSIONS ARE VITAL

First Principles

- The reception area is where visitors will form their first opinion of your organisation, albeit subconsciously
- Your reception area should convey your organisation's image and express your ethos and aspirations simultaneously
- Ask your design and fit-out specialist for examples of their work

Just as car parks are the first thing most visitors will see of your organisation, the reception area is where they will get their first human contact and where they will form an opinion of your organisation, albeit subconsciously. Those first few seconds are vital to make a positive impression. Your reception area should convey your organisation's image and express your ethos and aspirations simultaneously.

Your reception area also has to be practical of course, controlling access, enabling good flows of people and accepting deliveries, all while demonstrating your organisation's efficiency. In sum, your reception area design has to be a combination of visual attraction and practical efficiency, satisfying both your own staff and visitors.

Ask your design and fit-out specialist to show you examples of what they have achieved for other clients. Various elements like colour, branding, layout, and materials can make positive statements about your organisation.

If you and your design and fit-out specialist thoroughly plan each detail of your reception space, the right messages will be conveyed to your visitors and staff.

Do look at your reception area from the viewpoint of security, visitors, deliveries, staff and the people who work on the reception desk. Avoid designs that put visitors out of sight of the receptionist. Be aware that heating and cooling in the reception area can prove a problem when external air circulating through the entrance doors alters the internal temperature.

Large expanses of glass in the reception area can be a security risk and a source of heat loss, and sometimes heat gain, which makes it uncomfortable for those who work on the reception desk and waiting visitors. Ask your design and fit-out specialist for advice.

Please don't forget that whilst you might spend a small fortune on the best design for the reception area it is so important that the receptionist greets visitors with a friendly face and a warm welcome. First impressions are vital!

Jargon Buster

Façade engineering	Expert skills applied to designing the external parts of a building, with a focus on the main entrance and reception area
Iris recognition	A method of biometric authentication utilizing pattern recognition to provide representations of the iris that yield unambiguous positive identification of a person

47 BRANDING AND SIGNAGE

First Principles

- If your office reflects your brand, your staff will identify with it
- Visitors to your offices will judge your business by what they see
- First impressions are lasting
- You will only get ONE chance to make a first impression

An office relocation or refurbishment will often provide an opportunity to enhance and re-brand an organisation. Indeed it is often for this reason that a refurbishment takes place. It is therefore vital that the brand is carefully incorporated into the brief to enable the designers to provide a coherent interior, reflecting your image precisely.

If your overall budget for branding is limited, we suggest that the monies are focused in "customer facing areas" in order to have maximum impact. To allocate the budget too thinly will reduce the overall impression, to the point where the impact of your brand becomes lost.

Glass is a fantastic surface on which to project your branding. Unlike etching, applied filmwork which reflects your corporate brand can be changed or removed very easily. Alternatively painted surfaces, such as columns, can be used very effectively if coloured to reflect your corporate identity. It is important to ensure this is not over-stated. Subtle use of corporate colours, however, can enhance brand awareness.

Jargon Buster

Brand values	The attributes of your company that add together to form a brand
Front of house	The areas of your company seen by your customers
Logo	Your company's badge
Logotype	The way in which your company name is graphically represented

48 POST ROOM – A KEY HUB OF THE OPERATION

First Principles

- The mailroom is a vital hub of most organisations
- Some mailrooms are being outsourced
- The next step up from running a mailroom operation is a move toward integrated document management

The mailroom is a vital hub of many organisations, and needs to be as well planned and efficient as possible. It is not just about measuring the space that has been allocated and deciding what will fit where. Your fit-out specialist will be able to assist you in an holistic appraisal of your mailroom systems, which will cover every aspect of the operation.

This will include the systems required, the staff needs, health and safety issues, and aspects such as security, office storage, recycling and courier services.

In some organisations, mailroom functions are being outsourced. Mailrooms in large organisations are concerned with the receipt, opening, logging and distribution of all inbound and outgoing mail, which is something that can become an administrative headache. The outsourcing solutions on offer typically cover the implementation of a virtual mailroom function on or off-site. The inbound mail can be fully managed and scanned, logged and distributed via email or internet document access systems to individual desktops, within/against service level agreements.

These services reduce staff costs as well as capital and management costs in implementing a document management solution. Collating and photocopying can take place here. Workflows through the post room can be planned, with specific functions being allocated, such as lay out staff, print specialists and collating staff.

It is still early days, but the next generation for running a mailroom operation is a move in the direction of integrated document management, where all documents – unstructured and structured – are in the organisation's system. It is the large organisations who are tending to lead the way. Your fit-out specialist will be able to discuss your organisation's needs in the years ahead and the relevant strategies to consider.

Jargon Buster

Document management system	A computer system or set of programs used to track and store documents and/or images of paper documents; there is some overlap with the concepts of content management systems
Unstructured data	Data that does not have a data model or has one that is not easily usable by a computer program (handwritten notes, speech, brochures, etc)
Structured data	Data stored in fielded form in databases or annotated in documents

49 EVALUATE YOUR STORAGE PROVISION

First Principles

- Do not allow storage to accumulate unnecessarily
- Provide good, accessible archiving
- Minimise personal storage
- Provide the best scanning and data storage you can afford
- Costs of off-site storage typically work out at 33% of the costs of on-site storage

Obviously, documents which need to be kept should be stored in the cheapest way possible. Storage can consume valuable amounts of office space and much of it will often be unnecessary. Archiving systems that work well – whether physical or electronics based – allow your staff to strip out much of the office-based storage.

Most financial records need to be kept for around seven years at least, in case of HMRC inspection. Many companies have a retention policy as to how long other classes of record are kept. When disposing of old documents, be aware of the risks of data theft. Professional record disposal companies make light work of bulk shredding of obsolete paper records or CDs.

Implementing a new filing system will be easier if it is compatible with your existing filing solution. Many storage cabinets can double up as screens or dividers between people or departments. Such an arrangement can be utilised to great advantage if their positions are planned properly – your design and fit-out specialist can offer sound advice here. Do note that if the arrangement is wrongly set up, the result could completely ruin an otherwise fantastic looking interior.

The method by which staff access the storage can also have an impact. Tambour or retractable doors save space when compared with rigid hinged doors.

Storage systems such as storage walls can be extremely efficient but do remember that a compact filing system will be heavy. So check that your office floor loadings are adequate.

Documents or other filed material that are unlikely to be needed regularly should be transferred to a basement or off-site storage for whatever length of time is decreed by relevant laws. Typically, costs of off-site storage work out at some 33% of the costs of on-site storage.

Jargon Buster

Storage wall	A filing system using floor-to-ceiling cabinets
Tambour	A door made in slats that can curve or roll up when opened
Floor loading	The amount of weight a floor can take expressed in kilonewton per sq mtr

50 CONSIDER YOUR FURNITURE OPTIONS

First Principles

- Have sample workstations built and test them rigorously
- Do not opt for the cheapest, rather consider the cost of ownership over the useful life of the product
- Remember that workstations must comply with regulations
- Consider retaining your old furniture and adapting it
- Consider bespoke furniture for high profile areas

In most cases, the furniture you select for your office will influence its appearance and functionality more than any other element. Your furniture needs to integrate with your IT requirements and also has implications on health and safety issues. Thought should also be given to ergonomics including the use of laptops, which have proven notoriously difficult to set up in accordance with workplace regulations.

Your fit-out specialist should provide advice from his own in-house specialist on the features and benefits of current furniture ranges – they may have their own showroom, where you can view products and evaluate everything first hand.

Be wary of the cheapest and most flashy-looking products as they may not necessarily provide long-term value for money. You should seek clarification of supplier status, continuity of supply, and guarantees.

Many organisations are selecting furniture based upon the sustainability and recyclability of the products. This includes not only the production of the furniture itself but the environmental impact that stems from the treatment of the raw material used in the manufacture. Your fit-out specialist will be able to advise which manufacturers are best qualified and certified to provide options.

Have you considered bespoke – made to order – furniture, which would meet your precise needs and deliver exactly what your organisation wants? This could be for front of house, boardroom, reception and executive areas.

Or, it could be appropriate for you to consider furniture lease options, which have the advantage of offering the necessary project finance streams.

Other factors to consider include re-configurability of the product range and its simplicity of use in a cluster or stand-alone situation. Because your business will change, develop and evolve, you may find you need furniture systems that can be readily and easily reconfigured to help your organisation adapt to fresh market and business demands.

Jargon Buster

Workstation	The combination of desk, chair and storage
Demountability	The ability to be dismantled and reassembled easily
Cluster	A group of desks that are configured together
Churn	The number of people who relocate within a workspace within a year divided by the total number of occupants, times 100

51 THE OFFICE CHAIR

First Principles

- Never buy an office chair until you have trialed it
- Check the detail of the manufacturer's warranty and exclusions!
- Beware of cheap imitations of design classics

The office chair, known variously in the industry as a "task chair" or "work chair", is something we often take for granted. Yet the market for this ubiquitous product is worth £2 billion in the USA alone, where it is manufactured by more than 100 manufacturing companies, all making sure the mechanical pads we perch on are as high tech as the digital ones we type on! Seriously minded ergonomists have been improving and reinventing the office chair with each generation since the 1960s. As a result, often the chairs of today look more like fitness equipment than furniture, and comes with control panels, levers, instruction manuals and even special advisors so explain how to use them!

Office chairs originated in America in the mid-1800s, when the American westward railroad expansion created an unprecedented number of clerical and management positions and an urgent need for office seating that would promote productivity by discouraging clerks from leaving their desks.

Born from the industrial revolution, task chairs didn't change very much until the dawn of the computer heralded the office revolution. The 1950s and 1960s were the last time you could expect to find an office chair that looked lovely.

51

The ultimate expression of the office chair is arguably the 1994 Aeron chair, which allows a seated person to recline and sink backwards from the ankles. The other main design uses the forces applied to the backrest to hoist the seat forwards and upwards, opening the angle between the torso and legs. This was introduced by the 1991 Picto chair, but has since evolved through several other designs.

Much like automotive design, the shape of office seating is determined by a small, elite group of manufacturers and specialists. Recently, however, others have argued the case for a new approach. As the workplace changes dramatically to allow more flexible and informal environments in which workers are no longer so shackled to their workstations, we might see some considerable new shifts in the market in the near future.

Jargon Buster

Aeron   An ergonomic chair design by Bill Stumfp of Herman Miller with a mesh support system produced in 1994, it changed office seating forever

Sychro mechanism An office chair mechanism that allows the backrest to tilt and move relative to the seat in a fixed ratio (usually 1:2 or 1:3). This helps to open the pelvis to stimulate blood circulation in the lower back

Kneeling chair A chair designed to allow you to kneel at the desk and which is claimed to improve posture and movement

52 WHY SIT/STAND DESKS?

First Principles

- Sit/stand desks reduce the risk of back strain
- They are a legal requirement in some European countries
- They can be expensive

Backache, obesity, Type 2 diabetes – the outlook isn't all that healthy for those who spend long hours sitting down. Which is why flexible sit-or-stand desks are starting to make an impact on the market.

There is clear evidence that prolonged, unbroken sitting time is not only related to musculoskeletal aches and pains but also to peoples' risk of obesity and Type 2 diabetes. Our message is therefore; "Sit less, move more." Stern words indeed, but what can the Office or Facilities Manager do about it? Having furniture that you can both sit and stand at will reduce the time spent sitting and this has definite health benefits. Fortunately there are many options out there that tick this sit/stand box. Experts and ergonomists agree that the human body is simply not designed to sit all day. Enlightened businesses are providing a greater choice in not only where you work, but how you work. See *Chapter 43*.

52

According to a leading expert, 55,000 hours of our professional lives are spent in a sitting position so it's little wonder that back problems are the most common medical complaint among office workers and the health problem that leads to the most time off – sufferers take an average of 22 days off per year. To combat this, furniture manufacturers have produced the T-Lift desk. This sit/stand model encourages users to shift positions to "Keep the body in motion and keep thoughts flowing", according to its makers.

Indeed, whilst a break-out space or touchdown area may provide a change of scene, merely standing up at your desk may sometimes provide just as much inspiration. And it may provide less of a barrier for interacting with others than being sat down too. It is a fact that meetings conducted standing up can be quicker and often more efficient.

Certain technical requirements need to be taken into consideration, such as cable management and the location of telephone and power point. Behavioural training to adjust to this new approach may also help. There are various mechanisms for adjusting the height of a sit/stand workstation including manual, crank operation and electrical. Your choice will be largely influenced by your budget!

This is also about changing hearts and minds. The message needs to get out about the deleterious effects of prolonged sitting. People definitely need to change their behaviour. A new office is a great way to review you furniture options and this may appeal to the more adventurous!

Jargon Buster

Desk Raisers	Wooden block that can be fitted under the feet of desks to raise the height of the workstation
Posture	Usually means the intentionally or habitually assumed position

53 TEA, COFFEE, WATER AND FOOD - HOW TO KEEP THE STAFF ON-SITE

First Principles

- A healthy diet leads to a healthy workforce, meaning reduced absenteeism
- While not everyone wants to eat at work, everyone does need water
- Key to drinking and eating plans is to get your staff into a mood where they will not only want to come into work, but enjoy it as well

Long off-site lunch breaks and the stress caused by having to hurry back to work are potential pitfalls of not being able to offer your staff quality refreshments and food. Not being able to control your staff's diet could prove an issue as a healthy diet leads to a healthy workforce, meaning reduced absenteeism. Having no restaurant facilities mean you could be less likely to attract staff due to a lack of quality food at subsidised prices – and there will be nowhere to provide customer hospitality.

You could offer free breakfasts to attract staff on-site out of peak travel times, and make the workforce more productive. Whether you opt to install vending machines for hot/cold drinks in addition to self-made facilities and a cafeteria-style service could well be determined through a staff survey, subject to executive approval of course.

While not everyone will want to eat at work, everyone should have access to a quality water supply. Most workers tend not to drink enough water, according to research, and interestingly the amount staff drink is directly related to where the

water cooler is located. You should ensure your staff have access to a water cooler which is integrated into the workplace design. Your design and fit-out specialist can give guidance on these points.

Key to these drinking and eating plans is the intention to get your staff into a mood where they will not only want to come to work, but enjoy it as well. In addition, any restaurant type space can be used for impromptu meetings and break-out sessions.

The growth of café culture means that today's employees are far more discerning in their demands for a quality beverage experience.

Good coffee in the workplace is highly sought after by employees and coffee machines that deliver quality tastes that are closer to coffee shops are extremely popular.

As touched on in *Chapter 33*, the way to produce the optimum solution for your staff and organisation is to arrange a survey – ask your staff what they want by way of refreshment and sustenance. Some organisations have extended this service to their grounds, offering barbecues in the warmer months, as well as outside eating.

Sitting down to eat together is a good way to break down barriers, discuss problems and share gossip. Doing it in a well-designed environment is even better.

Jargon Buster

HACCP	Hazard analysis critical control point – caterers must have this written documentation in place
852/2004	Regulation applying to all food business activity from primary production through to sale to the end-user

54 WASHROOMS AND SHOWERS

First Principles

- Washrooms will reflect on the quality standards of your organisation
- Staff and visitors alike appreciate having access to clean washrooms
- Sustainable practices are increasingly being deployed

Washrooms may be accessed at any time of the working day by staff and visitors alike. Their appearance will reflect on the quality standards of your organisation. Clean and hygienic washrooms will demonstrate the regard you have for the safety of your staff and customers. Having hygienic and odour-free washrooms will improve the impression that your organisation provides to your customers. Showers are most likely to be used by staff cycling to work and those taking exercise or playing sport in lunch breaks, for example.

Washroom services companies offer many benefits, for example, regular contact with industry experts, guaranteed quality of service and access to the latest products. Going down this route, there are many financial benefits that will accrue to your organisation, for example, you will be able to cut supply, maintenance and capital costs immediately.

54

Many products are available for today's washrooms, including waterless urinals, air fresheners, dust mats, eco-friendly water management systems, grey water systems and hand dryers utilising the latest technology. Sustainable practices are increasingly being deployed.

Your staff and visitors will appreciate having access to clean washrooms, with showers as an added bonus. Your design and fit-out specialist will be able to discuss the various options suitable for your organisation, and the many regulations that cover them.

Jargon Buster

Grey water	Non-industrial wastewater produced from such domestic processes as dish washing, bathing, showering and laundry. Using grey water for toilet flushing saves paying the cost of metered water supplies
WHSWR	Workplace (Health, Safety & Welfare Regulations) 1992 contain much of relevance to washrooms, for example, water management, hand dryers, soap, paper and fragrance units

55 WHY HAVE PLANTS?

First Principles

- Review the plants and other decorative items in your offices
- Plants soak up ozone produced by office equipment and systems
- It is important to have a maintenance contract

Before a move or refit, it is a good time to consider the plants and other decorative items such as artworks in your offices. Today, having plants in your offices is concerned with impressing customers and motivating staff through having stunning displays in interesting containers.

It is well known that living plants contribute to a healthy atmosphere by absorbing carbon dioxide and the ions being emitted from display screens, photocopiers, printers, air conditioning units, ultra violet lights, and other electronic equipment. The plants soak up the ozone produced by many of these systems.

The ozone levels in offices and homes today are rated amongst the world's greatest public health risks. Indeed many people die each year from polluted indoor air, according to UN statistics. In tests in the USA, the most effective plants to counter the effects of ozone were found to be common blooms such as the spider plant, snake plant and Golden Pothos.

55

There is research which shows plants having a beneficial effect on counteracting "sick building syndrome" by absorbing negative ions in the atmosphere. Indeed the benefits are that staff in offices with plants tend to be healthier, more motivated, more productive and take fewer sick days than staff in offices without plants.

It is important to have a maintenance contract in place to ensure all the plants in your offices are kept in a healthy condition and remain aesthetically attractive.

Not all areas of offices are suitable for live plants. Where there is, for example, a lack of light, cold draughts or excessive foot traffic, consideration can be given to deploying replica and silk plants.

Jargon Buster

Sick building syndrome	A condition in which staff feel unwell without suffering from any specific illness; symptoms usually occur after spending lengthy periods inside sealed buildings
Golden Pothos	A plant also known as Devil's Ivy

56 RECYCLING AND WASTE MANAGEMENT

First Principles

- Recycling is good for the environment
- WEEE requires all electronic and electrical items to be recycled responsibly
- All construction projects over £300,000 must have a site waste management plan

Recycling is known to be good for the environment and has been warmly embraced by the national psyche. You will be aware of initiatives to recycle printer toners, cartridges, paper, plastics, cardboard, packaging and pallets. It is a good time to review your organisation's plans post fit-out.

If you are having new office furniture, your fit-out specialist may already have discussed the options open to you. Some organisations recycle chairs, desks and filing cabinets to local schools and charities. Carpets, carpet tiles, wood laminate flooring, blinds and screens can all be recycled.

The Waste Electronic and Electrical Equipment (WEEE) EU Directive requires all businesses to recycle their old IT and (tele)communications equipment, and other electronic and electrical waste responsibly. Energy-saving light bulbs have to be recycled responsibly due to the mercury they contain.

All construction projects in England which have a construction value of over £300,000 must have a site waste management plan, which provides a structure for waste delivery and disposal at all stages of the project. The plan usually identifies items such as who is responsible for resource management, the types of waste generated and how the waste will be managed. Your fit-out specialist will be able to help with this work.

Three options exist for waste disposal: reduction of waste generation; internal recycling of waste materials to provide new/different products; and/or passing the waste to a third party and making it their responsibility.

By examining what is in your waste, you can typically discover new ways to improve your internal business performance. Low costs typically devolve from responsible environmental management. Prudent housekeeping results in savings, as does investment in process design and/or research technology.

Jargon Buster

SWMP Regulations — Site Waste Management Plans Regulations 2008 are enforced by the Environment Agency and potentially both the HSE and local authorities – fixed penalty fines for not having a plan are £300, or court fines of up to £50,000 could be levied

WEEE Regulations — Applies to importers, producers, retailers and users, and to those treating or recovering WEEE, Waste Electronic and Electrical Equipment

57 ACCESS CONTROL AND SECURITY

First Principles

- Before deciding on a security strategy, perform an access risk analysis
- Access control is one option to maximise security around your offices
- ID badges need to be unique to your offices and not easily copied
- Intruder alarms are a good visible and audible deterrent
- Personal attack alarms serve to summon assistance in the event of an incident

On average business and internal criminal activity is at its highest rate with 64% of business reported to be victims of crime at a per annum cost of £2,900 for each business. It therefore is a serious consideration how to combat this crime and to provide effective deterrents.

Before deciding on your security strategy, perform an access risk analysis. Your fit-out specialist should be able to recommend some security consultants.

One of the options for seeking to maximise security around your offices is access control, while other options include CCTV, staff training and manned guarding. Access to your workplace needs to be a balance between convenience for your employees and visitors – and the denial of access to parts where people do not have a right/need to be. There has to be no blockage of escape routes in case of emergency or fire.

If it is part of your access control strategy, ID badges need to be unique to your offices and not easily copied. Contact-less electronic access control systems combine security with convenience – they enable doors to remain locked but to be automatically unlocked when a person wearing an authorised badge comes close.

57

Today's access control systems are as much a management tool as a security system. They can be used to monitor the movements and activities of personnel on the site, log hours spent in the building and indeed which rooms have been accessed. In the event of an emergency the system will enable a real time master report of precisely who is on site.

Biometric fingerprint recognition will typically be used to verify a person's identity and automatically eliminate the practice known as "ghosting" or "tail gating" where persons who hold doors open for others save them having to swipe to gain entry.

There are also voice entry, PIN pads into which numbers are keyed, contact systems such as magnetic stripe swipe systems, and technologies like biometric fingerprint recognition and iris reading systems.

Personal attack alarms are more of a deterrent – they cannot prevent aggression – but can be linked to CCTV or a means of alerting a security guard. These alarms can also be linked to a siren or flashing lights.

Asset protection is vital. Prime targets include your cash, stock, portable electronic equipment and computers. Clear security marking of your assets is a simple way to deter thieves and identify items if stolen. The need for physical security including data safes for critical data storage should be considered.

Increasingly and especially in city centres there is a need to have controlled access to company car parks. Systems can be linked to your access control system to allow selected employees to use the car park.

Jargon Buster

ID badges	Identity badges
CCTV	Closed circuit television video

58 ALARM SYSTEMS

First Principles

- Alarm systems are a worthwhile investment
- Use a reputable installer
- Consider who will monitor and maintain the system

Very few office buildings to not have security alarm systems these days and indeed most insurance companies insist upon it. Alarm systems for non-domestic insurance policies are categorised by a type – or grade – based upon the nature of the property, its contents and the profile of the likely in intruder. This starts with Grade 1 for low risk domestic to Grade 4 which usually applies to high risk properties such as banks. The majority of commercial systems are Grade 2.

Most alarms to commercial buildings are linked to the Police and/or a key holder in an approved Alarm Receiving Centre. If you want Blue response to an alarm then the system must conform to the relevant standards and usually requires more than one detector to be activated to generate police investigation. This helps to prevent "false alarms".

A recent survey showed that 35% of intruders came through a door, 26% through a window and 25% from unconventional entry points (wall or ceiling) and 14% failed entry altogether. This will give a good idea why windows and doors should be alarmed individually.

The alarm industry is heavily monitored by government agencies and you should ensure that any company installing an alarm has the appropriate membership of NACOSS which is the regulatory body. All suppliers should be able to confirm that they will install the alarm in accordance with BS4737.

Finally, make sure that wherever possible your installer conceals the cables neatly and with care for the architecture and finish of your building. There is nothing worse than cables that detract from your otherwise beautifully finished office!

Jargon Buster

BS6799	Code of practice for wireless intruder systems
Redcare	A BT product which provides a secure monitored communication service
ARC	Alarm Receiving Centre
SIA	Security Industry Authority
NACOSS	National Approval Council for Security Systems

59 LIGHTING SYSTEMS, CONTROL AND SHADING

First Principles

- Lighting accounts for 20% of total electricity consumption in the UK
- The cheapest and most natural form of lighting is daylight
- Buildings can be lit using a range of energy-efficient solutions

In recent years it has become increasingly accepted that controls for building services in general and lighting in particular are essential for achieving maximum energy performance. The reality is that it doesn't matter how efficient the lighting systems are designed to be – they will only realise full energy saving potential if controlled effectively.

One of the major breakthroughs in lighting control has been the DALI protocol which allows a high level of functionality and efficiency. However, most DALI systems will still use residual power when on standby – so selecting the latest zero-power DALI systems will provide an even greater energy saving.

The ability to dim lighting is spreading to areas where this traditionally has not been possible. The latest high-output T5 and LED lighting are now widely specified to allow a high level of controllability and can maintain 95% efficiency over 20,000 hours compared to traditional tubes which decline in efficiency by up to 35% and only last 10,000-12,000 hours.

Your fit-out specialist will be able to offer advice on these points.

Natural lighting has to be supplemented with artificial lighting, typically electric lighting. There are statutory requirements and health and safety issues relating to lighting for which your fit-out specialist should be able to provide guidance.

There is a range of energy-efficient solutions to lighting buildings today. Lighting specialists favour centralised control of all lighting in a workplace. These allow total control of each open-plan area, from a central control point and locally by PIR systems.

Automatic control interfaces with a building management system and provides energy-saving benefits, which go beyond lighting alone. Your fit-out specialist again will have guidance on these points.

For buildings with large areas of windows, which experience high levels of solar gain, there are various external and internal types of shading available, for example brise soleil. External aspects tend to be the domain of façade engineers, architects or building services engineers, but internal shading options can be addressed by your fit-out specialist.

Jargon Buster

Lux	Unit of luminance, equal to one lumen per sq mtr
LED	Light-emitting diode, aka solid-state lighting, operates with 40-60 lumen per watt output, with developments ongoing
DALI	Digital Addressable Lighting Interface
Brise soleil	Type of externally-mounted structural sunshade with slats, holes, etc to prevent sunlight from striking fully on a building
PIR	Passive infra-red sensor which detects motion and automatically turns on lights when someone is in a room

60 WORKPLACE CCTV

First Principles

- CCTV is an effective deterrent
- There are many regulations governing the use of CCTV
- Use high quality cameras if you want good definition

CCTV is an emotive subject. People in areas plagued by anti-social behaviour are quick to call for cameras, but CCTV on its own does not solve the problem: it tends just to shift it down the road. However there is no doubt that it is a very effective deterrent.

Some claim Big Brother is upon us, pointing to an estimate of 4 million CCTV cameras in the UK alone – that's 1 camera per 15 people! To curb the unbridled proliferation of CCTV, the Home Office CCTV Operational Requirement demands that organisations assess and state the purposes for each CCTV system in a policy document. In practice, CCTV system assessors routinely discover that few CCTV system users know about this requirement so you should appoint someone in your organisation to undertake this role.

Despite the number of cameras, CCTV tends to have poor eyesight. Around 80% of CCTV images are reported by the police as "not fit for purpose" (Home Office National CCTV Strategy report). The reasons for this are many. CCTV systems are complex, plus the technology is changing fast. Some equipment is old, badly positioned, or there are gaps in the management, operation or maintenance regimes.

Plus, poor presentation of film on courtroom equipment means even good quality CCTV evidence can fail to secure a conviction. Although this can easily be resolved with a video forensics facility to edit the footage for clear presentation in a court of law.

There are also issues around the security of CCTV images. Recognisable human images are as sensitive as personal information on a database. That is why these images are subject to the DPA. This means CCTV images must be held as securely as personal databases. That's particularly important now that most CCTV images are digital, so they are easily altered. There should be an audit trail that proves the tamper-proof nature of any CCTV footage that may be needed as evidence.

It is now generally accepted that 90% of CCTV systems do not fully comply with the requirements of the DPA (Source: CameraWatch). Many CCTV systems fail to comply with the DPA for minor reasons, such as adequate signage. But again, this is an area where there is widespread misunderstanding. The contact information on the signage allows people caught on camera to request a copy of their images, provided that he image has been captured on a CCTV camera operated by a business or organisation, and the request is reasonable, members of the public have a legal right to a copy of the footage.

CCTV is an excellent way to protect your premises, both internally and externally, but there are a number of issues which your fit-out specialist will be able to advise you on.

Jargon Buster

DPA Data Protection Act

Right of Subject Access Part of the DPA which allows you a legal right to request copies of your images captured on CCTV

61 DO I NEED A GENERATOR?

First Principles

- Receiving an uninterrupted power supply can no longer be taken for granted
- Access to a guaranteed source of power is mandatory for most organisations
- Today's diesel generators are reliable and robust enough to provide continuous power throughout any power outage
- For complete power protection the generators need to support an uninterruptible power supply
- What would your organisation do if it had no access to power?

The certainty of receiving uninterrupted power supplies can no longer be taken for granted. Media reports abound about supply problems, brown outs, and the need for green energy supplies. But green energy supplies alone – wind power, solar, tidal flows, biomass, waste incineration as well as combined heat and power – cannot make up the shortfalls expected in the years ahead. Increasingly, the issues of nuclear power and other non-coal-burning sources are being discussed, but it will take many years for these systems to be commissioned and fully implemented.

If your organisation has a critical element on which your business depends, for example, a server holding sales leads and key customer information, a need for constant power and light, the air conditioning, medical reasons, or any commercial reason, you will need access to a guaranteed source of power. Can your electricity supplier guarantee your supplies will be delivered at 100% rates all the time?

If your organisation needs unbroken access to key data held on a server, one solution is to utilise the services of a data centre or Internet service provider. That ensures the safety of your data, but you will still need access to power for the computers and terminals you utilise to access that data.

Looking at the market today, diesel generators are reliable and robust enough to provide continuous power throughout any power outage. However, for complete power protection, the generators need to support an uninterruptible power supply system, which in turn will constitute a key part of your business continuity system.

Only you can decide what plans you wish to deploy for your organisation and whether you will need a generator. It is a good idea to discuss this with your design and fit-out specialist, as the location of generators and ways of designing in cable runs, power sources and relevant furniture can be accommodated. Most of the systems in your offices cannot work without power.

Ask yourself – what would you do if your organisation had no power for several hours?

Jargon Buster

UPS	Uninterruptible Power Supply
Brown out	Reduction or cutback in power because of a shortage, mechanical failure or overuse by users

62 IT AND TECHNOLOGY

First Principles

- IT hardware manufacturers aim to double the power of their components every year, as do software companies
- Wireless technologies abound
- Beware the hacker – online, in-house and even on mobiles
- Although data cables can be replaced with optical fibre, power cables cannot

The IT business moves at a ferocious rate, and it is often only months before recently-installed technology becomes out-of-date (but not redundant). Few other industries would tolerate the antics of this industry, where for example "patches" have to be applied to new software after it's been bought to bring it up to par. Any system will only perform as well as its weakest link, and this is often the data cabling. Ample provision of bandwidth significantly increases the future-proofing of your IT system.

Data storage is evolving equally fast and you should provide spare data storage capacity, either via on-site servers or by using off-site data centres. Installing telephone and data lines can have notoriously lengthy lead times – ensure you have a sufficient order period prior to fixing your occupation date.

The way in which power and data are distributed will also have an impact on your design. Simple underfloor trunking systems with floor boxes are flexible and enable you to relocate power and data to suit your requirements. To help you provide for your future IT needs, we suggest you retain a qualified consultant who is conversant with current technology and what's on the technology horizon.

62

For example, there is talk of buildings in the future featuring only one IP-based backbone cable, which would carry everything – data, video, graphics, voice, TV, radio, security and control – and be accessed at will. The upcoming chapters discuss these topics in detail.

The cloud provides many business benefits such as cost savings, flexibility and so on. It also provides threats and risks that must be considered and mitigated. Security is defined as confidentiality, integrity and availability and if you choose to put your business data on the cloud you need to be sure of a highly resilient network connection. You need to find out who has access to your data and what protection there is against hackers. What would happen if they sold your data to you opposition?

Cybercrime cost the UK an estimated £27 billion last year according to the Office of Cyber Security & Information Assurance (OCSIA), so it pays to investigate and make your choices wisely!

Many organisations are resolving the situation by creating hybrid clouds that combine private and public services; sorting applications into those that can be entrusted to the public cloud and those that must be kept securely in-house.

Jargon Buster

Cloud computing	A style of computing in which dynamically scalable and often virtualised resources are provided as a service via the internet
Virtualisation	The creation of a virtual (rather than actual) version of something, such as a server, storage device, network, etc
Grommet	Rubber or plastic protection for the rough edges of a hole through which cables pass
Floor box	A box in the floor for power, data and phone outlets

63 COMMUNICATIONS, VOIP AND TELEPHONE SYSTEMS

First Principles

- VoIP is an IP telephony term for sending voice data over the Internet
- VoIP will run over any type of network
- IP telephony is a win-win situation for everybody
- More customer satisfaction and increased productivity throughout your organisation guaranteed; and you reduce costs

VoIP (Voice over IP) is an IP telephony term for a set of facilities used to manage the delivery of voice information over the Internet. VoIP involves sending voice information in digital form in discrete packets rather than by using the traditional circuit-committed protocols of the PSTN. A major plus-point of VoIP and IP telephony is that it avoids the tolls charged by ordinary telephone service. However, there are occasions when voice patterns can break up due to signal problems and network conditions. In time, such issues are expected to be overcome.

Contrary to belief, VoIP will run over any type of network – it's not just restricted to the internet. Users can access their accounts on the VoIP network by a desktop phone, wireless IP phone (similar to a mobile phone), or soft screen dial pad on a laptop/desktop computer. With this arrangement, users can move to another location of their office building (or even across the country) without having to forward their calls to a new telephone – it's all portable. Further, they can access the web from their IP phone – it's as if there is a pocket PC and mobile phone combined, specifically designed for their network.

63

Key for getting support for any move to IP convergence is convincing the decision makers that it is the right way to go. The best way? Focus on convergence as a cost-effective solution to an expensive problem.

Reasons for your organisation to switch to IP telephony include, you can: receive all the traditional telephony features plus many new features and communications applications; manage data applications and IP-based telephony and videoconferencing systems; manage everything running over your local and wide area networks; manage telephony and data networks together; and reduce costs.

Today's technology allows home workers to connect with clients as if they were in the office. They can see the office wallboard, instant chat and speak with colleagues just as they would in a normal office environment. Session initiation protocol (SIP) promises further improvement in customer support and service by combining IP telephony with media streaming for richer communication sessions with customers. This allows you to push graphics and email to customers whilst on a call.

IP telephony is theoretically a win-win situation for everyone. More flexibility and faster response times should translate into more customer satisfaction and increased productivity throughout your organisation. We suggest you discuss all these points with your fit-out specialist's IT and communications adviser.

Jargon Buster

PSTN	Public Switched Telephone Network
CTI	Computer-Telephony Integration
IP	Internet Protocol

64 CABLING – FUTURE PROOF WITH CAT 5E OR CAT 6/6A OR CAT 7

First Principles

- Cabling systems are categorised in terms of the data rates that they can sustain effectively
- Cat 6/6A offers more than double the throughput of Cat 5E
- Cat 7 is a standard that offers well over double the throughput of Cat 6 and also handles full-motion video

Cabling systems are categorised in terms of the data rates that they can sustain effectively. The specifications describe the cable material, as well as the types of connectors and junction blocks to be used in order to conform to a category.

While longer connections for Gigabit Ethernet use optical fibre, it is intended that the Cat 5E twisted-pair wiring networks most organisations already have in place will be utilised for connecting up all desktops and workstations.

The Cat 6 specification improves on Cat 5E in terms of things like balance of signals and bandwidth. According to IEEE, most new installs in the mid-part of the decade were Cat 6, which offers more than double the throughput of Cat 5E, at 250 megahertz (MHz). Cat 6 cable is a cable standard for Gigabit Ethernet and other network protocols that are backward compatible with Cat 5E. There is not much Cat 5 cable in use today.

64

Category 6A, or Augmented Category 6, is defined at frequencies up to 700 MHz which is twice that of Cat 6. It supports Cat 7 workloads but at shorter distances.

Category 7 (Cat7) and Category 7a (Cat 7a) are the newest cable standards for Ethernet and other interconnect technologies and can support full motion video with speeds up to 600 Mbps (up to 1000Mbps for Cat 7a) and Ethernet applications up to 10 Gigabits. Cat 7 and Cat 7a can be used for backbone connections between servers with a data centre and are an alternative to fibre optic cabling. Both Cat 7 and Cat 7a provide superior immunity to interference from other adjacent cabling systems reducing the effects of crosstalk and EMI.

Confused? You are not alone. Many people become bewildered with techno-speak. Any issue can be logically explained. We suggest you discuss your organisation's plans for the foreseeable future of your IT and communications strategy with your fit-out specialist's IT and communications adviser.

Jargon Buster

IEEE	Institute of Electrical and Electronic Engineers
Crosstalk	Disturbance caused by the electric or magnetic fields of one telecommunications signal affecting a signal in an adjacent circuit
Noise	Another word for electrical interference on an electronic transmission line or cable. Usually due to a lack of effective shielding

65 SURVEY THE AIR CONDITIONING

First Principles

- Air conditioning systems are technical machines and can go wrong
- Regulations call for regular inspections
- Maintenance is vital for optimum performance
- Systems tend to be expensive to repair
- This is one of the most complained-about elements in any office

Many commercial buildings have air conditioning systems. If your selected building is air conditioned, make sure you have it surveyed properly before you sign any lease. Mistakes and/or oversights can be costly and they will most likely be your responsibility once you have signed a lease.

Regular inspections are now mandatory for all air conditioning systems with a capacity of over 12 kilowatt. The systems have to be carefully maintained and managed so that they do not consume too much energy. The trigger for these inspections is the size (the effective rated output) of the system, not the type of building. Inspections are done by accredited energy assessors and include an assessment of efficiency, review of sizing, and advice on improvements or replacements and alternative solutions.

Air conditioning systems vary in complexity and effectiveness. The most cost-effective and common is the fan-coil system, where fans blow air over the heat exchangers, providing heating or cooling.

VAV systems can be more complex to install and adapt. They deliver air from central heat exchangers. They are usually quieter than other systems and can often give more control.

65

Heat recovery captures waste heat energy and reuses it by returning it to its source system or process, which may include heating space and water. Heat recovery may give you substantial long-term energy savings. Often the need to generate heat initially is reduced, providing further energy and cost savings for you.

It is often difficult to provide a balanced and appropriate air conditioning system and only a competent mechanical and electrical consultant should be advising you on a solution. In a multi-tenanted building, your landlord's maintenance contractor may be required to carry out works on the air conditioning so as not to disrupt systems in adjacent demises – do remember to check your lease, as indicated earlier.

Time has now run out for existing chillers using R22 refrigerant, with the production halted by 2010. Some air-conditioning chillers can be adapted to run on other refrigerants but this may not be efficient long term.

The Carbon Reduction Commitment, now called the "CRC Energy Efficiency Scheme", allows organisations that purchase qualifying equipment to reduce their allowances based upon the carbon emissions. The financial incentives for reducing energy are thus greater than ever. See *Chapter 27*.

Jargon Buster

ACSEA	Air Conditioning System Energy Assessor
Comfort cooling	Cooling only from units above the ceiling or around the walls
VAV air conditioning	Variable air volume changes the amount of air delivered
Chill "Beams"	A form of cooling in offices often used where there is a low floor to ceiling height and electrical interference

66 AUDIO VISUAL AND VIDEO CONFERENCING

First Principles

- Get good advice from an AV specifier
- Obsolescence is not far away. Design AV and VC as part of an overall room package
- Decide who is going to provide training and technical support

"A picture paints a thousand words" – states the aphorism.

Visual presentation aids can be an essential part of giving speeches, presenting ideas and winning sales pitches. When used correctly in business they can drive home key points and enhance persuasive speaking.

According to the US Government office of Training and Education "retention of information three days after a meeting or other event is six times greater when information is presented by visual and oral means than when the information is presented by the spoken word alone". The combination of sight and sound along with written hand-outs is a necessary component of information retention and can be found in every successful training organisation.

Since communication is key to modern business it is no surprise that increasingly sophisticated AV aids are being promoted in meeting rooms, auditoriums, video conferencing suites and commercial meeting space.

Before rushing out to purchase the latest technological gadgets it is essential to examine what the actual users require both now and in the long term. This will help to form a brief that can be developed in to a deliverable solution by a technology specialist.

Key factors to consider in this process are ease of use, flexibility, available support, hidden costs and the need for staff training.

AV equipment tends to be expensive especially if it utilises "cutting edge" technology and it is worth consulting a specialist who can not only specify the right equipment but also advise on the best installation procedures. There is nothing so frustrating as installing a large plasma screen only to find that direct sunlight from a nearby window causes reflection on the screen.

Many companies are considering carefully the business case for video conferencing to reduce travel costs, reduce carbon emissions and save time. There are also new ways to use video to do business. At the high end, multi-screen tele-presence systems provide superb face-to-face experience. In the middle, a single broadband supply with a single screen can be good for team meetings. At the entry level desktop and mobile conferencing is feasible thanks to better cameras built into laptops and increasingly smart phones and tablet devises. These days you can dial-in with Google Talk, Skype and have video on your screen whilst talking.

Jargon Buster

AR	"Augmented reality" is a term for a live direct or indirect view of a physical real-world environment of which elements are augmented by virtual computer generated images
OLED	"Organic light emitting devices" are area solid state devices composed of thin films of organic molecules that create light through the amplification of electricity
Web 2.0	The buzz word for a web application designed to facilitate collaboration and interaction by allowing users to contribute to a site's content
VC	Video Conferencing

67 HUMIDITY AND INDOOR AIR QUALITY

First Principles

- Good air quality inside buildings ensures health and well-being, plus maximum productivity
- Optimum levels of humidity are necessary for worker efficiency and staff health and comfort
- Air conditioning can produce low humidity levels

For staff health and comfort, the optimum adequate level of humidity is considered to be about 50% Relative Humidity (RH) and not less than 40%. HSE recommends for worker efficiency that humidity is maintained in the range 40-70% RH (warm offices should be at the lower end of the range) while British Standard 29241 recommends 40-60% RH for office terminals.

You have a duty of care to comply with this legislation. You are also under an obligation to identify symptoms resulting from low humidity in your staff – headaches, dry eyes, dry throats, dry skin, cold and flu-type conditions, and tiredness and lethargy. Static electricity is a conclusive indicator the humidity in your workspace is too low. Low humidity is caused through the volumes of electronic equipment around us – photocopiers, computers, display terminals and dust. The remedy is to install humidifiers, but do seek professional advice. Your fit-out specialist should be able to help you.

67

It is vital that air quality inside buildings is maintained to ensure health and well-being, plus maximum productivity in the workplace. Research has shown most of us spend up to 90% of our time inside a building. Poor air causes or exacerbates asthma, eye irritations and nausea, for example. Oddly, there is no legislation on this area in the UK, nor are there any guidelines. CIBSE however has set standards for indoor air quality, which are mainly based on comfort levels. Many electronic devices produce harmful ozone, and *Chapter 55* shows a preferred way to counteract this.

Staff should have easy access to a quality water supply, typically via a water cooler, see *Chapter 53*. Workplaces should be comfortable and ventilated by fresh or purified air. BRE recommends natural ventilation is used wherever possible – although hermetically-sealed and double/triple glazed environments cause trade-offs to be made. Opening windows causes energy wastage and ingress of pollutants and traffic noise.

Jargon Buster

RH	Relative Humidity
CIBSE	Chartered Institute of Building Services Engineers
BRE	Building Research Establishment
HSE	Health and Safety Executive

68 GETTING THE FIT-OUT UNDERWAY

First Principles

- Identify clear lines of communication from the outset
- Never allow anyone without authority to instruct the fit-out specialist
- The site will look worse before it gets better
- Your staff must respect the site rules

Your fit-out specialist will commence the site set-up procedure upon the agreed access date to the site or work area. The procedure will include Health and Safety, fire precautions, welfare facilities and protection of the existing building fabric, where necessary. Once the works have started, your own project co-ordinator should have regular contact with the project manager or site foreman.

It is important to identify clear lines of communication from the outset. Never allow anyone without authority to instruct the fit-out specialist. This will only cause confusion and unnecessary cost.

If you have taken on the lease of a Cat A specification building or one that has been newly refurbished, the work area may rapidly begin to look like a construction site. Your fit-out specialist will take up floors and some of the suspended ceilings may be removed to allow access to services. Similarly, the carpets that looked so good on day one may have to be removed. The site will look worse before it gets better.

68

Staff will probably be inquisitive and you should advise them of the dangers and the need to comply with the requirements of the CDM Regulations. The F10 certificate will be on display and HSE can appear at any time to inspect health and safety issues.

Everyone in your organisation needs to understand that a working site is a potentially dangerous place. No one may enter the site without authorisation or without the appropriate protective clothing and equipment. It is vital that your staff respect the site rules.

Jargon Buster

PPE	Personal protective equipment, such as hard hats, luminous jackets, steel toe capped boots, etc
CDM	Construction (Design and Management) Regulations 2007 comprise one set of regulations to govern the construction industry, and ensure safe working practices and long-term design integrity
F10	Before construction work starts, the nearest HSE office to the proposed site has to be notified using form F10

69 CDM REGULATIONS

First Principles

- CDM Regulations ensure projects are designed and built safely
- CDM Regulations require the client to provide sufficient management arrangements
- The CDM co-ordinator manages the flow of health and safety information

The Construction (Design and Management) Regulations 2007 replace the 1994 CDM Regulations entirely and also incorporate the Construction (Health, Safety and Welfare) Regulations 1996, so giving one set of regulations to govern the construction industry. The regulations are supported with an ACoP: Managing health and safety in construction. Their purpose is to ensure that the construction work is designed and built with safe working practices and long-term design integrity.

CDM Regulations 2007 apply to all construction projects and so there is no longer any exemption for small construction projects employing less than five operatives. You will need to make sure procedures are in place for all refurbishment works, new build, maintenance and repair works, regardless of the number of operatives involved. If the construction phase lasts over 30 days or 500 person-days, it will be notifiable to HSE on Form F10. These notifications enable HSE to arrange its inspection visits. Local authority environmental health practitioners may also enforce the regulations, for example if construction work areas are not segregated from any work area during internal alterations and redecoration works.

69

The responsibility to coordinate the CDM Regulations rests with the client – which means you. Indeed you must employ a CDM coordinator to take responsibility. Duty holders within the Regulations are the client (you), designers, CDM co-ordinator, principal contractor and contractors.

There is a significant benefit in engaging with a CDMC early in the project since the eventual coordinator's work can be seriously compromised if they are unable to influence the early work of designers or to be in a position to advise on the competency of the chosen designers before an appointment is made.

Your fit-out specialist will be able to discuss with you the necessary requirements of these Regulations and you should take expert advice from a fully-qualified health and safety co-ordinator to make sure your responsibilities under the Health & Safety Regulations are met.

Jargon Buster

ACoP	Approved Code of Practice
CDM co-ordinator	The person who manages the CDM process
Planning supervisor	Term used in the CDM Regulations prior to April 2007 – now no longer used; replaced by the CDM coordinator
HSE	Health & Safety Executive, see *Chapter 36*

70 KEEP COMMUNICATING

First Principles

- Increase the level of communications as the works commence
- Staff may be experiencing some disturbance
- Plan your moves carefully and keep staff informed

If your refurbishment is being undertaken in an occupied building, your communication with staff and adjacent occupiers is critical as the contrast between last week's quiet and this week's noise will be quite marked. Your neighbours need to be reminded that it is only a short-term inconvenience and that normality will soon be resumed. Increase the level of communications as the works commence. There can never be enough communication of information.

During the programme, staff may have to be moved around, either to accommodate the work or to move into a completed workspace. Staff must be given clear instructions as to when to pack boxes and/or crates, and how to label them.

It is a good idea to display progress photos online and in the office, to keep everyone on the staff informed, and to reduce the inclination of staff to make unnecessary visits to the site to view work in progress.

70

To quote from *Chapter 33*, communication with your staff about the project must start early and be sustained throughout the life of the project, to influence their buy-in and approval. The staff are your most valuable asset. Indeed communication and consultation with staff is a pre-requisite to ensure an effective office relocation.

It has been proven many times over that if this process is handled correctly and with due consideration for staff needs, the results can be extremely productive and work for the good of the organisation. This will become apparent as the works progress.

Jargon Buster

Handover	Taking over the building from the fit-out specialist at PC
PC	Practical completion – the time from when the project can be used effectively by the client (but the works are not necessarily entirely finished and snagged)

71

CASH FLOW AND STAGE PAYMENTS

First Principles

- You should consider the impact of the works' progress on your cash flow throughout the project
- You must agree a payment plan with your fit-out specialist
- Alternatively payments could be based on progress on site

Your project may draw heavily on your financial resources. Your fit-out specialist will require payment for the work as it progresses. You must agree with him how these payments will be triggered.

A normal procedure is where you agree with your fit-out specialist a series of stage payments based on reaching certain defined progress milestones. Frequently these payments are a percentage of the contract value.

It is normal practice for your fit-out specialist to require some form of mobilisation payment or deposit. This will cover the high initial site set-up costs and fees for surveys. It is important that this is paid well before the date when work on site is intended to start, to enable your fit-out specialist to place orders for materials and labour.

For any variations, see *Chapter 72*, which arise during the project, a running total of extra and reduced costs is kept by the project consultant. The net cumulative value is generally invoiced on practical completion of the project.

Alternatively, valuation of work is sometimes handled on a monthly basis. The process involves inspecting the site and agreeing the value of all work that has been carried out in the preceding month, including the value of any materials that have arrived on site since the last valuation and any materials that are being stored off-site. This valuation forms the basis for payment.

Jargon Buster

Valuation	An assessment of the value of work carried out to date and any materials purchased and stored on or off-site
Certification	The formal issue of a valuation which places an obligation on the client to pay the contractor
Stage payment	The payment of an agreed amount when an agreed stage of the project has been completed
Cash flow	The difference between cash revenues and cash outlays in a given period of time, not including non-cash expenses

72 COST CONTROL AND VARIATIONS

First Principles

- The cheapest contractor is sometimes ultimately the most expensive
- Keep a record of all variations
- Keep a cumulative cost plan, in order to control your budget
- Contingency sums can only be spent with your authority
- The cost of a variation should be agreed before it is actioned

Sadly, it is sometimes the case that the cheapest and apparently most cost-effective fit-out providers turn out to be extremely expensive and inefficient.

The basis of their additional costs often lies in inaccurate or vague specifications and a lack of adequate detailed surveys at the quote stage. Inevitably, this results in numerous requests for additional works to complete the project. This can be financially embarrassing for you and is often the reason used by inexperienced contractors to justify late or extended programmes.

Your fit-out specialist should provide you with a fixed price for any variations for you to authorise. This enables you to keep control of your budget. Variations should be documented weekly and a cumulative cost summary provided to you regularly.

It is a verified fact that variations tend to be more expensive than the same work carried out as part of the original contract. This is because materials may have to be ordered in small quantities, labour may not be readily available or work may have to be done out of sequence. For this reason, it makes sense to spend longer in getting the specification right from the outset, rather than finalising essential details after the works have started.

Jargon Buster

PC Sum	An amount of money included in the contract to cover the cost of an item where the exact cost is not known
Gantt Chart	A bar chart that illustrates a project schedule, showing start and finish dates in blocks over time

73 SITE PROGRESS MEETINGS

First Principles

An agenda for a site meeting should include:

- Meeting date and time, attendees, and a review of previous meeting notes
- Health and safety update
- Environmental concerns
- Review of programme
- Finishes
- Design amendments
- Variations/cost changes
- Progress payments
- A walk about the site

A regular site meeting is an extremely effective tool for monitoring the project and an agenda for such a meeting should include as a minimum the items listed above. The fit-out of your office will progress very quickly and you should remain firmly in control of the project at all times. This does not mean hands-on project management. It is important that all instructions as to the works are channeled through the fit-out specialist's project consultant.

Commitment to a regular site meeting is an excellent way to control the flow of information and keep you informed. In addition, your presence at the weekly meetings provides an incentive to ensure that all promised milestones are satisfactorily achieved.

Site meetings should be enjoyable, with a team spirit prevailing. A good fit-out specialist will conduct site meetings in a professional and co-operative manner, taking detailed minutes for subsequent circulation and approval.

The site meeting could include relevant specialists such as IT, removals or M&E consultants to ensure that all and any technical aspects are understood.

Jargon Buster

Minutes	Records of site meetings
Site instructions	Instructions given to the contractor on site; these should only be given by an authorised client representative to the project consultant and they should be recorded in writing
M&E	Mechanical and electrical

74 SNAGGING

First Principles

- Snagging should be completed as the project progresses
- Final commissioning may have to be completed following occupation
- It is how snagging items are dealt with that makes the difference
- Only agree to release your final payment once the snagging is finished

Any reputable fit-out company will insist on snagging being completed as the project progresses. Indeed it is a sign of poor management where large amounts of rectification work are not addressed and have to be dealt with following the practical completion of the project. This can prove to be disruptive and disturbing, as you may well be in occupation at this time.

In order to be sure that wherever possible, the snagging will be implemented during the project, we recommend you make enquiries as to how your chosen fit-out specialist rectifies snagging issues.

A good site foreman will not allow snagging items to remain and will often correct them prior to a weekly site meeting. It is not your job, as client, to identify snagging items – it is the job of the fit-out specialist.

You should expect to receive a one-year warranty, although some items such as furniture will carry a longer warranty. In order to retain the advantage of a warranty, you may be required to service and maintain equipment in accordance with the manufacturers' recommendations. These warranties are normally inserted into the O&M manuals which will be handed back to you on completion of the project by your fit-out specialist.

Jargon Buster

Snagging	The listing and correction of defects
Defect	An element of the work that needs rectification
Defects Liability Period	The agreed period for which the contractor remains responsible for correcting defects after practical completion – usually one year
O&M manuals	Operation and Maintenance instructions

75 FIRE SAFETY – THE KEY FACTS

First Principles

- Your business needs to manage fire safety through fire risk assessments
- You have to carry out a fire risk assessment appropriate to the workplace
- In case of a fire, staff should be able to proceed safely along a signed route to a place of safety

The Regulatory Reform (Fire Safety) Order 2005 – effective from October 2006 – consolidates a range of fire safety legislation into one enforceable order and allows fire authorities to adopt a consistent approach to fire safety needs. Businesses such as yours need to manage fire safety by way of fire risk assessments.

Fire safety is now concerned with a risk-based approach and risk assessment applies to all workplaces. Fire certificates have now been abolished. The risk-based approach applies equally to non-employees. You have to designate a "responsible person" to comply with fire safety legislation.

It is important to carry out a fire risk assessment appropriate to the workplace – and involve staff as they may have identified a potential fire risk of which people higher up the organisation might not be aware.

There are five steps in the approach to fire safety:

- Identify fire hazards,
- Identify the location of people at significant risk in case of fire,
- Evaluate the risks,
- Record the findings and the action taken, and
- Keep the assessment under review.

Once staff are aware of a fire, they should be able to proceed safely along a signed escape route to a place of safety – this should be practised rigorously and regularly in a fire safety drill. All staff should be aware of the location and use of escape routes, the location of their assembly point, how to use the fire equipment provided, and how to summon the fire service.

Anyone given responsibility to manage fire safety or to react in the event of a fire should be competent to carry out the tasks allocated (for example, they must have adequate knowledge, training and experience of the building and environment). Following a refurbishment or relocation, fire marshals should therefore be given fresh training.

Jargon Buster

Fire notice	Clear instructions on the action to be followed in case of fire to be prominently displayed throughout the workplace
Emergency lighting	Lighting required when there is insufficient natural light for people to make their way out of the building safely if primary lighting should fail

76 BUSINESS MOVES AND RELOCATIONS

First Principles

- Organisation of the move is critical
- Aim for a minimum downtime – a smooth transition
- Most business moves are scheduled to take place out of hours, but this does cost more

The relocation of your business assets and personnel can be a challenging proposition. With this in mind, it makes sense to engage only the best companies to assist you in this process.

A detailed survey and inventory should be carried out of your existing equipment to be relocated. This inventory will include existing furniture, IT systems, storage, etc. Your relocation manager will be able to co-ordinate and oversee the project and keep your staff aware of the timetable and identify potential problems and bottlenecks.

Your IT and (tele)communications equipment is key to the continued running of your business and the decommissioning and relocation of these items should be considered before anything else, see *Chapters 62, 63 and 64*. It should not be obvious to your customers that your IT capability has been relocated. Ensure you have a competent IT team to ensure that this is so, and that all your systems will be operational when you are up and running in your new location.

One option to consider is to utilise a data centre services provider to take over your IT systems for a period around the relocation. Alternatively you could inform your key customers that there will be a period of a few hours of restricted service while you are transferring to a new location.

Office equipment such as photocopiers, mailing and vending machines may be leased and it is often only the leasing company that can relocate these items. It is important to liaise at an early stage with your relocation specialist to agree the relocation of such items.

Do not finalise your move until you can be sure your telecommunications requirements can be accommodated.

Jargon Buster

Downtime	The duration for which your company cannot operate normally
Phased move	Moving departments individually or in groups as areas of work are completed
Office move specialist	A company that deals with the relocation process

77 POST FIT-OUT REVIEW AND AFTER THE PROJECT

First Principles

- The relationship with your fit-out specialist does not end when you move in but carries on as your business develops
- You should review the success of your project with your fit-out specialist
- Publicise your move or refit, and add the finishing touches
- Show your staff how to use their new offices and equipment
- Arrange maintenance contracts

Following your relocation or refit, it is essential that you review what you have achieved and measure this against your original objectives. You should evaluate how well your partnership with the fit-out specialist has worked. A successful project, completed on time, will reflect well on your judgement and you should be prepared to congratulate your fit-out specialist for contributing to the result. Equally you should communicate any poor performance or suggestions for improvements, so they can be addressed.

You embarked on a process that was intended to bring business benefits to your organisation. It is important, therefore, to discuss these with the team that advised you. There may be further (quick and simple) enhancements you can make that will further improve your working environment. Any teething problems for your staff, for example, can be identified through a simple questionnaire and rectified.

Once you are enjoying your new working environment, it is an opportune time for publicity as you have something exciting to show your clients. Invite them to visit your new offices to see the investment you have made in your staff and clients. If appropriate, you may consider that an upbeat PR message could promote good publicity and awareness of your company's relocation.

The staff will also need to know how to use the new offices, and a welcome pack may be appropriate for such things as where the stationery is located, how to use the telephones and instructions as to how to set up the task chairs, for example. Your fit-out specialist will provide O&M manuals for advice on the products and services provided, including the maintenance requirements for the equipment.

Jargon Buster

Drains up	A post project meeting that openly examines what went well and what could have been handled better
Partnering	Creating a working relationship with a company that goes beyond the initial project
O&M manual	Operation and maintenance instructions
Welcome pack	An instruction manual for the staff

78 CRISIS/RISK MANAGEMENT

First Principles

- Some risks are worth taking while others are not
- Risk can be split into natural risk and business risk
- A threat assessment is only a snapshot at a specific point in time
- Managing risk is totally linked to quality – reduced quality can lead to heightened risk, and vice versa

There are three phases of crisis/risk management – analysis, assessment and mitigation: the process of working out things that can go wrong, likelihood and consequences; appropriate action to minimise the probability of the risk occurring; and the preparation of plans, identification of management teams and assignment of responsibilities for managing the process.

Risk is minimised by removing or reducing hazards. HSE defines "hazards" as those things which have the ability to cause harm, while "risk" is the likelihood that harm will occur. "Harm" occurs when your organisation has to divert from a predetermined plan to react to unforeseen circumstances.

Your business can be diverted for many reasons, outside your control or within it; those outside your control require business continuity measures, see *Chapter 79*, and insurance policies to be instigated; for those within, legislation usually determines minimum levels of risk management. Risk can be split into natural risk and business risk.

Natural risk includes nature's effects (flood, storms, fire), technical events (equipment failure), personal issues (sickness, injury, theft, negligence). Business risk includes the impact of/changes in new technologies, social impact (changes in customer expectation), economic impact (inflation, budget constraints) and political impact (imposition of government policy).

Your senior management committee is responsible for identifying, monitoring and reviewing risk. Since 2001, the London Stock Exchange (based on the recommendation of the Turnbull Committee on corporate governance) has required that quoted company reports should comply with certain key recommendations relating to risk management. If a quoted organisation suffers through failing to manage risk, including digital risk, as well as possible, the way is open for shareholders to sue the board of directors individually and personally. Is your senior management committee aware of this?

Jargon Buster

Turnbull Report	Published by the Institute of Chartered Accountants to the Stock Exchange, recommending all quoted companies should have a risk management strategy
Risk	The likelihood that harm will occur

79 BUSINESS CONTINUITY

First Principles

- Is your organisation prepared for a disaster?
- Business continuity management is concerned with the whole business
- Test, test and test your plan, then test it again
- Are you really prepared?

Is your organisation prepared for a disaster? Disaster refers to any incident that prevents your organisation from operating as usual – from microchip theft to computer virus outbreaks, not just large incidents such as fires, floods, terrorist activity, storm damage. Business continuity management is concerned with ongoing preparation of the whole business for an incident whereas disaster recovery focuses on recovery and back-up plans following an incident, such as loss of a major customer or supplier or key staff, a burst water main, transport or postal strike and power failure.

Business continuity management is "the ongoing process of ensuring the continual operation of critical business processes through the evaluation of risk and resilience, and the implementation of mitigation measures."

Business continuity represents an investment which rather than just reducing the impact of disaster on your business can increase employee, investor and shareholder confidence in your organisation.

79

The ultimate aim and effective strategy is for a cost-effective and focused business continuity infrastructure for your organisation. Draw up a plan, if possible with a business continuity consultancy, and publish it throughout your organisation. Rehearse your plan, test it regularly (there can never be enough testing) and update it whenever necessary. Consider outsourcing your mission-critical IT and (tele) communications elements to a disaster recovery specialist. This could be concerned with critical servers, PCs, and could include standby facilities, buildings and even people.

Business continuity insurance may form part of your strategy but to obtain a reasonable premium you will need to demonstrate that mitigation measures are in place. Do not fall into the trap of saying "it won't happen to us" – do you know what all your neighbours do? If an incident occurs, the police/fire/security services may throw a cordon around the focal point, meaning you could have no access to your offices. Are you prepared? Really?

The occasion of a relocation or office fit-out is an opportunity to make infrastructure provisions to help the business survive a crisis.

Jargon Buster

BCM	Business Continuity Management
BS 25999	Business continuity standard, two-part publication that describes activities and outcomes of establishing a BCM process

80 WHY CONTACT OFFICE PRINCIPLES?

Because of our commitment to our clients:
We are diligent and professional
We have character and creativity
We deliver clever ideas and brilliant interiors

- If you need office interior design solutions that work
- If you don't want hassle, but admire true partnering
- If you want experienced project management
- If you hate wasting time, but want results
- If, having read this book, you would like to know more...

Contact: Cyril Parsons
Tel: +44 (0)118 913 1818
Email: cyril.parsons@officeprinciples.com

80

How to find us

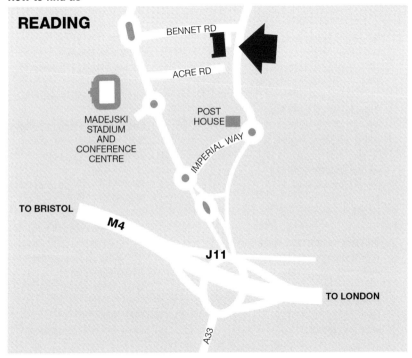

READING

BENNET RD

ACRE RD

MADEJSKI
STADIUM
AND
CONFERENCE
CENTRE

POST
HOUSE

IMPERIAL WAY

TO BRISTOL

M4

J11

TO LONDON

A33

USEFUL CONTACTS, WEBSITES AND SOURCES OF INFORMATION

Association of Security Consultants
web: www.securityconsultants.org.uk

**Automatic Vending Association
of Britain** (AVAB)
tel: 020 86611112
web: www.ava-vending.org

British Council for Offices
tel: 020 7283 4588
web: www.bco.org.uk

**British Security Industry
Association** (BSIA)
tel: 01905 21464
web: www.bsia.co.uk

**Building Owners and Managers
Association** (BOMA International)
web: www.boma.org

Building Research Establishment (BRE)
tel: 01923 664000
web: www.bre.co.uk

**Building Services Research and
Information Association** (BSRIA)
tel: 01344 426511
web: www.bsria.co.uk

Business Continuity Institute (BCI)
tel: 0870 603 8783
web: www.thebci.org

Carbon Trust
tel: 0800 085 2005
web: www.carbontrust.co.uk

CCTV User Group
For model code of practice and procedural
manual
web: www.cctvusergroup.com

Chartered Institute of Building (CIOB)
tel: 01344 630700
web: www.ciob.org.uk

**Chartered Institute of Building Services
Engineers** (CIBSE)
tel: 020 8675 5211
web: www.cibse.org

**Combined Heat and Power
Association** (CHPA)
web: www.chpa.co.uk

CHP Club
web: www.chpclub.com

Energy Systems Trade Association (ESTA
Building Control Group
web: www.esta.org.uk/bcg

European Commission
tel: 020 7973 1992
web: http://ec.europa.eu/index_en.htm

Health and Safety Executive (HSE)
HSE Infoline: 0845 345 0055
tel: 0870 154 5500
web: www.hse.gov.uk

Heating, Ventilation and Air Conditioning Manufacturers' Association (HEVAC)
web: www.hevac.com

H&V Contractors' Association (HVCA)
tel: 020 7727 9268
web: www.hvca.org.uk

Institution of Engineering and Technology (IET)
Formerly IEE (Institution of Electrical Management Engineers)
tel: 01604 620426
web: www.theiet.org

Institution of Fire Engineers
tel: 0116 255 3654
web: www.ife.org.uk

Lighting Industry Federation (LIF)
web: www.lif.co.uk

National Security Inspectorate
tel: 01628 637512
web: www.nsi.org.uk

Office Furniture Advisory Service (OFAS)
tel: 01344 779438
web: www.ofas.org.uk

Royal Institute of British Architects (RIBA)
tel: 020 7580 5533
web: www.architecture.com

Royal Institution of Chartered Surveyors (RICS)
tel: 020 7222 7000
web: www.rics.org

Security Industry Authority
web: www.the-sia.org.uk

Ska
web: www.rics.org/ska
web: www.ska-rating.com
web: www.ska-tool.rics.org

Society of Light and Lighting
web: www.lightandlighting.com

Chartered Institution of Wastes Management (CIWM)
web: www.ciwm.co.uk

The Environment Council
tel: 020 7836 2626
web: www.wasteguide.org.uk

The Stationery Office
web: www.tso.co.uk

USEFUL TERMINOLOGY

Accountability 21
A non-profit, tax-exempt organization founded in 1998 by Beatriz Casals to support and expand global efforts to curb corruption in government and the private sector.

Adaptive technology
Products which assist people who cannot utilise regular versions of products, mainly people with physical disabilities such as limitations to vision, hearing and mobility. It promotes greater effectiveness for people with functional limitations or disabilities by enabling them to perform tasks they were formerly unable to accomplish, or experienced difficulty accomplishing.

AHU
Air handling unit – the part of an HVAC system responsible for moving air, which may also clean, heat or cool the air.

Biomass
A renewable energy source – touted as the most efficient of green energies – it is biological material derived from living or recently-living organisms such as wood, waste and alcohol fuels. It is commonly plant matter grown to generate electricity or produce heat.

BREEAM
BRE Environmental Assessment Method (BREEAM) is a measurement rating for green buildings that was established in the UK by the BRE (Building Research Establishment). Since its inception it has grown in scope and geographically, being exported in various guises across the globe – equivalent benchmarks include LEED in North America, Green Star in Australia and HQE in France.

Brise soleil
A type of externally-mounted structural sunshade with slats, holes, etc to prevent sunlight from striking fully on a building.

Business Continuity and BS 25999
BS 25999 is the world's first standard for business continuity management (BCM). Achieving certification to the standard by an independent third party BSI Management Systems provides assurance to stakeholders that an organisation complies with BCM best practice. See web: **www.bsi-global.com**

CAFM
Computer-aided facilities management – about the support of facilities management by information technology.

CFL

Compact fluorescent lamp, also called a compact fluorescent light or energy-saving light (and less commonly a compact fluorescent tube, (CFT), is designed to replace an incandescent lamp and can fit into most existing light fixtures formerly used for incandescent bulbs. Compared with general-service incandescent lamps giving the same amount of visible light, CFLs generally utilise less power, have a longer rated life, but a higher purchase cost.

CIBSE

Chartered Institute of Building Services Engineers.

CMMS

Computerised Maintenance Management System, also known as Enterprise Asset Management and Computerised Maintenance Management Information are systems that schedule, track and monitor maintenance activities and provide cost, component item, tooling personnel and other reporting data and history CMMS can interface with production scheduling and cost systems, and be utilised to follow preventive maintenance policies.

Chilled beams

Three types of chilled beam exist: chilled ceilings, passive chilled beams, and active chilled beams. A, chilled uses water, not air, to remove heat from a room – a one-inch diameter pipe of water carries the same noise reduction, significant energy savings and increased occupant comfort. amount of energy as an 18x18-inch duct of air. Advantages of the systems include noise reduction, significant energy savings and increased occupant comfort.

Chlorination

The process of adding chlorine to water as a method of water purification to make it fit for human consumption as drinking water; also chlorinated water helps to prevent the spread of disease.

CHP

Combined Heat and Power or cogeneration is a system that involves the recovery of waste heat from power generation to form useful energy like useable steam. CHP is also the production of electricity and thermal energy in a single integrated structure.

CTS

The Carbon Trust Standard is a mark of excellence awarded to organisations for measuring, managing and reducing carbon emissions over time.

USEFUL TERMINOLOGY

Disability Equality Scheme
Ensures that disability equality is not reliant on the commitment of a few individuals but instead is fully integrated as part of an organisation's daily business.

EMS
Environmental management system which provides your organisation with a framework through which its environmental performance can be monitored, improved and controlled.

Ground source heat pump
Also known as a geothermal heat pump, this is a central heating and/or cooling system that pumps heat to or from the ground. It uses the earth as a heat source (in the winter) or a heat sink (in the summer). This design takes advantage of the moderate temperatures in the ground to boost efficiency and reduce the operational costs of heating and cooling systems, and may be combined with solar heating to form a geosolar system with even greater efficiency.

Hot work permit
This is used to control the potential ignition hazard associated with cutting, welding or other "hot work", which is defined as any temporary activity that produces sparks, heat or flame. Examples of hot work include welding, cutting, grinding, soldering, brazing, torch-applied roofing, etc.

HSE
Health and Safety Executive.

IEE/NICEIC
Acronyms for the Institution of Electrical Engineers and the National Inspection Council for Electrical Installation Contracting. The IEE Wiring Regulations have become a standard for the UK and many other countries while the NICEIC is the industry's independent, non profit making, voluntary regulatory body covering the UK The IEE became the Institution of Engineering and Technology (IET) in 2006, see website at **www.theiet.org**

LEED
Leadership in Energy and Environmental Design – a Green Building Rating System developed by the US Green Building Council (USGBC) which provides a suite of standards for environmentally sustainable construction.

Lien
A lien is a type of security interest granted over an item of property to secure the payment of a debt or performance of some other obligation. The owner of the property, who grants the lien, is called the lienor and the person who has the benefit of the lien is called the lienee.

Lifestyle logistics
The process(es) of removing clutter from an office environment, organising space, arranging filing and defining administrative solutions.

Obsolescence management
Activities that are undertaken to mitigate the effects of obsolescence (itself a state of being which occurs when something or somebody is no longer wanted even though it could still be in good working order).

PEEP/GEEP
Personal emergency egress plan/Generic emergency egress plan – part of fire safety planning.

Plenums
Air compartments or chambers including uninhabited crawl spaces, areas above ceilings or below a floor, including air spaces below raised floors of IT centres, or attic spaces, to which one or more ducts are linked and which form part of either the supply air, return air or exhaust air system, other than the (occupied) space being conditioned.

ROI
Return on investment.

Sick Building Syndrome (SBS)
A combination of ailments associated with a place of work (office buildings for example) frequently ascribed to flaws in the HVAC systems, or contaminants from volatile organic compounds (VOCs), mould, ozone as a byproduct of some office systems.

TIA
Telecommunications Industry Association.

Virements
Transfers of financial funds.

VOCs
Volatile organic compounds – long-term exposure to VOCs in an indoor environment can contribute to sick building syndrome. Building materials such as paint, adhesives, wall boards and ceiling tiles emit formaldehyde which irritates the mucous membranes and can make people irritated and uncomfortable. New furnishings, wall coverings and office equipment also give off VOCs.

WAHR
Work at Height Regulations (falls are the biggest killer in the workplace).

INDEX
a route to key words and terms

THE **BLACK BOOK**

INDEX
a route to key words and terms

THE **BLACK BOOK**

INDEX

a route to key words and terms

THE **BLACK BOOK**

INDEX
a route to key words and terms

THE **BLACK BOOK**

INDEX
a route to key words and terms

THE **BLACK BOOK**

INDEX
a route to key words and terms

THE **BLACK BOOK**

KING ST.

Set Three
BOOK 5

The Lottery

The Lottery
King Street: Readers Set Three - Book 5
Copyright © Iris Nunn 2014

Text: Iris Nunn
Editor: June Lewis

Published in 2014 by Gatehouse Media Limited

ISBN: 978-1-84231-130-1

British Library Cataloguing-in-Publication Data:
A catalogue record for this book is available from the British Library

It was Friday night.
Jane had been at work
on the tills.

Jane worked
at the local supermarket.

She was tired,
but it was a fine evening.

Jane walked slowly
down the road.

As she walked,
she looked in the shop windows.

She looked at clothes for the twins.
She looked at clothes for Mark.
She looked at clothes for herself.
She looked at things for the house.
She looked at things for the kitchen
and things for the living room.
She looked at the carpet shop.

The twins' room was so shabby.
When she and Mark had got married
they could not afford new things,
so they had got second-hand.

Mark's mum had given them
an old sofa.
They had got a second-hand TV
and Mark had put up some shelves.
The carpet in the living room
had come from her sister.
She was getting a new one.

The twins were at school now.
When they were small
they did make a mess,
but now they didn't.

Jane wanted a carpet
for their room.
She wanted a good fitted carpet.

"If they have a carpet in their room
they will play up there,"
she said to herself.

Jane stopped at the carpet shop.
There was the carpet she wanted,
but it cost too much.
She could not afford so much.

When she got home
she made the tea.
She kept thinking about the carpet.
The twins had gone to watch TV
and she and Mark were having
a cup of tea.

She told Mark about the carpet.

"It is dark green
and just what we need
for the twins' bedroom -
the floor is so hard!"

"No way," said Mark.
"We have bills to pay."

Jane shut up and felt sad.

The twins sat side by side
in front of the TV.

"Have you got a lottery ticket, Mum?"
they yelled to Jane in the kitchen.

"Not this week," said Jane,
"but Dad will get one later."

Jane had to work
on Saturday morning.
She was so tired when she got in.
She was cross too.
It had been a hard day at work.

After tea they all sat down
in front of the telly -
Mark, Jane and the twins.
They liked to watch the lottery.
But Jane was so tired,
she fell asleep.

Suddenly she was woken by a shout.
Mark was jumping up and down
and waving something about
in the air.

"Mum, Mum!" shouted the twins.
"Dad's won some money!"

Mark had got a lottery ticket
and he had won - not the jackpot,
but £1000!

"Jane, you can have your carpet now!"